The Reasonable Man

The Reasonable Man

Trollope's Legal Fiction

Coral Lansbury

Princeton University Press
Princeton, New Jersey

Copyright © 1981 by Princeton University Press

Published by Princeton University Press, Princeton, New Jersey
In the United Kingdom: Princeton University Press, Guildford, Surrey

All Rights Reserved

Library of Congress Cataloging in Publication Data will be
found on the last printed page of this book

Publication of this book has been aided by a grant from the
Paul Mellon Fund of Princeton University Press

This book has been composed in Linotron Sabon

Clothbound editions of Princeton University Press books
are printed on acid-free paper, and binding materials are
chosen for strength and durability

Printed in the United States of America by Princeton
University Press, Princeton, New Jersey

For Acki and Pauli

Table of Contents

	Preface	ix
	Acknowledgments	xi
I.	The Legal Structure of Trollope's Fiction	3
II.	Order and Vision	26
III.	Society Examined: The Travel Books	48
IV.	Success and Personality: Autobiography and Biography	69
V.	Society and the Language of Law	82
VI.	*The Macdermots of Ballycloran*	112
VII.	The Single Transaction—Conscience and Society: *The Warden*	129
VIII.	The Single Transaction—Guilt and Society: *Cousin Henry*	144
IX.	The Multiple Transaction—Social Contracts—Law and Justice: *Orley Farm*	157
X.	The Multiple Transaction—Social Contracts—The Rebels: *Mr. Scarborough's Family, Ayala's Angel*	172
XI.	The Extended Multiple Transaction—The Rights and Duties of Barchester: *The Warden, Barchester Towers, Doctor Thorne, Framley Parsonage, The Small House at Allington, The Last Chronicle of Barset*	190
XII.	The Extended Multiple Transaction—Privilege and Power in Politics: *Can You Forgive Her? Phineas Finn, The Eustace Diamonds, Phineas Redux, The Prime Minister, The Duke's Children*	212
	Index	225

Preface

Every critical sensibility is offended when the source of literary creativity is found in the humdrum and commonplace. It is customary these days to note the influence of Middleton, Thackeray and Cicero upon Trollope, and then refer to the secondary inspiration of Defoe and Fielding. But it is the purpose of this work to demonstrate that Francis Freeling and his Post Office report did more to shape the structure of Trollope's novels than did any writer. To a generation with a justified abhorrence of all government prose this statement alone should provoke a certain measure of cynical disbelief.

Trollope wrote as much for the Post Office as he did for his reading public, yet no one has bothered to examine the reports in which he took such pride. Certainly, it has not seemed likely that what was written in the service of the government should have any bearing on the novels, and no one would hold that Trollope consciously and deliberately set out to adapt the bureaucratic forms in which he had been trained to suit the structure of his fiction. In more ways than most of us would care to know, the routine procedures to which we have become accustomed in formative years serve to influence the conceptual and imaginative modes we employ for other purposes. However incongruous it may seem to those who love the art of Trollope it may well be that he unconsciously used the Freeling report, derived from a legal declaration, as a model for his novels.

All Trollope's novels are transactions involving money and marriage and all can be comprehended within the structure of the report. The latter imposed a form that helped Trollope define his themes and also permitted him to exclude areas of his experience that he found too painful to express in fiction. Children, for example, do not play any significant role in

Trollope's world and there are none of the coincidences, lost relatives, and unexpected inheritances that provide the stock devices of so many Victorian novels. Trollope described a rational world that is expressed within a legal form and may be analyzed as legal rhetoric.

By no means should this be read as a brief for Trollope as a lawyer. He was a civil servant who both resented and embodied the legalistic procedures of the Post Office. Indeed his art is often characterized by the antagonism between accepted authority and independent opinion. His novels are the result of the paradoxical conflict between the bullying martinet of the Post Office and a man possessing an extraordinary ability to identify himself with the minds and feelings of others.

The Post Office under Francis Freeling and Rowland Hill was noted for its speed, efficiency, and handsome annual profits. When Trollope spoke of his virtues as a novelist he used the same terms in his own praise. He described his novels as sermons, but if they were sermons it was law that inspired the lesson, not religion. Moreover, the audience to which they were directed was neither the sinner nor the seeker of vicarious emotions: it was personified in that legal fiction, the reasonable man, who should judge for himself by the canons of common sense.

In describing a society governed by reason, Trollope created a legal ideal and then convinced the world of its reality. That may yet be the greatest tribute to his genius.

Acknowledgments

It is customary, and a matter of common courtesy, to pause occasionally in a work of literary scholarship and acknowledge one's debts and obligations to others. I have failed to do this, not because I am unaware of what I owe, but simply because there is no time in a work of this kind to acknowledge all those who have made my critical task less arduous. *Hiatus valde deflendus.* In extenuation let me plead that this is a new interpretation of Trollope, using new material, and, in arguing my own case, I have frequently disregarded the opinions and interpretations of others. Yet this book would never have been written had I not been led to my own conclusions by Ruth apRobert's moral reading of Trollope, James Kincaid's and U. C. Knoepflmacher's theory of Trollopian comedy, John Halperin's and Juliet McMaster's sense of historical values, Robert Tracy's discussion of analogical plots—these among many others. Certainly, I cannot omit mention of the late Lord Snow who mentioned in his own study of Trollope that Post Office records "contain surprises. . . . They might yield more, on further examination." Many of the subtleties of the Civil Service were clarified for me in conversations with him.

Above all else I must thank Mrs. Jean Farrugia, assistant curator of the Post Office Museum. Her fine editorial hand can be discerned in all the chapters dealing with postal matters. Without her help I would never have found my way through the labyrinth of postal records. In many ways this book is as much the result of her scholarship as it is my own.

John Hall allowed me to use the unpublished Trollope letters; Mrs. Mary Leahy of Bryn Mawr College let me see the fine collection of books from Trollope's library that fills so many gaps in the Victoria and Albert Museum's collection. At Princeton, Mrs. Coffin permitted me to read in the Robert

H. Taylor library and I am grateful for the kind assistance given me in the Morris L. Parrish holdings. Miss Arnold led me to the Drinker manuscripts in the Biddle Law Library of the University of Pennsylvania. Similar courtesies were shown me in the Bodleian, and at the Folger Library.

My colleague John Paul Russo read the work, and his literary comments were invaluable. Six lawyers then read it like a brief: Russell Fairbanks and Jay Sigler of Rutgers University; Malcolm Turnbull of Brasenose College, Oxford; Roberta L. Jacobs of Philadelphia; Robert Ferguson of the University of Chicago; and, pre-eminently, Gertrude Leighton, professor and formerly chairman of the Caroline McCormick Slade Department of Political Science at Bryn Mawr College. Combining the qualities of lawyer and literary scholar, Miss Leighton brought a legal file to the work: "Limae labor et mora." Its legal refinements are hers, and I confess to a certain confidence in her defense of my case. Finally, I should like to thank Mrs. Arthur Sherwood for the spirit of "deep reasonableness" in which she edited the work.

Despite friends and family, the book would never have been finished without an NEH Fellowship and the Research Council of Rutgers University.

The Reasonable Man

Chapter I

The Legal Structure of Trollope's Fiction

A miserable childhood of pain and rejection would seem the prerequisite for a successful novelist in the Victorian period. Certainly, Anthony Trollope had experienced refinements of humiliation that surpassed the brutal shock of the young Charles Dickens set to pasting labels in a blacking factory. The ingenious torments of childhood were expressed with considerable resourcefulness by the masters and pupils at Winchester and Harrow when Trollope, shabby and dirty, awkward and ugly, shortsighted and dull, "became a Pariah" in their midst. With more time on their hands, the public school boys could maintain a bloody-minded oppression with far greater persistence than Dickens' cockney workmates. At least it was possible for Dickens to cherish the belief that he was a gentleman, cast down by fortune into a company that was alien to his nature. It was rather more difficult for Trollope to assert his proper station in society when gentlemen of all ages seemed bent on rejecting him. If his home and family had ever provided a refuge, a measure of consolation for the grief of childhood, it is possible that Trollope would have become neither so troubled a man nor the most judicial and pragmatic novelist of the age.

Trollope was twelve in 1827 when his mother went to America with his younger brother Henry and his two sisters. It was a journey that later produced a literary profit after the financial disaster of Frances Trollope's attempt to establish a cultural and commercial bazaar in Cincinnati where the resident natives could buy European gewgaws and acquire a little artistic polish. Social philanthropy as a result of capitalist enterprise was highly approved then and later, but few had attempted it with such flamboyance and slender means. Undoubtedly, the moral improvement of the Americans would have justified the Trollopes' descent into trade, but they were not to enjoy the satisfaction of doing good and making money at the same time. It was the record of this failure, *The Domestic Manners of the Americans*, published in 1832, which gave the family a momentary financial stability. The book was acclaimed by the conservative opposition to the Reform Bill as testimony to the folly of a democratic suffrage. The blame of failure for the Cincinnati bazaar was now satisfactorily accepted as the natural consequence of Radical enthusiasm and American crassness.

Trollope admired his mother's industry and fortitude throughout the agonies of illness when she later wrote her novels and nursed and buried all her family save Anthony and her eldest and best-loved son, Thomas Adolphus. However, Anthony's sympathies were tempered by an awareness that he had always been overlooked, and when not neglected, then made the whipping boy for many of the family's misfortunes. It seemed to him that his mother's gaiety in the face of disaster was more a reflection of her inability to accept facts than a reasoned optimism. His own misery as a child was made more painful by this disregarding cheerfulness. He was always seen as difficult and sullen, a boy whose cloddish mind was manifest in his ungainly appearance. Yet the dullard was capable of a brilliant commentary on Burke's *On the Sublime* when he was at Harrow, revealing on paper his power to test motive and act against social forms.[1] No doubt it was part of Trollope's mode of critical enquiry at this age but it received neither attention nor commendation. It was not in tackling Burke that the young scholar received his laurels, but from an exhilarating encounter with a Greek threnodist.

[1] Susan L. Humphreys, "Trollope on the Sublime and Beautiful," *Nineteenth Century Fiction*, 3, No. 2 (September 1978), 194-214.

Legal Structure

When he wrote his autobiography as an old man, Trollope remembered how at Winchester his brother Thomas had flogged him every day: "Hang a little boy for stealing apples, he used to say, and other little boys will not steal apples."[2] There had been no stolen apples, just a failure to construe, and Thomas's own satisfaction in being able to inflict pain with the righteous authority of age and intellectual superiority. It was an attitude that he attempted to maintain over his brother throughout his life, gleefully pouncing on inaccuracies in Anthony Trollope's *Commentaries of Caesar* and *Life of Cicero* and commending his mother as a merry angel of delight after Trollope had noted, in his posthumously published *Autobiography*, that her enthusiasm had been balanced by an equal measure of insensitivity. Clearly, for Thomas, Anthony saw his childhood "too much en noir."[3] Anthony had never known that darkness to be made light by a brother's presence.

Loneliness had been the measure of Trollope's youth. One summer he spent in his father's chambers in Lincoln's Inn:

> There was often a difficulty about the holidays,—as to what should be done with me. On this occasion my amusement consisted in wandering about among those old deserted buildings, and in reading Shakespeare out of a bicolumned edition, which is still among my books. It was not that I had chosen Shakespeare, but that there was nothing else.[4]

Loneliness can result in a stupor of mental and physical inaction; it may become the source of contending symbolic fictions within the mind. Shakespeare has kindled less active imaginations than Trollope's. As a child Trollope knew both the torpor of loneliness and the absorption of creating a fictional world. There was no comfort for him in family or

[2] *An Autobiography*; the text used throughout is *The World's Classics* with an introduction by Michael Sadleir (Oxford, 1953), ch. 1.

[3] This was Thomas Adolphus Trollope's reaction to his brother's description of the farmhouse at Harrow Weald in *What I Remember*, London, 3 vols., 1887-1889, vol. 1, p. 228.

[4] *An Autobiography*, ch. 1.

friends at school. His father, once a brilliant barrister, now shambled in moods of neurotic depression either cuffing Latin into his sons or, in more genial moments, reading *Sir Charles Grandison* aloud as the evening's entertainment.

The brief flurry of financial success after *The Domestic Manners of the Americans* was soon buried in the customary debts. Like the Micawbers, the Trollopes could no longer afford to live in England as gentlefolk. They left for Bruges in a moonlight flit, barely managing to rescue a few belongings from the bailiffs who were about to take possession of "Julians," that blighted residence at Harrow, and all its contents. In Bruges Trollope's father and his brother Henry were to die and be buried. Thomas Adolphus had gone schoolmastering, but there seemed no occupation possible for Anthony save a wild suggestion of a post in an Austrian cavalry regiment. It was obvious that the awkward Anthony could not expect a straight and easy road to success. Returning to England, Frances Trollope remembered her dear friend, Mrs. Clayton Freeling, whose father-in-law, Sir Francis Freeling, was Secretary to the Post Office and the employer of many young men as clerks in his thriving service.[5] A letter was sufficient, and Anthony Trollope became a junior clerk on November 4, 1834, in the Secretary's office, "in the room of Mr. Dizzle resigned."[6] That unfortunate gentleman had, in fact, been dismissed. Trollope was to be given ninety pounds a year and lodging found for him in Northumberland Street in Marylebone.

Freeling, born in Bristol, had begun his long and illustrious career in the early 1770s, as an assistant to another young man destined for fame, John Palmer, a theater proprietor of

---

[5] Frances Eleanor Trollope recalled: "This Post-Office appointment was obtained through Mrs. Trollope's old friends the Freelings. Sir Francis Freeling was at this time Secretary to the Post-Office, and his daughter-in-law, Mrs. Clayton Freeling, was a dear friend of Mrs. Trollope's." *Frances Trollope*, London, 2 vols., 1895, vol. 1, p. 235.

[6] Pkt. 887, 1, A minute to the Postmaster General, November 4, 1834. POR. Sadleir's photostat of the oath that Trollope signed at the time of his appointment gives the unfortunate Dizzle as "dismissed." Michael Sadleir, *Trollope A Commentary* (London, 1945), p. 119.

Bath. Together they had worked on Palmer's plan to speed the mails by armed mail coaches and, the success of Palmer's plan assured, Freeling had become in 1787 head of the Post Office's corps of Riding Surveyors—men responsible to London for the supervision and efficient working of local postal services. The Post Office relied on the eyes and ears of these men, and the varied nature of the surveyors' duties proved an invaluable training-ground for men with the ability and energy of Freeling. By 1798 he had won, to some extent by patronage, but certainly by merit, the top appointment of Secretary to the Post Office. From that date until his death in 1836 he was in control of the Post Office, supervising the construction of the new headquarters and central sorting office near St. Paul's; extending rural posts where profitable; and regulating the Post Office's transition from the slower days of sailing packet and mounted postboys to the hurtling progress through the night of armed mail coaches on all the major post-roads and, later, into the new age of steampower over seas and by rail.

Without a university education and dependent upon patronage for his own post, Freeling was happy to oblige friends with positions for likely lads without the means of entering a profession. In his day this was the way appointments were made, with the requirement of an entrance examination no more than a gesture to the reforming zealots of the community. Freeling's ideal was the creation of a profitable postal service of surpassing excellence, and no aspect of it escaped his personal care, not even the welfare of a morose young clerk in the general office.

As in his formative years as a Postal Surveyor, Freeling wrote continually: official minutes and reports to the Postmaster General, the political head of the Post Office; missives berating the drunkard who had a habit of spending more time at the pub than delivering the mail, letters of condolence with the odd fiver to a letter-carrier's widow; and minutes insisting that prisoners had as much right to a regular postal service and fair postage as other citizens of the realm.[7] It was his

[7] Freeling's life and work remains unrecorded although there is adequate material for a significant biography. *Inland Mails* Post 98/4 POR is a selection

boast that he knew, personally, every letter-carrier in London, and no doubt he did. Of course, he was fortunate that he did not have to work with long-established and entrenched rules of governance. The Post Office was still small enough for one man to run and its traditions were to be of Freeling's own making. His administration was benign, authoritarian, and, occasionally, idiosyncratic. It was also remarkably effective.

In his minute recommending Trollope's appointment, Freeling had generously described him as being "well educated," but this was not evident in the lad's variable spelling and eccentric grammar. Trollope had acquired a smattering of Latin and Greek at Winchester and Harrow, but he was essentially self-educated and as unprepared for civil service as Charley Tudor in *The Three Clerks*. Nevertheless, in Trollope's day the survival of intelligence despite a public-school education was an accomplishment in its own right. In the *Autobiography* Trollope exaggerated his ignorance at this age in order to magnify his later success. As he had demonstrated in his commentary on Burke he was, like most young critics, pompous, opinionated, and obscure, but with the difference that marks originality from mere talent, he had already discovered his own voice. In his ability to measure received views by experience, Trollope was refining his perception to become the compass of honesty that set the course for his life and work. For example, he always affirmed that it was influence, not competence, which gained him a post in government.

In London, as at Harrow and Bruges, loneliness was as much self-imposed as actual. Genteel poverty is the worst poverty of all and Trollope felt that his place on the threshold of gentility was very precarious indeed. Gentlemen went to university like his brother Tom (even Henry had managed a term at Caius) or, better still, they inherited property and lived on an income not earned across a counter. It was socially acceptable for gentlemen to enter the public service after ca-

---

of Freeling's private letters. In them he is regularly found sending money from his own pocket to postmen's widows, including the widow of John Barrett, the last man hanged in England for any post-office crime. The execution took place February 13, 1832, and was opposed by Freeling.

Legal Structure

reers in the military or with a university degree, but now it was the lower middle class that was pushing its way into government departments and blurring the standards that separated a gentleman from the ordinary run of men. Trollope detested the monotony of his work and the tepid dissipations of his leisure hours. It was no fine thing to ape the heavy swell in a chophouse in Butcher Hall Lane, and he refused invitations from his mother's friends in London because he felt he had neither the manner nor the means to mix with gentlefolk.

The work at the General Post Office at St. Martin's-le-Grand was stupefyingly dull for the ungainly youth. He resented the servitude of regular hours from ten to four and complained about them as bitterly as any Manchester mill hand confined to his loom from dawn until dark. The right to leisure and the authority to regulate the hours of work was becoming a major distinction between the gentleman and the worker. At this stage of his career Trollope considered himself a drudge. Later he was to adjust his work to accommodate his passion for hunting, the confirmation of the rights of the gentleman over the duties of the civil servant.

After Waterloo it was the military officers who made excellent public servants.[8] These were men accustomed to discipline and not afraid to exact it from others. Trollope felt oppressed under Freeling, but when Colonel Maberley was appointed Secretary at Freeling's death in 1836, life became a rebellious misery for the young clerk. Maberley was a blustering autocrat who treated his clerks like batmen and his colleagues like junior officers. Trollope resented being treated like a slovenly conscript and felt that he had been forced back into the slavery of his school days without the physical shame of being flogged.

At Harrow and Winchester Trollope had found a refuge from the daily stumble through classical texts in a world of his imagining. Now at the Grand he sought the same means of escape from copying minutes and reports and writing official letters. There was a crucial difference. Under Maberley

[8] Oliver MacDonagh in *Early Victorian Government 1830-1870* (London, 1977), pp. 4-5, writes:

at the General Post Office he found only a slight variation from the brutal tedium of school. However, whereas at the latter he learned little, at the Grand he was taught to write English and write it well. The seven years in the general office before he accepted a position as a postal surveyor's clerk in Ireland were to provide the structure for all Trollope's fiction. It was the conjunction and the conflict between the official factual report and the realm of fiction that created the novels.

If Trollope had not sought and found a world of his own design, just as the Brontës had fashioned Angria and Gondal at Haworth, it is possible that he would have committed suicide or succumbed to that worse death in life which gives the mind to inaction and the body to sloth. "But, ah! how well I remember all the agonies of my young heart," he recalled as an old man, "how I considered whether I could not find my way up to the top of that college tower, and from thence put an end to everything."[9] And as a boy he had written in response to Burke's reasoned aphorisms that the pleasure of melancholy is a component of grief: "NO ONE CAN LIKE GRIEF." When Burke stated that no man would choose a life of perfect pleasure at the cost of a death in torment, Trollope's comment in the margin was terse and from the heart: "I would."[10] At school he had not been permitted to play cricket or squash rackets. His few friends were the despised solitaries like himself. Only the solace of his daydreams enabled him to survive.

These dreams were not the panting fantasies of sexual heroism that inspire most lads, but an ordered and genial society

---

The administration also inherited two material legacies from the revolutionary and Napoleonic wars. One was a considerable mass of statistical and social data and still more the skills and casts of mind which had been developed in these inquiries. The other was a great body of officer-veterans. These supplied a high proportion of the new officials of 1815-40; and their experience of working within a vast hierarchical and centralized organization patently prepared them for the new field work and the new form of executive corps.

[9] *An Autobiography*, ch. 1.

[10] Quoted in Susan L. Humphrey's "Trollope on the Sublime and Beautiful," p. 210.

in which he was neither famous nor heroic, simply bright and popular:

> I coveted popularity with a coveting which was almost mean. It seemed to me that there would be an Elysium in the intimacy of those very boys whom I was bound to hate because they hated me. Something of the disgrace of my schooldays has clung to me all through life.[11]

Trollope hungered to be liked by all, to exert the unconscious charm of a Phineas Finn or a Harry Annesley; instead the pariah of Harrow had become the misfit of the Post Office, writing letters, copying reports.

It was not Colonel Maberley who had projected the form and style of the reports that Trollope initially found as dull as Greek syntax, but Sir Francis Freeling, who had given him a job and then tried fruitlessly to befriend him. Freeling's work at the Post Office has been largely forgotten, obscured not by Maberley's "military governorship" that lasted eighteen years, but by the much-acclaimed success of Rowland Hill and his system of uniform penny postage of 1840. Yet it was Freeling who had already set the pattern the postal service was to follow throughout Hill's subsequent administration, even down to the end of the century and beyond—speed, efficiency, and a reasonable profit. It was the working of the internal bureaucracy of the Post Office that had most clearly reflected Freeling's determination to make it the most efficient, best regulated, and—of paramount importance in Freeling's day, when the posts were a major source of revenue—the most profitable department of government.

Freeling's industry had been prodigious. He did not publish, like his friend, Sir Henry Taylor at the Colonies. His life was the Post Office. One of Freeling's reforms was the change in the structure and style of all letters, minutes, and reports in the Post Office. Throughout his long term of office all submissions to the Postmaster General were written by Freeling himself, in his own hand. Some two hundred bound volumes

[11] *An Autobiography*, ch. 1.

and nearly seven hundred large boxes crammed with his original reports still remain in Post Office records as witness to his industry. Invaluable to the historian—whether his field is local, economic, social, or political history—these detailed records of Freeling's administration provide a unique and comprehensive picture of communications throughout the empire.

Priding himself on clarity and precision, Freeling would often recast a sentence in a more simplified form in his draft reports. He took pains to avoid all metaphors and official jargon. This was not the case throughout the rest of the civil service, where Trollope's Mr. Alphabet Precis could always be found mutilating the language:

> Mr. Precis' peculiar forte was a singular happiness in official phraseology. Much that he wrote would doubtless have been considered in the purlieus of Paternoster Row as ungrammatical, if not unintelligible; but according to the syntax of Downing Street, it was equal to Macaulay, and superior to Gibbon. He had frequently said to his intimate friends, that in official writing, style was everything; and of his writing it certainly did form a very prominent part. (*The Three Clerks*, ch. 6)

What satisfied the circumlocutory gentlemen of Downing Street would not have been tolerated by Freeling at the Grand.

Today a government report is often a verbose leviathan dragging its subordinate clauses to a dubious conclusion, but this was not generally the case with reports in the first half of the nineteenth century. Most reports were well written at this time, but an extraordinary variation in form and style can be found in different departments. Sir Henry Taylor's *The Statesman* had set out the main requirements of an official style. Having already shown the world his literary prowess with spangled images in the verse play *Philip van Artevelde*, Taylor could never be accused of wearing drab because he could not afford velvet. Taylor insisted that in official works

> The leading rule is to be content to be commonplace,—
> a rule which might be observed with advantage in other

writings but is distinctly applicable to these. Any point of style is to be avoided by a statesman which gives reason to suppose that he is thinking more of his credit than of his business.[12]

This was not a style that required fine flourishes and Attic salt. To write well at the Post Office meant to write plainly without any evidence of personality. Taylor had continued:

His style therefore, though it should have the correctness and clearness which education and practice impart to the writing of a man of good understanding, should not evince any solicitous precision beyond what may be due to exactitude in the subject-matter, much less any ambition of argument for its own sake, and less still of ornament or pungency in like manner gratuitous.[13]

As one might guess from this sentence, Taylor did not always himself conform to these requirements for the commonplace and purely correct, but Freeling did. Being in control of the Post Office, he had the opportunity to impose both style and method upon his subordinates, who learned to write like Freeling or found another occupation.

Simplicity of utterance is apparent in Freeling's earliest reports, but their structure begins to change after 1823 when the influence of legal form can be discerned. It was at this time that Freeling came to know the young barrister and legal writer, John Frederick Archbold. Like Freeling, Archbold was a bibliophile and attended the Roxburgh Club, which Freeling had helped to establish at St. Alban's in 1812. Unlike many advocates writing hard lawyer's law for their peers, Archbold sought a wider audience and found it among the growing numbers of civil servants. His first work before being called to the bar from Lincoln's Inn in 1814 was a new edition of Blackstone's *Commentaries on the Laws of England*.[14] Arch-

---

[12] "Of Official Style," *The Statesman* (London, 1836), p. 39.
[13] *Ibid.*, p. 40.
[14] *Commentaries on the Laws of England, In Four Books*, Sir William Blackstone, notes and additions by Edward Christian, analyses and an epitome of the whole work, John Frederick Archbold (London, 1811).

bold's preface defines his purpose of making "the study of the law more pleasing and less difficult,"[15] in accord with Blackstone's own statement from his Vinerian lecture at Oxford "On the Study of the Law:

> For I think it an undeniable position, that a competent knowledge of the laws of that society, in which we live, is the proper accomplishment of every gentleman and scholar; an highly useful, I had almost said essential, part of liberal and polite education.[16]

A knowledge of the law was regarded as an important part of a gentleman's general education in the eighteenth century, when the gentry regularly undertook legal duties that were later appropriated by lawyers. Douglas Hay has argued in "Property, Authority and the Criminal Law" that the English gentry were confirmed in their authority by their control of the criminal law.[17] The country gentleman knew that it was as much his duty to serve as a magistrate as it was to preserve foxes. Country libraries of this period are distinguished by the considerable number of legal works on their shelves, and Blackstone was simply confirming common practice in his statement at Oxford. Blackstone and the Bible protected a man from the dangers of this world and the fears of the next.

Blackstone's implied rebuke in the Vinerian lecture was to those who regarded the classics as more valuable than the law in the making of a gentleman. Law for Blackstone was the cement that bonded the innate infirmities and fears of mankind into an ordered society.[18] The classics were a mere social or-

---

[15] The complete passage, p. iii, from Archbold's preface reads:
Still however, in my opinion, there remained much to be done; not perhaps in rendering the work more complete, but in attaining that which seems to have been the principal object of the learned author of the Commentaries in their first publication,—the rendering of the study of the law more pleasing and less difficult to the student.
[16] *Ibid.*, p. 3.
[17] *Albion's Fatal Tree*, New York, 1975, pp. 49-53.
[18] But, though society had not its formal beginning from any convention of individuals, actuated by their wants and their fears, yet it is the *sense* of their weakness and imperfection that *keeps* mankind together, that

Legal Structure

nament. In the nineteenth century Blackstone enjoyed a lesser regard because of the efforts of the legal profession to protect itself from amateurs, particularly the civil servants who seemed bent on being more lawyerlike than the lawyers. To many lawyers it was clear that the civil servants were presumptuously attempting to assume the legal function in government that the gentry enjoyed in the country.

Freeling prided himself on his knowledge of the law and Archbold's many works were in his library. The most valuable for his purposes at this time was Archbold's digest of the law relating to pleading and evidence which sets out the form of a declaration, published in 1821.[19] It was to remain Archbold's most famous work. In the preface Archbold announced that he was not going to employ arcane terms intelligible only to the initiate, rather: "The style in which the Work is written, will be found plain, simple and unadorned."[20] Throughout the discussion of the form that a declaration should take, Archbold affirmed that "general words are sufficient." He did not avoid Latin but he did not use it where English words would suffice. To this day Post Office reports follow the requirements of Archbold's declaration: three parts, a Commencement, the Statement of the Cause of Action—and the Conclusion.[21] Outlining the form of the Commencement,

---

demonstrates the necessity of this union, and that therefore is the solid and natural foundation, as well as the cement, of civil society.
Commentaries, "Of the Nature of Laws in General," p. 43.

[19] *A Digest of the Law Relative to Pleading and Evidence in Actions Real, Personal and Mixed.* (London, 1821.)

[20] *Ibid.*, p. viii.

[21] *Ibid.*, p. 71. Trollope follows the form of the declaration, now also known as a complaint, and its terminology in *Orley Farm*. The declaration was the first of the pleadings, a series of alternate responses intended as Archbold shows, to inform the court of the precise issue in dispute. Put in motion by the plaintiff, the declaration stated the proper form of action (the remedy for the plaintiff's alleged wrong: breach of contract, debt, trespass, as the case might be), the cause of action (setting out in detail the facts that had occurred which were legally sufficient to support the case for the plaintiff), and a conclusion (affirming the injury sustained by the plaintiff as a result of the defendant's conduct and claiming, in consequence, satisfaction).

This was followed by the defendant's reply. Other rejoinders and counter-

Archbold emphasized the particular need to state "the parties' names, the mode in which the defendant has been brought before the court and the form of action adopted."[22] His setting out the precise enumeration of admissible facts was invaluable to a man like Freeling who found himself continually at odds with local authorities over municipal rights. Archbold provided a model which could be reproduced in a report to give the appearance of authority and responsibility, and might provide a defense against legal action. Abstract speculation had no part in this. The department was increasingly called upon to establish new post offices or lines of posts, even where these seemed neither workable nor profitable. It had to deal with differing tariff rates constantly under challenge. It had to protect mail from robbery within England and overseas, and to prevent illegal infringements of the Post Office's monopoly. There was no room for theory in these multiple tasks. Although no disciple of Bentham, Freeling was a practicing utilitarian for whom Archbold's practical manual confirmed the everyday conduct of business.

The substance of Archbold's advice was that the "essential qualities of a statement of the cause of action in a declaration are, that it be certain, positive, and true."[23] It was his rule that

---

rejoinders might follow until disclosure of the exact issue of fact between the parties. At the ensuing trial the burden would fall upon both parties to introduce evidence to prove the facts each had alleged in the pleadings. *Archbold*, pp. 14, 21-24, 79, 81-82, 149-150, 191, 310-312, 329. A great number of Archbold's cited cases read like Trollopian plots, but this coincidence is accidental: a general result of the formal requirements of the declaration and the pleadings as well as the common subject matter—property, inheritance, money and marriage.

[22] *Ibid.*, p. 79. Trollope developed a passion for accurate facts. In his introduction to *The Commentaries of Caesar* (London, 1870), p. 3, he stated his faith in the authority of facts:

It is no doubt that if we did but know the facts correctly, we could refer back every political and social condition of the present day to the remotest period of man's existence; but the interest fails us when the facts become doubtful, and when the mind begins to fear that history is mixed with romance.

[23] *Archbold*, p. 98. One has only to open the pages of his work to appreciate the value of this advice, to discern the extraordinary complexity and rigor

the parties, the place, and the time be clearly set out, and that the summing-up should indicate a precise line of action. This form, and Archbold's injunction that "general words are sufficient," prescribed the mode for everything written in the Post Office, and remained so long after Freeling's death because nothing better could be found to replace it.

Freeling's adaptation of the declaration to the report did not require an ingenious manipulation of form. As Blackstone had defined it, the declaration was the most narrative, and occasionally discursive, legal form capable of incorporating both the charge against the defendant and the plaintiff's probable case.[24] If a legal model had been sought to serve the purposes of a bureaucratic report, nothing would have come more readily to mind than the declaration. The possibility for its further transference by Trollope to the structure of his novels is explicit in Blackstone's own definition of the form: "The first of these [the pleadings] is the *declaration, narratio* or *count*, antiently called the *tale*. . . ."[25] And what had once been known as the tale was to become the novel with Trollope.

Copying letters, minutes, and reports at the General Post Office demanded a disciplined, logical, and limited form of writing that served its purpose. Day after day Trollope set his pen to it, returning to his lodgings at night to write the journal

---

of common-law pleading. The slightest error in a statement of fact in the declaration or other pleadings could lead to irretrievable results such as the loss of the plaintiff's case in the pleadings or even at the trial, or a judgment against the defendant without submission of the issues to a jury. *Ibid.*, pp. 96, 318-320.

[24] This declaration always concludes with these words, "and thereupon he brings *suit*, &c." "*inde producit sectam, &c.*" By which words, *suit* or *secta, (a sequendo)* were antiently understood the witnesses or followers of the plaintiff. For in former times the law would not put the defendant to the trouble of answering the charge, till the plaintiff had made out at least a probable case. But the actual production of the *suit*, the *secta*, or followers, is now antiquated; and hath been totally disused, at least ever since the reign of Edward the third, though the form of it still continues. *Commentaries on the Laws of England*, Book the Third Tenth Edition, London, 1787, p. 295.

[25] *Ibid.*, p. 293.

which he said he kept until he was twenty-five. Later, in 1870 he read over those volumes

> and, with many blushes, destroyed them. They convicted me of folly, ignorance, indiscretion, idleness, and conceit. But they had habituated me to the rapid use of pen and ink, and taught me how to express myself with facility.[26]

Trollope neglected to mention the hours spent every day writing in accord with the style and to the form required of the Post Office. The journal may well have been indiscreet, passionate, and full of extravagant fancies: the writing at the Post Office was the very antithesis of this—"certain, positive and true." These two literary muses were to direct Trollope throughout his life: the imagination that created a society after its own desire, and the genius of official order that presided over every desk at the Grand. Trollope continued to dream, but his dreams became ordered and sequential even as he chafed under the regimen of daily work:

> For weeks, for months, if I remember rightly, from year to year, I would carry on the same tale, binding myself down to certain laws, to certain proportions, and proprieties and unities. Nothing impossible was ever introduced,—nor even anything which, from outward circumstances, would seem to be violently improbable.[27]

This is not the occasion to embark on a discussion of genre criticism but a few tentative points should be made. A legal form resembles a literary genre in its definition of the boundaries of human experience, for although its requirements are less flexible and its content more uniform, there is a similarity in its relationship to experience as a kind of geography that can be charted and defined. The morphology of literary kinds is a disputed and inexact area of scholarship; still, there is general agreement that the traditional genres are not the arbitrary creation of critics with a passion for stuffing literature into pigeon-holes. Genres do, in effect, refer to literary forms

[26] *An Autobiography*, ch. 3.   [27] *Ibid.*

Legal Structure

and nonliterary phenomena, as Northrop Frye has shown us. Because life is so often tragic we respond to certain emotions in tragedy whether the form is that of prose or verse, novel or drama. We do not expect to weep when contemplating a comedy—there is a general agreement that certain moods and emotions and not others will be generated by a work. However, a legal form works within a more rigid boundary and its relationship to experience is more exact. The greenest lawyer would not confuse a lease for a last will and testament. Legal writing can be graceful and lucid but it moves within defined precedents. Archbold's declaration was Aristotelian in form, and Trollope's description of his "castle in the air" reflects both Archbold and Aristotle. Unity, proportion, and propriety governed by probable impossibilities rather than improbable possibilities are the measure of his dreams.[28]

Yet the lawyer is daily confronted with improbable possibilities: they are unlikely facts which must be accepted and then interpreted in accordance with the legal tradition. Only the novelist can make reality itself subservient to art. The lawyer cannot hope to attain this degree of artistic congruity in his work. Responding to the creator of fiction the lawyer would state that if the law is an ass it is because it expresses the will of a society of donkeys. Real events are often absurd but they must be made to conform to the requirements of a legal method based on the assumption of common sense and reason. All too often the lawyer is confronted by the disjunction between real content and legal form in which one seems designed to confound the other, as though a troupe of painted clowns had arrived to play Hamlet. Moving an action from one class to another may be a partial solution to the problem, but if it is occasionally permitted the lawyer to make a tragicomedy of his tragedy in court he cannot alter the evidence. The lawyer may be forgiven a certain sour rejoinder to critics who rail against the law's "codeless myriad of precedent" when he contemplates the irrational gyrations and inconsequential accidents that constitute everyday life. Lost wills,

[28] *Poetics*, XXIV:10.

lotteries, and fortuitous deaths are deplored in the Victorian novel as narrative and stylistic contrivances, but they crowd the courts and perplex the lawyer who has to coax and bully them into some semblance of legal form. Unlike the artist who can always select what he wants from the real and imaginary world, the lawyer is challenged by events which have then to be interpreted by the rules of evidence and precedent.

Law reflects the necessary compromises of society but art is largely comprehended by an aesthetic of the ideal. Nevertheless, Archbold as a contender against the surging emotions of the young Anthony Trollope was a worthy opponent. Certainly it permitted a zealous public servant and a novelist to exist in the same person. There was to be argument and often violent controversy between the two, but the legal form allowed Trollope to suppress and exclude certain parts of his own experience, whereas his imagination and dreaming gave the legal structure of the novels an extraordinary tension and vigor.

Implicit in Freeling's version of Archbold's declaration is the reliance upon a complete and honest rendering of the evidence. Freeling was not an opinionated man, and his reports reveal the subject, not the mind and art of the enquirer. Trollope was never able to acquire the temperate rationality of his employer, nonetheless he did try to make reason the arbiter of his fiction in the person of his reader—a reasonable man who could be relied upon to bring in a just verdict from the given facts. Even as a legal declaration and Freeling's reports are open-ended, looking to an expected act beyond the stated conclusion, so Trollope's novels echo to one phrase and appeal: "The reader must judge for himself." Freeling's reports were meant to be read by reasonable men; Trollope's novels relied upon the judgment of reasonable readers.

Of course it can be maintained that Archbold was misused by civil servants like Freeling, who so often found himself at odds with county clerks and local magistrates as the Post Office extended its services. There was a certain disdain in legal circles for a man who spent so much of his life educating those who should have used their time more wisely in con-

Legal Structure

sultation with a good solicitor. But Archbold was always a Blackstonian, believing that no person could play a responsible part in society without some knowledge of the law. He was never appointed to the bench although his reputation as a special pleader stood high and his legal writings were described by Holdsworth as "voluminous." His style was not commended by contemporary jurists, who suspected that his readers were the very men so often in contention with them. Holdsworth dismissed Archbold's *Pleading* as one would a useful grammar: "it is a severely practical book. But it is clear, well arranged, terse and complete."[29] It was precisely those qualities which made it so valuable to Freeling and his successors, who continued to use the form of the declaration in their reports even when they were no longer aware of its source.

At this early period of his literary career Trollope was being disciplined by a form of writing which he at first found tedious but later a source of great satisfaction and pride. He regarded himself not simply as a novelist but also as a writer of fine reports. Official writing was to influence the structure of his novels just as legal modes of examination and evidence came to define his narrative art. It has always been overlooked that Trollope wrote as much for the Post Office as he did for his reading public. In his *Autobiography* he maintained that his reports aroused official disfavor by their originality, but there is no evidence of this. He wrote that:

> Through my whole official life I did my best to improve the style of official writing. I have written, I should think some thousands of reports,—many of them necessarily very long; some few in which a spark of indignation or a slight glow of pathos might find an entrance. I have taken infinite pains with these reports, habituating myself always to write them in the form in which they should be sent,—without a copy. It is by writing thus that a man can throw on to his paper the exact feeling with which

---

[29] Sir William Holdsworth, *A History of English Law*, ed. A. C. Goodhart and H. G. Hanbury, vol. XIII, p. 465.

his mind is impressed at the moment. . . . I had learned so to write my reports that they who read them should know what it was that I meant for them to understand. But I do not think that they were regarded with favour. I have heard horror expressed because the old forms were disregarded and language used which had no savour of red-tape.[30]

In the succeeding passage, with all the honesty of his own contradictions Trollope finds himself unable to supply a single instance of a report's being received with disfavor. Instead, he relates the occasions when his correspondence was regarded as offensive and objectionable. If Trollope had written his letters to Rowland Hill with the same official discretion that governed his reports it is unlikely that he would have found the years before his retirement from the Post Office in 1867 quite so contentious.

Trollope's reports are superb examples of the Archbold-Freeling style—laconic, informed, and objective. He leaves us with the impression that he was the rational spirit of reform in all matters stylistic at the Post Office, as much a master of the official report as Alaric Tudor in *The Three Clerks*. It is not unknown for the memory to gild the dross of past ac-

---

[30] *An Autobiography*, ch. 8. The most readable of Trollope's reports are those filed under *Packet Minutes* in Post Office Records; viz., Conveyance of Indian Mails through Egypt Port, Pkt. 10041/1858. Ref. Post 29. 86. Proposals for improvement of West Indies mail service. Pkt. 204L/1860. 93. Transfer of Jamaican Post Office to local control. Pkt. 531L/1860. 96. Malta Post Office. Report. Pkt. 860M/1861. Transit rates in British closed mails sent across Panama Isthmus, Pkt. 1105M/1861. Bags substituted for boxes for Indian, etc., reports. Pkt. 256 R/1866. 126. Mission to U.S.A. in connection with negotiation of Postal Convention Pkt. 949T/1868. 152. The most interesting of the internal reports is 685 K/1814, Minute file 49A of England which sets out Trollope's reasons for setting up letter boxes at St. Helier in Guernsey. The cause is given in the first lines: "There is at present no receiving office at St. Helier, and persons living in the distant parts of the town have to send nearly a mile to the principal office." The report then continues with the plan in France of fitting up letter boxes at the roadside, it examines the practical worth of this scheme and, in the conclusion, recommends its adoption in Guernsey.

tions—although Trollope was more honest than most in this respect. A successful writer generally insists upon the singularity of his work. No writer has ever blushed to own the influence of Homer or Shakespeare. Bulwer-Lytton was always happy to pay homage to Virgil and Pindar in his novels when Sterne and Fielding would have been more appropriate.[31] But no creative writer is likely to avow indebtedness to an official report and a legal handbook. What Trollope did not observe, and would not have accepted if he had, was the remarkable uniformity in the surveyors' reports at this time. By 1860 surveyors like Beaufort, Creswell, Milliken, and Godby, who were responsible for the management of postal services in their areas, were writing like Trollope. Indeed, everyone within the Post Office, including Trollope, was following the Freeling style.

Particularity of detail is essential in a legal declaration and Freeling's reports were never deficient in this respect. Throughout his *Pleading* Archbold stresses the need for specificity; the name of the plaintiff must be correctly stated, the relationships between the parties to the action stated, and the time and place of the action defined exactly. At first this demand for minutiae made Trollope feel like a Gulliver tied to the ground with red tape. Yet his later novels, often dictated, were to follow the legal form more closely than his earlier works and their style was as "plain, simple and unadorned"

---

[31] It is also the convention for critics to locate a source of influence upon a writer in literary works. Thus, Robert Tracy in observing the analogical nature of Trollope's plots:

> In the more complex novels, those of multiple plot, Trollope is exploiting structural devices he apparently found in the plays of the Elizabethan and Jacobean dramatists, which are often constructed with double or multiple plots, and were well represented in Trollope's library. They were his favorite reading during the seventies, when he left 257 of them carefully annotated.

Trollope's Later Novels, Berkeley, 1978, pp. 9-10. Trollope's collection of Elizabethan and Jacobean dramas is held by the Folger Library in Washington. His interest in character and motive can be observed from the annotations, however the actual construction of the plots clearly does not seem to have interested him.

as Archbold and Freeling would have wished. The Post Office report was to shape Trollope's writing without his ever being consciously aware of its influence. He admitted that he learned to write letters well at the Grand and was not found remiss in copying minutes and reports, but it was drudgery, and his laziness and temper brought him to the point of dismissal on more than one occasion. In 1840 his name led the list of indolent clerks "through whose neglect the accompanying cases of increased expenditure have been withheld from the Accountant General."[32] Notwithstanding the displeasure of his superiors and his own rankling aversion to the work, Trollope retained his post at the Grand. Debt and embarrassment darkened his life and there seemed less chance of success than when he struggled alone down muddy lanes to school. Yet those seven years were to discipline and train the young writer. His dreams were no longer reveries but sequential stories. His mind grew more accustomed to detail as Freeling's reports began to design the architecture of his visions. Hope for Anthony Trollope came in the form of exile.

The following chapters will suggest ways in which legal forms and legal reasoning serve to shape and inform Trollope's published work. Although this influence operated at the level both of language and of structure, Trollope developed an antipathy for the professional lawyer and allowed his fictional world to be governed by an ethic wholly different from that which the law was assumed to defend. His was a vision of a social order in which individuals knew success or failure as a result of free decisions reached in circumstances unaffected by external contingencies. This was not evident in his travel books, where Trollope presented objective analysis of the societies he visited, but even here, as in the actions of his fictional characters, the final judgment lay with the reader. Trollope's own character and ideals as implied by his autobiography and revealed by his associations with others as well as by his novels, betrayed an insecurity for which the popular acclaim

[32] Minute signed by I. Campbell, 10 November 1840. Trollope was cited for three instances of neglect, the others only once. 685 K/1814 File 49A of England POR.

enjoyed by some of his heroes served as anodyne. Using legal language for his own ends, he structured his plots round single and multiple transactions initially concerning property and marriage and then extending into the institutional roles his characters were obliged to play.

Moreover, there came to be an intimate connection between the structure of the declaration and the antiphonal development of Trollope's typical plots, for they, like the trial that followed the pleadings are spun from testimonial voices that alternately carry forward the burden of proof with respect to the evidence offered to prove or disprove the facts alleged or "stated" in the declaration.[33] Blackstone's ancient tale lived on to become the Trollopian novel.

[33] I owe much to Gertrude Leighton of Bryn Mawr College for clarifying this point.

Chapter II

Order and Vision

After he left London, Trollope's work for the Post Office deepened his antagonism against lawyers while strengthening that lay version of the legal mind the professionals themselves detested. His personal insecurity can be detected both in his official relations with his inferiors and his private encounters in club, drawing room and hunting field. These were the experiences that led him to formulate a fictional world very different from that in which the lawyer made his calling the guarantee of social order. It was a world where conservative acceptance of convention was justified by a different kind of equity. This private vision was imbued with a rationality that discounted the accidental and unforeseen, and Trollope felt obliged to depict it in a circumscribed mode, imposing order by enumeration.

It was Ireland which gave Trollope a taste for facts at the same time that it permitted him to exercise the authority he had always resented. In debt, sullen and suffering from poor health, with a number of unsatisfactory romances behind him, Trollope seized the opportunity to fill the post as surveyor's clerk at Banagher, King's County, in August 1841. The salary was "one hundred pounds a year, with an additional fifteen shillings a day for every day spent away from the surveyor's base and sixpence for every mile travelled on postal business."[1] This could mean around four hundred a year, a very handsome income indeed, particularly in Ireland, provided a man were prepared to spend the greater part of his days on foot or

---
[1] James Pope Hennessy, *Anthony Trollope* (Boston, 1972), p. 70.

horseback. Of course, a post in Ireland was rather like choosing voluntary exile in Siberia, but there was no alternative for Trollope. Colonel Maberley disliked him as much as Trollope hated his work at the Grand. It was no more than a choice between Ireland or dismissal. Everyone predicted ruin, even Trollope's family solicitor, who lent him two hundred pounds to clear his debts before he could leave London. Colonel Maberley attempted to insure an appropriate reception for Trollope by sending an accompanying letter stressing Trollope's shortcomings and misdoings. At Banagher, the writer of reports and the dreamer of ordered visions commenced the dialogue that took the form of the subsequent novels.

No department of government at this time was more assiduous than the Post Office in its emphasis on the systematic collection and assessment of numerical facts. Mail routes had to be precisely measured and speed of delivery was made the object of every post. There could no longer be the casual arrangements of the old country service when every great house would receive a post daily and a neighboring village seldom or not at all. Postmen had to be given regular runs and reasonable hours. They had to be made sober, industrious civil servants, not itinerant porters. There was a demon at the elbow of every surveyor urging him to make his mail service the fastest in the kingdom, and no one drove his messengers with more righteous ferocity than Trollope.

For the first time in his life Trollope found himself in authority, no longer the butt of bullies but with a chance to do a little bullying himself. There is no evidence that he ever restrained himself. The miserable lad who had slunk to school in grime and patches was now an official who could berate the idle and call upon every postmaster in the area to open his books. If the surveyor at Banagher had not been so reluctant to travel, Trollope would not have been able to shout and bluster his way around the country while still only a clerk. His new-found energy, his assiduity in compiling and writing his own reports made his promotion inevitable.

One reason for the Post Office's astonishing efficiency at this time was the power given to the local surveyors. Within their districts the surveyors were like subordinate secretaries, with the right to hire and dismiss, subject to appeal. The surveyor kept his own order book set out in regulation form in which all the business of the district was recorded in the same manner as at the General Post Office. The surveyors Foxall and Spofforth were both approving in 1952 of the Banagher Order Book of 1850 in which Trollope himself set out the requirements for new local services and dealt with disciplinary cases. They noted almost in passing that "All communications from the Surveyor to the Postmaster were of a strictly formal construction."[2] After seven years at the Grand, the Freeling mode was second nature to Trollope. In the *Autobiography* he noted that he had learned to write a report without the need for a rough draft, although accuracy and speed had been achieved only at the cost of "infinite pains." It was not a tyro or an imitator of his mother's style who later wrote his first novel, but a writer who had mastered a literary form that could unconsciously provide an effective structure for the novel.

Trollope was regarded with less than affection by those in his employ. His literary and social contemporaries enjoyed a testy, loyal, and noisy friend in Trollope: the postmen who served under him as clerk and later surveyor found him a tyrant, shouting his orders, smashing open desks and threatening instant dismissal for insubordination. In his own words Trollope seems a parody of the officious surveyor Mr. Cochrane whom Flora Thompson describes in *Lark Rise to Candleford*, who arrived to inspect Miss Lane's post office in "a top-hat and an immaculate morning suit." It is not an appealing picture, but it is the logical progression of menial to master. The journal of the General Post Office, *Blackfriars* and later *St. Martin's-le-Grand*, contains many reminiscences of postmen and some women who remembered Anthony Trollope, the surveyor. The boy whose only boast at school was that he had been "flogged oftener than any human being

[2] J. T. Foxall, and A. O. Spofford, O.B.E., *Monarchs of all they Surveyed* (London, 1952), p. 32.

alive"³ was now a terror to rural postmen. J. G. Uren's account of Trollope is typical of many:

> It was at Falmouth I made the acquaintance of the late Mr. Anthony Trollope. He had been sent into Cornwall, I think in 1849 or 1850, to "revise the Rural Posts" a task about as easy for a stranger in those days as to lay out a post road on the Upper Congo. I remember his stalking into the office, booted and spurred, much to the consternation of the maiden lady in charge. He seemed to us then the very incarnation of a martinet, though I have since heard that he really was a kind-hearted man, and that this was the way he had of showing it. At any rate, he frightened the unfortunate rural messenger, whose walk he was about to test, almost out of his wits.⁴

The stories never vary: bluster and shouting, stamping and roaring, with a half-hearted admission by the unfortunate recorder of the incident that the man may not have been as rough as he seemed. Thus Robert McFerran, who later became mayor of Hurley in Wisconsin, recalled his encounter with Trollope in Ballycarry:

> On the outskirts of the village, his carriage passed a young boy who was carrying a mail bag. Trollope ordered the carriage to stop and, leaning out, asked to see the contents of the bag, but the boy refused, and, taking to his heels, fled through the fields, pursued by Trollope. Having caught the boy, he enquired breathlessly, "You young rascal, why didn't you give me the bag in the first place?" The boy, Robert McFerran, answered simply, "Because I didn't know who you were." Trollope, highly pleased with this answer, saw to it that Robert was commended for his action.⁵

---

³ *An Autobiography*, ch. 1.
⁴ J. G. Uren, "My Early Recollections of the Post Office in the West of England," *Blackfriars* IX (July to December 1889), 157-158.
⁵ Avy Dowlin, *Ballycarry in Olden Days*, Belfast, 1963, p. 73.

Punctilious attention to duty and immediate information were what Trollope wanted, and he delighted in an unheralded inspection of a country post office clad in his hunting pink and brandishing his riding crop. He learned to interrogate his trembling postmen with all the rigor of Mr. Chaffanbrass putting Undy Scott through his paces in *The Three Clerks*. It is with some relish that Uren records the one instance to his knowledge when Trollope was sent packing. The postmistress at Penzance, Miss Ellen Swain, told Trollope that he was "no gentleman" and later described him as "a cross between a country farmer and a whipper-in."[6] Trollope's status as a gentleman was never questioned in Ireland, where class distinctions were felt to be inherently English and the whole concept of the gentleman extended from the aristocracy to the man who could ride well, hold his liquor, and carry his debts with insouciance. It was a different matter altogether in England, where Trollope was regarded as something less than a perfect gentleman by others beside a local postmistress. Inevitably it is the servant who determines the respect to be paid the master. Since Trollope never possessed the genial assurance of Freeling that won him the affection and regard of his staff, he exacted deference by the traditional means of the school bully. He enjoyed catching out the postman in a defection of his duty or threatening the postmaster with instant dismissal. Authority for Trollope was always compensation for his uneasy sense of social identity. He both resented it and rejoiced in being known as the most authoritarian of all the surveyors.

He came to accept cruelty as part of his own nature and that of humanity in general. In *The Three Clerks*, the most autobiographical of all his novels, he observed that: "Mankind in general take pleasure in cruelty, though those who are civilized abstain from it in principle" (ch. 38). To those who complained about the grinding hours of service, walking country roads in all weather, Trollope would always reply that he had walked farther and at an average of six miles an hour,

[6] *Ibid.*, p. 158.

Order and Vision

which was more than the Post Office demanded of any of its messengers.[7] As he wrote in his *Autobiography*:

> Our law was that a man should not be required to walk more than sixteen miles a day. Had the work to be done been all on a measured road, there would have been no need for doubt as to the distances. But my letter-carriers went here and there across the fields. It was my special delight to take them by all short cuts; and as I measured on horseback the shortcuts which they would have to make on foot, perhaps I was sometimes a little unjust to them. (ch. 5)

He could always justify the pain of others by boasting that he had suffered more himself. And this singular bully could then identify with his victim and often send a gift afterward to a man he had intimidated and threatened.[8]

If the Post Office required facts then he would be a Gradgrind of surveyors, noting more, observing more, always ready with submissions for an improved service. It was not his introduction of the first post boxes at St. Helier which was remarkable but the enquiry and research that prompted his report to the secretary.[9] He had obviously learned how to read and assess reports on foreign mail services, particularly

---

[7] A postmaster recalled in 1904:
I was attached to a country office in South Wales when he strode in one day, fresh from a tramp over the heather, just as Professor Wilson—Christopher North—was wont to do in surprising his students. No other description could well be applied to the gait of Trollope. About the first remark he made was, "I have walked up from Cardiff"—a distance of 24 miles. "Any hotels here; which is the best?" I directed him; and, as he marched out, still at a six-mile-an-hour stride, he said, "back soon, going to have a raw beef steak." He left me pondering over his powerful build, his physical go, and his reference to the "underdone." . . .
St. Martin's-le-Grand, October 1904, pp. 453-454.

[8] "I had the honour of serving under Anthony Trollope, then surveyor of the Northern District. He was brusque in manner, certainly, but he had a kind heart . . . he was held out to the juniors in the service as a terror." R. S. Smyth, "The Provincial Service Fifty Years Ago," *St. Martin's-le-Grand*, October 1903, p. 374.

[9] Minute file 49A of England, 685 K/1814. POR.

those in France where letter boxes had just been introduced. He then interviewed the local Guernsey folk, making precise notes on how far they had to walk to post a letter. His accuracy was not questioned in the light of the evidence he presented.

He prided himself on his skill in examining recalcitrant postmasters, eliciting the truth by means of brusque interrogation and threats. It was not a lawyer's mode of examination but it was legalistic and it assumed an important function in the dialogue of the novels. In his old age he retained the same instinctive love of enquiry. On a trip to Iceland in 1878 he wrote of the postmaster at Faroes: "I should have liked to ask this gentleman what was his salary, and what his duties, and whether there ever came an inspector from the head office in Denmark to look after him."[10] Clearly Trollope had cast himself in that role of Danish chief inspector. Surveyors were trained to question and examine and there were few parts of his employment that he enjoyed more. Long after his reports had been shelved at the Post Office he continued the same mode of ascertaining facts. His reports were accurate: his novels were sustained by a continuing, often discreet, system of evidence.

Trollope's detestation of authority remained even as he chivvied his postmen on their country walks. Rank and bureaucracy tasted of the rod to him and he rejoiced in belittling his superiors and the service although he sought to embody its very spirit. There is seldom any real harmony in the human personality, and Trollope's character was more paradoxical and incongruent than most. A very shrewd old woman, Susan Gay, recalled the Trollope she remembered as a girl:

> No more repose was left in the house when he awoke in the morning. Doors slammed, footsteps resounded, and a general whirlwind arose as he came to and returned from his bath, or walked out in the garden, and from that time until nightfall he was as busy as a man could be. He had a scorn of everything in the way of pretension—even of justice to time-honoured institutions—and

---

[10] *How the "Mastiffs" Went to Iceland* (London, 1878), p. 14.

slurred over his family history and belittled "the service" right royally. "Post-Office"—he always omitted the "General" or departmental style and title—he would write with a little "p" and a little "o" as though it were a village sub-office retailing stamps with tobacco and onions. . . .[11]

This was the same man who could write in 1865 to an unhappy young postman who wanted to leave and find another job, that it was necessary "to teach yourself not to regard the service with dissatisfaction."[12]

Trollope had become the model surveyor. He worked in Ireland and England and made his first foreign trip on Post Office business to Egypt in 1858. The minutes and reports he sent back to the Post Office were formal, detailing the difficulties in securing an agreement with the Viceroy of Egypt that would enable the mails to go from Cairo to the Red Sea in a possible eighteen hours. Trollope not only tested the speed at which a camel could travel by riding one for long distances himself, he also sent covert letters back to the Grand accusing the agent of the Peninsular and Oriental Company of deliberately trying to prevent the rapid transit of the mail.[13] These accusations were not made part of the report—as facts they were unproven and therefore not admissible evidence. The report had to withstand scrutiny and examination, and could not contain anything supposititious. There was clearly so much Trollope would have liked to say about the P. and O. but the report was inviolate. He chafed against its restrictions but he abided by them, having taught himself not to regard them with express dissatisfaction.

The negotiations over the Indian Mail Service in 1858 were the first of many Trollope undertook for the Post Office, culminating in the Postal Convention of 1868 arranged by Trollope between the United States and the General Post Office

---

[11] *Old Falmouth: the Story of the Town from the Days of the Killigrews to the Earliest Part of the Nineteenth Century* (London, 1903), pp. 216-217.
[12] "The Provincial Service Fifty Years Ago," p. 374.
[13] Pkt. 84.1. regd Nos. 1012/58 3. 928/58. POR.

in the year after his retirement. The travel books often written in consequence of these duties would incorporate material that could never be permitted in a report. So close was the relationship between the report, the travel book, and the novel that Trollope blended the three forms in *The Bertrams*, in which his Egyptian experience provided a chapter.

It was not the restriction on evidence and interpretation which irritated Trollope in the Post Office report so much as his belief that it could not encompass the full reality of a situation. He was convinced that the legal model of presentation not only restricted the truth, it distorted it. Trollope was not the first to accuse the lawyer of defending the law at the expense of truth. Others have made the charge more reasonably, few with so much passion. In *The New Zealander*, Trollope's unpublished response to Carlyle's *Latter-Day Pamphlets*, the novelist challenged the lawyer, personified as Mr. Allwinde. Trollope proposes a hypothetical case of murder and then sets himself against Allwinde, whose major achievement is to confuse a bewildered witness into mistaking his right hand for his left. Trollope as the protagonist of truth and common sense is all for summary justice. The novelist knows the murderer is guilty since he has created the character and the crime, but the lawyer who is restricted to reality has to prove the murderer's guilt by means that Trollope finds devious and theatrical. Trollope accuses the lawyer of making inept fictions and cruel sport at the expense of a living man. And still there was a part of him that warmed to the sport and applauded the hunter:

> A spectator unaccustomed to such scenes cannot but think that the wretched man upon whose brow drops of agony are standing is the real criminal. The judge frowns at him from his bushy eyebrows, and with thick hoarse voice bids him beware of himself. Mr. Allwinde tosses him to and fro and turns him in and out, till he hardly knows himself whether or not he be the perjured villain that they are calling him. The jury look at him uncomfortably and whisper among themselves all but audibly.

Order and Vision

> The younger bar watch the scene with laughing eyes and ears erect; it is to them a treat as much as a battle of rats in which the famous dog Badger is backed to kill his twenty rats in the hour.[14]

It is difficult for Trollope to conceal the admiration in this vociferous denigration.

Trollope's own knowledge of the law was acquired in county courts and from the daily procedure of preparing and writing reports. Like most civil servants he regarded himself as a model of probity and fair dealing, quite capable of ordering the troubled affairs of society, whereas lawyers dealt in evasion when not actually engaged in falsification. As he wrote in *The New Zealander*:

> But our lawyer will not admit this. It is not that he fails to look on the truth as excellent; it is not that he is less averse to murder than another; it is not that he would have crime escape unpunished; but the habits of his education, of his trade, and his life will not allow him to see clearly.[15]

This is the substance of Trollope's complaint—the lawyer is blinded by precedent, the novelist can see to the very heart of a crime. Thus when Undy Scott is dismissed from the court in *The Three Clerks* because there is no law by which he can be charged and convicted, Trollope enters as *amicus curiae* and thunders out his denunciation of the villain:

> Fate, however, and the laws are averse. To gibbet him, in one sense, would have been my privilege, had I drunk deeper from that Castalian rill whose dark waters are tinged with the gall of poetic indignation; but as in other sense I may not hang him, I will tell how he was driven from his club, and how he ceased to number himself among the legislators of his country. (ch. 49)

---

[14] *The New Zealander*, ed. and with intro. by N. John Hall (Oxford, 1972), p. 58.
[15] *Ibid.*, p. 56.

Trollope regarded himself as a very unusual artist who could regulate society more effectively than the lawyer because the latter worked with archaic fictions, as little pertinent to the delineation of truth as though the tailor were given a bag of rags from which to cut his coat.

At this point it cannot be emphasized too strongly that Trollope's view of the law was not a lawyer's but a legally minded layman's. He was quite capable of holding two contradictory opinions of the lawyer in his mind at the same time: one as a manipulator of facts, crafty and deceptive, the other as an inflexible narrow-minded pettifogger. Trollope never forgot the occasion when he caught a postman suspected of theft in possession of a marked half-crown. Cross-examined by Sir Isaac Butt, Trollope almost exploded with rage when asked if he had placed the marked coin into the prisoner's pocket.[16] This was law at its worst in Trollope's opinion. From the conflict between authority and liberty, legal strictures and artistic freedom, came the narrative voices of the novels. The moral ambiguity so often observed in Trollope's work reflects his changing stance as he takes one side of the argument and then another. Within a single chapter Trollope can speak for order and tradition and then propose its change. It is not only the novelist who conducts the narrative commentary but a legal advocate. The latter attempts to present the story in accord with regular form whereas the artist, by evading official procedure, strives for a higher truth. If only Trollope had been able to sweep away the trappings of justice at the trial of Alaric Tudor and impose the sentence of death upon Undy Scott! And afterward, when both voices have stated their case, the final arbiter is, of course, the reasonable reader.

In the novels Trollope was free to select his characters and events. In the reports he was always being confronted with the impossible and absurd. Once in County Cavan he was called upon to visit a bored gentleman who wrote endless letters of bitter complaint to the Post Office. After some ques-

---

[16] Lawyers writing on Trollope never fail to note this incident, viz., Henry S. Drinker, Jr., *The Lawyers of Anthony Trollope*, mss. Biddle Law Library. AD3-3780, p. 8.

tioning, he admitted to Trollope that writing abusive letters to civil servants was his hobby, nothing more. Trollope's only response was: "But, what am I to say in my report?"[17] His plaint echoes the lawyer constrained by the requirements of a difficult brief who uses the footnotes to provide explanation and emendation. It is not permitted to call a witness a liar in the context of the brief, but a footnote may well say that and a good deal more. The gentleman from County Cavan would have slipped comfortably into a novel of Dickens or Lever, but he was an intractable figure in an official report.

Throughout the novels Trollope can be seen contending with the writer of reports over the nature of admissible and nonadmissible evidence. Trollope was of the opinion that lawyers had the easier job since they had only to impose order on reality, not create that order. In *Castle Richmond* Trollope challenged his legal self in the archaic hortatory language he reserved for a special address to the court:

> Had it perchance fallen to thy lot, O my forensic friend, heavy laden with the wisdom of the law, to write tales such as this of mine, how charmingly might not thy characters have come forth upon the canvas—how much more charmingly than I can limn them! While, on the other hand, ignorant as thou now tellest me that I am of the very alphabet of the courts, had thy wig been allotted to me, I might have gathered guineas while to thee perhaps they come no faster than snow-drops in the early spring. (ch. 43)

This is Trollope bluntly accusing the lawyer of peddling cheap fictions disguised as justice. He, as an honest novelist accustomed to the practice of a far more difficult art, could beat the lawyer at his own game if he chose and show a handsome profit. It was not only Mr. Scarborough in *Mr. Scarborough's Family* who knew he could set the law on its head if once he set his mind to it. Trollope always regarded the lawyer as part of his own being, his official self, a lesser practitioner of justice than Trollope the novelist.

[17] *An Autobiography*, ch. 4.

38   *Order and Vision*

   He never forgot that his brothers had been given the chance to attend university, to study for law if that had been their wish. He read law assiduously but he always remained that hybrid person, the civil servant who prides himself on his legal knowledge and both admires and despises the professional lawyer. Not every lawyer he portrayed was a trimmer: some like Apjohn in *Cousin Henry* are as honest and courageous as any postal surveyor. When Apjohn voices his simple delight in seeing justice vindicated, he echoes Trollope's own sentiments in *The Three Clerks*: "The truth is, Brodrick, the whole of this matter has been such a pleasure to me that I don't care a straw about the costs. If I paid for it all from beginning to end out of my pocket, I should have had my whack for my money." (ch 23).
   The Post Office gave Trollope financial security and a little authority to bolster his lack of self-esteem. Thackeray always doubted his own work and voiced his fears publicly, an act Trollope deplored even though he could sympathize with it.[18] But there was no assurance in Trollope's work as a civil servant that he had acquired the rank of a gentleman, much less that he could be regarded as popular among his fellows. In London he had felt himself as much an outcast as at Harrow. Those desperate times of anguish at school were never recalled in his fiction; they never provided a Dotheboys Hall or a blacking factory in which the past could be exorcized in the form of fiction. These passages of his life were excluded by the structure of the report which sustains all his novels and which enabled him to define the content. But misery remained a companion throughout his life, occasioning moods of despondency and melancholy. The *Autobiography* records:

> I was wretched,—and sometimes almost unto death, and often cursed the hour in which I was born. There had

---

[18] Of Thackeray, Trollope wrote:
He was not a man capable of feeling at any time quite assured in his position, and when that occurred he was very far from assurance. I think that at no time did he doubt the sufficiency of his own mental qualification for the work he had taken in mind; but he doubted all else.
Thackeray (London, 1882), p. 15.

> clung to me a feeling that I had been looked upon always as an evil, an encumbrance, a useless thing,—as a creature of whom those connected with him had to be ashamed. (ch. 4)

Susan Gay remembered him slurring over his family and belittling the service after the fashion of a man who rejects that which he desires most.

Duty was the restorative of the Victorian's flogging spirit and Trollope learned to write fiction as he composed his reports: not as the spirit moved, but in order to fulfill a daily provision of words. Just as he had advised the young postman, Trollope believed that you could train yourself to bear pain and suffering with equanimity. Nothing reads more strangely to a modern sportsman than Trollope's account of his dedication to hunting. There are cricketers who approach their game as though it were a religion but they can, and frequently do, give reasoned accounts for their addiction. Trollope wrote simply:

> I have ever been constant to the sport, having learned to love it with an affection which I cannot myself fathom or understand. Surely no man has laboured at it as I have done, or hunted under such drawbacks as to distances, money, and natural disadvantages.[19]

In the season he spent at least one day a week hunting, regarding it as much duty as pleasure. Hunting was not simply a favored sport, a means of exercise and recreation; it was an obsession he had taught himself to love, even as he had trained himself to write reports and serve the Post Office. He continued: "Nothing has ever been allowed to stand in the way of hunting,—neither the writing of books, nor the work of the Post Office, nor other pleasures." Few people have spoken of a chosen sport in quite this way, not even champions express their dedication to training with such grim fervor. What did

---

[19] *An Autobiography*, ch. 4. In his *Hunting Sketches* (London, 1865), Trollope makes out a better case for "The Man Who Hunts and Doesn't Like It" than he does for "The Man Who Hunts and Does Like It."

hunting mean to Trollope when it dominated his later life and became a means of revealing character in so many of his novels?

First, it was an authoritarian, disciplined sport governed by a man, the Master of Fox Hounds, a despot by popular acclaim. "There are some positions among mankind which are so peculiarly selected by Providence for happiness on earth in a degree sufficient to raise the malice and envy of all the world around."[20] This could have been Jorrocks proclaiming the quality of an M.F.H.[21] Second, Trollope ached for popularity. He could invade a country post office demanding instant accounts but he could never know the pleasure of welcoming smiles and glad greetings wherever he went. Yet this is what he craved and this is what his favored heroes possess above all else, petted by the world like Arthur Fletcher, "liked at his club, and courted in the hunting-field, and loved at balls and archery meetings, and reputed by old men to be a rising star. . . ."[22] This was the persona Trollope had created for himself in those ordered daydreams wherein his greatest glory was to be clever and popular.

Trollope knew and affirmed in every work he wrote that "Whatever may be our walk in life, no man can walk well who does not walk with the esteem of his fellows."[23] Sport has always been a traditional means of acquiring popularity. It is often extraordinary what will be tolerated in a person's character provided he has sporting prowess. And in every group sport there is a certain camaraderie evoked by people of disparate nature brought together for a single object. Never having known the fraternity of the cricket club or the football field, Trollope found a substitute for it in the hunt. And no one was more punctilious about the rules than Trollope, never trying to get ahead of the hounds, governing and guiding his

---

[20] "The Master of Hounds," *Hunting Sketches*, p. 99.

[21] " 'Of all situations under the sun none is more enviable or more 'onerable than that of a master of fox-'ounds! Talk of an M.P.! vot's an M.P. compared to an M.F.H.?' " R. S. Surtees, *Handley Cross* (London, 1843), ch. 11.

[22] *The Prime Minister*, ch. 15.

[23] "The Hunting Parson," *Hunting Sketches*, p. 83.

Order and Vision

horse, never forcing a jump. The exuberant good-fellowship of a hunt delighted his spirit, dispelling the dark depressions and glowering rages that tested the few friends he owned. The rules of the hunt fulfilled the part of his nature which responded to discipline, and the cruelty of the exhausted fox finally torn apart by the hounds satisfied the savagery which Trollope regarded as inherent in man. In this case the cruelty was not only permissible, it was socially approved. Nevertheless, Trollope had an instinctive sympathy for the fox, and as he cried halloo with the best of them, he could still find pity for "the poor beast." The raucous clamor of the hunt made him forget the disgrace of his school days, the misery of being an object of derision for a pack of bloody-minded little boys at Harrow.

Nobody was noisier than Trollope: everyone who knew him remarked on his voice and how the table shook when he emphasized a bellow with a thump. It was as though he abhorred silence, and certainly he took pains to make sure that he was never alone. He learned how to fill his solitary hours with voices and people, at first the ordered day dreams, afterwards with the world of his novels:

> At such times I have been able to imbue myself thoroughly with the characters I have had in hand. I have wandered alone among the rocks and woods, crying at their grief, laughing at their absurdities, and thoroughly enjoying their joy. I have been impregnated with my own creations till it has been my only excitement to sit with the pen in my hand, and drive my team before me at as quick a pace as I could make them travel.[24]

This was the company he took with him on the long rides between post offices, a group of people who were as real to him as the surly messengers and bellicose country squires he did business with every day. Silence was the doorway to memory and a past that he could never forget or dispel in fiction as Dickens and Brontë had done. The suffering of childhood

---

[24] *An Autobiography*, ch. X.

remained with him always, but he subdued the pain with the force of will rather than by an act of imagination. He remembered "a daily walk of twelve miles through the lanes" to Harrow: as a man he would walk three times as far and take pride in the distance. Because he was clumsy and poor as a boy he could not play games; as a man he chose to ride to hounds with gentlemen. Poverty had scarred him in his youth; as a man he gloried in his ability to write for money, gaining income and social prestige at the same time. He was physically ungainly, so he learned to please women.

Trollope was not a womanizer although he took great pleasure in the company of women and they in his. He had many friendships with young women throughout his life, but although he loved Kate Field dearly she was never his mistress. If he found it difficult to be popular with men this was not the case with women. The spluttering bully would sit tranquilly for hours while they confided their secret fears to him. Like Samuel Richardson he not only found it easier to converse with women but he found them a constant source of inspiration. Women saw a different Anthony Trollope from the noisy and argumentative clubman. It was his air of calm, his benign respectability, which led the young black girl to speak to him in the parlor of the inn at Port Antonio in the West Indies. As he noted himself: "I am not a very young man; and my friends have told me that I show strongly that steady married appearance of a paterfamilias which is so apt to lend assurance to maiden timidity."[25] Josephine confided her story of love used and abused to Trollope and later he wrote:

> There was not about my Josephine all the pathos of Maria; nor can I tell my story as Sterne told his. But Josephine in her sorrow was I think more true to human nature than Maria. It may perhaps be possible that Sterne embellished his facts. I, at any rate, have not done that.[26]

And it was much the same when he met a young Washington beauty, Constance Beale, who recalled him talking to her at

---

[25] *The West Indies and the Spanish Main* (London, 1859), p. 36.
[26] *Ibid.*, p. 41.

Order and Vision

their home in Bloomingdale. Constance was entranced when Trollope promised that she would be in his new novel, "which pleased her very much."[27] Trollope's next book was *He Knew He Was Right* and we must assume that Constance became Caroline Spalding and not the American poet known as the Republican Browning, Miss Petrie.

Trollope acknowledged his good fortune in marrying a woman with whom he lived happily to the end of his days. Rose Heseltine traveled with him, copied out his work, and approved his romantic and imaginative attachments to young women. It is unfortunate that we know so little about Rose Trollope, for undoubtedly she helped him understand women and sharpened his perception of clothing and dress. Unlike some writers who punish their fictional women for the women they have known in life, Trollope never failed to sympathize with the plight of women in society. From his own experience he knew how society could give freedom to some and crush and restrict others. It is his women who speak out with most vehemence against a society that made marriage the only acceptable career for a woman. There are some very jolly spinsters in Trollope's novels, like Miss Todd, but they can live as they please because of large private incomes, the passport to independence in any age. Without money a woman had to find a husband in Trollope's world or become the appendage to the nearest relation prepared to support her. It is not men but women who complain about the social order, and their criticism comes from the heart. In *He Knew He Was Right*, Dorothy spoke of women as nobodies whose very existence was by courtesy of men:

> A man who is a nobody can perhaps make himself somebody,—or, at any rate, he can try; but a woman has no means of trying. She is a nobody, and a nobody she must remain. She has her clothes and her food, but she isn't wanted anywhere. People put up with her, and that is about the best of her luck. If she were to die somebody

---

[27] "A Reminiscence of the Life of Edward F. Beale," June 1921. Permission to quote from the MS. from Mrs. Francis Randolph, Philadelphia.

perhaps would be sorry for her, but nobody would be worse off. She doesn't earn anything or do any good. She is just there and that's all. (ch. 51)

Even the ethereal Ayala rages against her helplessness, crying out to her sister in *Ayala's Angel*: "But what is the good of talking about it, Lucy? You and I have no voice in it, though it is all about ourselves. As you say, we are like two tame birds, who have to be moved from one cage into another just as the owner pleases." (ch. 10)

Trollope himself believed that women found their greatest happiness in marriage and continued to advise his young American friend, Kate Field, to settle down with a good husband. His fictional women often feel quite differently and may choose not to accept the crowded nursery and a lover who inevitably dwindles into a domestic partner at the best and a tyrant and bully at the worst. Trollope knew that a wife had to accept the same kind of humiliation and pain that had darkened his childhood. He never wrote of children in his novels except as incidental to issues of property and inheritance. The formal legal structure of his work effectively excluded them as active participants in the narrative. But, as he revealed in the *Autobiography*, he had never forgotten the muddy lanes to Harrow, the misery of loneliness and the anguish of being daily abused and flogged. A wife had to accept grief as part of her lot. Marriage for a woman always brought with it a measure of disappointment, often neglect, sometimes physical brutality. A single woman could protect herself against a man's recurrent anger by refusing to see him again. A married woman did not have this choice. She had to endure being beaten even as Trollope had known stick and cane as a child.

If he could not bear to write of children and find release for suffering in the confession of fiction as Dickens had done in *David Copperfield*, he could at least project that pain onto a surrogate. Women as victims provide an emotional substitute for Trollope's childhood. Dorothy in *He Knew He Was Right* saw herself and all women as potential nobodies; Trollope at nineteen had described himself as "an idle, desolate hanger-on" without money and prospects. Miss Mackenzie in the novel of that name is one person with money, and quite another without. It requires a very strange perversity of nature to enjoy being flogged (some public-school boys like Swinburne could appreciate it). Trollope raged when he recalled that he had often been scourged five times in a single day at Harrow. Only a wife could know the same mortification of body and spirit. In *Can You Forgive Her?* Trollope wrote:

> What woman can bear a blow from a man, and afterwards return to him with love? A wife may have to bear it and to return. And she may return with that sort of love which is a thing of custom. The man is the father of her children, and earns the bread which they eat and which she eats. Habit and the ways of the world require that she should be careful in his interests, and that she should live with him in what amity is possible to them. But as for love,—all that we mean by love when we speak of it and write of it,—a blow given by the defender to the defenceless crushes it all! A woman may forgive deceit, treachery, desertion,—even the preference given to a rival. She may forgive them and forget them; but I do not think that a woman can forget a blow. And as for forgiveness,—it is not the blow that she cannot forgive, but the meanness of spirit that made it possible. (ch. 56)

In this instance the blow was struck by George Vavasor, and his sister Kate suffered a broken arm in consequence. The passage in tone and passion echoes Trollope's references in the *Autobiography* to his brother with whom "habit and the ways of the world" later engendered a qualified affection. The friendship of adult life was no compensation for the flogging that Thomas Adolphus had inflicted upon his young brother as "a part of his daily exercise." He could teach himself to accept the neglect of his parents and the obvious preference of his mother for her eldest son. He even came to pity and understand his mad, disappointed father: he could never forgive those who had scourged him as much for sport as for punishment. Women spoke for that pain and sense of outrage in his novels.

Trollope accepted society and its ways with few complaints. He chose to write Post Office without capitals but he prided himself on being the best writer of reports in a department that esteemed itself in this regard. Trollope knew that children suffered in society, and so did women, but this was no reason to cry revolution and seek radical change. In his mind society was law: it could be appealed, but it should not be overthrown. The same charge of muddled and insensitive conservatism has been leveled against Trollope that Bentham brought to bear against Blackstone. Bentham railed against Blackstone for composing what he regarded as a servile apologia for a flawed society and then accused him of hypocrisy in attempting to equate common law and divine providence.[28] For Trollope it was not the sovereignty of law but the sovereignty of society which had to be maintained and respected. For this reason Trollope defended some apparently indefensible institutions and events in the societies he examined.

The concept of submission to the law despite its shortcomings has been a constant in legal theory. "It is certainly not the case that every law is the extension of morality," Samuel Stump wrote,

> Law in the making often reflects the weakness, selfishness, and predatoriness of which men are capable. There is no guarantee that the law will be made in accordance with man's moral insights or the requirements of his moral nature. But even where a law has been made in violation of a moral right the law is subject to criticism only because there is this discrepancy between the law as it is in fact and what the moral right indicates that it ought to be.[29]

Trollope's works provide a continuing confirmation of this attitude. It is not a bland acceptance of the *status quo* but a

---

[28] *The Sovereignty of the Law*, ed. and with intro. Gareth Jones (Toronto, 1973), p. xxviii.

[29] *Morality and the Law* (Nashville, 1966), p. 238.

reasoned social philosophy that finds its fullest expression in Plantagenet Palliser's vision of a future society. Underlying it is a profound skepticism regarding the goodness of human nature. All utopias, all plans for perfection must necessarily fail when one constructs them on the frailties of men and women. It is this point that Trollope is determined to emphasize in his one venture into science fiction, *The Fixed Period*. Contrary to general critical opinion of the Victorians as social optimists or Carlylean catastrophists, he was a cautious pessimist, believing neither in the perfectibility of man nor in some inevitable form of evolutionary progress.

The official Post Office report satisfied a psychological need for discipline and restraint in Trollope. It expressed the authority that he both resented and embodied. Certainly the report shaped the structure of his fiction and provided a model for his travel books. He continually chafed against it just as he challenged the concept of the law and all it represented. In this contest he used his fiction to present a system of equity that could be ranged against his definition of the common law. To his way of thinking it was not the lawyer who could best determine and order the affairs of society but that responsible and informed novelist, Anthony Trollope. All his work was a demonstration of that conviction.

Chapter III

Society Examined: The Travel Books

In contrast with the vision of an ordered society underlying his fiction, Trollope's travel books were objective analyses of actual societies. This was not merely the result of the difference between the genres: it was also because the underlying suppositions of the novelist applied primarily to the English gentry. When examining the manners and problems of alien communities Trollope was closer to the persona he adopted in the Post Office: the practical expositor of issues that others chose to ignore or were too blind to perceive. But the material he collected on his travels was quite unlike the subject matter of his official reports. In approach and style his descriptions of foreign lands occupied a middle ground between his administrative and fictional writing, though the deep structure of all three forms had much in common. Trollope abroad was anxious to collect evidence on all sides of disputed issues, and to allow his reader to form his own conclusions. Certainly, this dispassionate manner was not reflected in his attitudes toward his superiors in the Post Office in those last critical years of his public service, when he sought high office and also embarked upon his successful career as a novelist.

Trollope was a successful administrator abroad and in the field. This cannot be said of his life when he returned to the Grand. He was a rancorous colleague, impetuous in argument, intemperate in his correspondence. Although his reports were always well written and carefully researched, he was unable to adapt to the bureaucratic impersonality of the Post Office. Size and the extension of its services made the new postal

Society Examined 49

service under Rowland Hill a very different institution from the paternalistic department run so agreeably by Francis Freeling. Trollope was outraged at what he regarded as continuing attacks upon the authority of the surveyors. To him it was rather like the contentions between field and staff officer with the power given to the latter and the actual work done by the former. As early as 1859 he had organized the surveyors, who signed a petition to the Secretary for an increase in pay.[1] It was refused and as a result Trollope's sense of being exploited and misused grew by the month. His attitude was regarded as inexplicable by his superiors. They, after all, permitted Trollope to hunt once and often twice a week, and knew that he was spending a great deal of his time writing novels. It was not these activities or his failure to secure the post of Under-Secretary that occasioned his resignation. Rather, he chose to leave because he could no longer accept the authority of men he disliked.[2]

In 1864 he had again petitioned for a higher salary for the surveyors and complained about the "special allowances" that were given to some of his colleagues. Entrance into the Post Office was now to be determined by official examination, and promotion by merit—the process he described in *The Three Clerks*. Failing to receive a courteous response from the Secretary, he wrote in considerable anger and with some incoherence and repetition to Lord Stanley, the Postmaster General, defending himself against the Secretary's accusation of impertinence:

> I am now an old servant of the Crown and can refer to my services for a great many years to prove that such is not my nature. I have endeavoured to pull well with the men at work with me, both above and below, and can boast that I have always obeyed the orders given to me to the best of my ability. But I think that it is due to me

---

[1] Memorial submitted to Rowland Hill, 27 May 1859, for an increased scale of salary. Hill to surveyors, 23 June 1859, stating that the improved scale was not warranted. File IV of England, 3174/59. POR.

[2] Rowland Hill in particular.

in return for such service that I should be heard when I complain,—especially as I have not been prone to complain,—and that any serious allegation made by me should meet with consideration.[3]

Trollope was charged, with some justification, of undertaking to speak for all the surveyors without consulting the men he held himself to represent. His views on promotion by merit about which he wrote and lectured publicly[4] were regarded as being personally motivated without consideration for the welfare of the service as a whole. When he spoke on the civil service as a profession and his detestation for promotion by merit it did seem that the "old servant of the Crown" was pushing his own barrow. Age and experience often guaranteed incompetence in the Civil Service, but Trollope would never accept this. It was not that he was against improvement or that he considered promotion should be determined by age without respect to ability, it was his firm opinion that merit simply meant the judgment of one fallible man upon another: "The best man is the man whom somebody thinks to be the best man."[5] Trollope's lack of faith in the judgment of his superiors did not go unnoticed.

Trollope certainly represented those whose only claim to higher office was age, but it could hardly be regarded as a popular cause amongst the higher officials of government. As early as 1832 Henry Taylor had argued against the efficacy of promotion by seniority.[6] The difficulty for the Post Office

[3] 18 July 1864, File IV of England, 3174/68. POR.

[4] "The Civil Service as a Profession" in *Four Lectures,* ed. Morris L. Parrish, London, 1938.

[5] *Ibid.,* p. 21.

[6] "On the Best Mode of Constituting Public Offices," Henry Parris, *Political Studies,* June, 1961. Taylor vigorously opposed seniority, maintaining that any man who had spent a long apprenticeship as a clerk was unfit for higher office:

The discipline of such establishments was of too gentlemanly a character to enforce industry and the consequence was that the men grew old in idleness, and when seniority at length gave them an opportunity of exercising their intellectual faculties, if any such faculties belonged to them, the power of exertion was gone and the habits of life were invet-

now was that whenever Trollope chose to speak he was accorded the attention given a popular novelist. It was not unnaturally resented when he put himself forward as the spokesman of the Grand, lecturing and offering opinions contrary to those of the Secretary. For the conclusion of a lengthy series of complaints he reserved his most scathing denigration for the whole merit system, describing it as "thoroughly Utopian."[7] For Trollope, all Utopias were based on coercion, ensuring the happiness of the many at the expense of the few. It might be thought that the merit system would produce the opposite effect, but Trollope saw no inconsistency. He hammered home his view of utopianism in the person of John Neverbend in *The Fixed Period*, who wants to enforce a theory of limited population growth that runs counter to the natural fear of death and the desire to live. Trollope saw merit as a mechanical process that would result in a demoralized service of "broken-hearted men."[8] It was far better to condone a pervasive inequality in an organization and accept a degree of inefficiency that reflected human fallibility than to attempt to impose an unnatural and theoretical hierarchy of talent.

Civil servants do not live comfortably with the reputation for disruption that Trollope had acquired at the Grand. The gray, efficient anonymity of the new bureaucracy defeated him and, almost in despair, he wrote to his old friend, Christopher Hodgson in 1867:

> It is not so much that the office is no longer worth my while, as you say, as that other things have grown upon me so fast that I feel myself beginning to neglect the office and I am sure you will acknowledge that when that is the case it had better be given up.[9]

---

erate. One principal remedy, therefore, for the inefficiency of these establishments is to get rid of the system of seniority (p. 182).

[7] Trollope to Rowland Hill, 24 May 1863. File No. XVIII No. 3849/63. POR.

[8] *Ibid*.

[9] This letter is by courtesy of N. John Hall, editor of Trollope's correspondence.

No one had ever accused Trollope of neglect since he had taken up office as a surveyor's clerk in Ireland. He was beaten by his own inability to conform, to hold his tongue and keep in step. He could not endure the authority that he enjoyed exercising over others. It was true that he had learned to discipline himself and his writing throughout those years in the postal service, but the discipline of his superiors recalled those days of bitter servitude as an adolescent. Perhaps it was fortunate both for literature and for those who served the Post Office that Trollope was not appointed Under-Secretary in 1864.

As a surveyor Trollope had learned how to examine a problem of the post and resolve it to the satisfaction of the public. He could, when dealing with the local gentry, be a model of compromise and tact. It was his conviction that a family had as much right to letters delivered in time for breakfast as it did to expect hot tea and buttered toast. There were no jokes made about late deliveries of the post in Trollope's day. A *Punch* cartoon showed a young woman at the doorway of a country house holding a letter between stained fingers and complaining that the ink was still wet, to which the dour postman replied that the service took pride in its speed of delivery. A joke incomprehensible to the modern reader but to the approving taste of Trollope and the British public. Unlike some government departments that seemed divorced from human problems, the Post Office dealt with the public's daily needs. It required neither theory of state nor constitutional tradition to sustain it, but merely the desire of people to communicate as cheaply and as quickly as possible. In his travels, as on his postal surveys, Trollope never looked beyond these basic concerns to wider issues. He worked for a bread-and-butter service and carried its principles abroad with him. It is one reason why his travel books remain of such interest. Social theorists, unless of exceptional brilliance, tend to have as short a public life as French literary critics. Trollope looked first to see if a society worked: if it was functioning economically and to the common good then it was worthy of commendation.

Travel books were extraordinarily popular in the nineteenth century—every conscientious traveler was expected to keep a journal as evidence that pleasure had been tempered by duty. Trollope's travel books fall midway between his official reports and his novels: occasionally a novel like *The Bertrams*, the Irish novels, and the less successful ventures into a European background show varying forms of conflation between the two. His first attempt in the genre of the travel book was a guide to Ireland. It was never published and the manuscript has been lost.[10] Later he was to write novels about conditions in Ireland during and after the Famine but a nonfictional depiction of the country that he knew so well would have been equally illuminating.

In *The Bertrams*, written in 1858 during the negotiations for the Indian Mail Service and published in 1859, Trollope used his Egyptian experience to deflate the current furor over Richard Burton's journey to Mecca disguised as Al-Haj Abdullah and the subsequent rage for all things Arabian.[11] Burton had given the world the Arabia of mystery and high romance, Trollope presented the actuality of travel to the sacred pyramids:

> A man who goes to Cairo must see the pyramids. Convention, and the laws of society as arranged on that point, of course require it. But let no man, and, above all, no woman, assume that the excursion will be in any way pleasurable. I have promised that I will not describe such a visit, but I must enter a loud, screeching protest against the Arab brutes—the sheikhs being the very worst of the brutes—who have these monuments in their hands. Their numbers, the filthiness of their dress—or one might almost say no dress—their stench, their obscene indecency, their clattering noise, their rapacity, exercised without a

---

[10] Trollope sent the manuscript of his guide book to John Murray, who returned it unopened. In the *Autobiography* Trollope recalled: "I 'did' the city of Dublin, and the county of Kerry, in which lies the lake scenery of Killarney, and I 'did' the route from Dublin of Killarney, altogether completing nearly a quarter of the proposed volume" (ch. V).

[11] Burton's *Personal Narrative*. . . . was published in 1855.

moment's intercession; their abuse, as in this wise: 'Very bad English-man—dam bad—dam, dam, dam! Him want to take all him money to the grave; but no, no, no! Devil hab him, and money too.' This, be it remembered, from a ferocious, almost blackened Arab, with his face within an inch of your own. And then their flattery, as in this wise: 'Good English-man—very good!—and then a tawny hand pats your face, and your back, and the calves of your leg—him gib poor Arab one shilling for himself—yes, yes, yes; and then Arab no let him tumble down and break all him legs—yes, yes—break *all* him legs.' And then the patting goes on again. These things, I say, put together, make a visit to the Pyramids no delightful recreation. My advice to my countrymen who are so unfortunate as to visit them is this: Let the ladies remain below—not that they ever will do so, if the gentlemen who are with them ascend—and let the men go armed with stout sticks, and mercilessly belabor any Arab who attempts either to bully or to wheedle. (ch. 38)

This was Trollope's answer to all the enchantment of Araby and as far removed from Burton's heightened experience as homespun from gossamer. With regard to the needs of the ordinary traveler, Trollope's account was probably more useful. He was at pains to establish himself as the realist, the man unclouded by romantic visions on the one hand or pettifogging conventions and "the laws of society" on the other. As a traveler he set a steady course between the shoals of romance and the cliffs of preconception. It would not be a very exciting journey but there would be the assurance of swift and safe delivery to port.

Even Jerusalem fell short of his expectations although he could appreciate the irony of Miss Todd and her friends eating cold ham in a Jewish burial ground. Burton never saw himself reflected in the society around him—it was sufficient to wear a disguise and speak the native tongue to feel that he had lost all his English identity and become an Arab. It was a theatrical tradition to be followed by many subsequent Englishmen.

Trollope always remembered that he was a tourist and often an intruder, and continually reminded his readers that they were the same. Throughout all his journeys he never lost this sense of himself, an English gentleman abroad, just as he had never forgotten his office of surveyor when traveling all through England and Ireland. Others, like Miss Todd in *The Bertrams*, conformed with the social conventions of the English traveler and felt conscience-stricken and ridiculous as a result:

> Miss Todd was somewhat ashamed of this. Here, in England, one would hardly inaugurate a picnic to Kensal Green, or the Highgate Cemetery, nor select the tombs of our departed great ones as a shelter under which to draw one's corks. But Miss Todd boasted of high spirits; when this little difficulty had been first suggested to her by Mr. M'Gabbery, she had scoffed at it, and had enlarged her circle in a spirit of mild bravado. Then chance had done more for her; and now she was doomed to preside over a large party of revelers over the ashes of James the Just. (ch. 8)

Trollope respected religious institutions but deplored enthusiasm and questioned the validity of spiritual experiences no matter how time-honored and holy the place. So when George Bertram believes he has a religious calling on the Mount of Olives it becomes little more than an essay in self-deception induced as much by tradition as by actual experience. If there is an instance of supposed revelation in Trollope's work, it does not lead to an awareness of a reality beyond material things, but to an appreciation of the proper value and significance of such mundane and material things as a comfortable home, good food, and pleasant surroundings. This is the understanding that comes to Mr. Arabin in *Barchester Towers* who "had to own to himself that he was sighing for the good things of other men on whom in his pride he had ventured to look down." (vol. 2, ch. 20) It was indeed only convention and false pride that enabled people to take pleasure in dirt and find virtue in poverty. Trollope always looked for creature comforts in society and was inclined to measure the worth of that society to the degree those comforts were enjoyed by all. Poverty was never picturesque in his opinion, and physical discomfort need not be a prerequisite for spiritual or aesthetic delight.

In his travel books Trollope was able to express what was inconceivable in an official report. Not only could he examine a social problem and resolve it to his own satisfaction, but he could speak in his own voice, setting himself against the landscape and the people he had chosen to evaluate. Scenery never impressed him and he always seemed able to contrive that fog or rain should obscure a famous view admired by all. Land existed for people and it was humanity at large that interested Trollope. A mountain had no more value for him than a stone unless it played some part in the lives of men and women. His perception was more analytic than descriptive, so that the reader learns less about the appearance of a country than he does about the sensation of living there. And Trollope never fails to remind one that what may be agreeable for some people would not suit an English gentleman at all.

He was not deficient in prejudice and received opinions. He has been termed a racist but there is no question that the Arab and the French receive more abuse in his work than the Kafir. He never doubted that an English gentleman was the finest work of creation and the existence of the empire seemed to provide adequate confirmation for this conviction. Nonetheless, he was always aware of the incongruity of the Englishman in an alien context and concluded that not every country was improved by an English presence. All his travel books should be read in the context of his final major study on South Africa, a work of prophetic insight. Never an idealist, he accepted a society on its own terms, suggesting improvements, noting that his own criticism was frequently the result of bias.

He traveled on official business and also on his own behalf, aware that his travel books would always be measured against the enormous popularity of his mother's *Domestic Manners of the Americans*. Unlike his mother, who cheerfully imposed her own presence upon people and places, Trollope characteristically expressed two often contradictory views. This is not deliberate ambiguity. It resembles the lawyer's insistence on seeing not one solution to a problem, but several. (The layman has always lamented the lack of left-handed lawyers.) Trollope was adept in suggesting the complexity of a situation even if he proposed a simple resolution of it.

He denotes these differences through statement and comment or by means of an illustrative anecdote that reveals the speaker both as narrator and subject. For example, he found the blacks of Kingston to be less deferential than the English lower classes and to have curious notions of the mode of address to be used between master and servant:

> "Halloo, old fellow! how about the bath?" I said one morning to a lad who had been commissioned to see a bath filled for me. He was cleaning boots at the time, and went on with his employment, sedulously, as though he had not heard a word. But he was over sedulous, and I saw that he heard me. "I say, how about that bath?" I continued. But he did not move a muscle. "Put down those boots, sir," I said, going up to him; "and go and do as I bid you."
> "Who you call fellor? You speak to a gen'lman gen'lmanly, and den he fill de bath."
> "James," said I, "might I trouble you to leave those boots, and see the bath filled for me?" and I bowed to him.
> "Es, sir," he answered, returning my bow; "go at once." And so he did perfectly satisfied. Had he imagined however, that I was quizzing him, in all probability he would not have gone at all. There will be those who will say that I had received a good lesson; and perhaps I had. But it would be rather cumbersome if we were forced to treat our juvenile servants at home in this manner—or even those who are not juvenile. (p. 26)

It is an incident like this that sets the interrogatory tone of the work. This is not an infallible observer but a fallible being who brings with him the foreigner's customary jaundiced eye.

Because he does not claim the moral and cultural authority of a Froude or an Arnold abroad, it is possible for voices other than his own to be heard. In all Trollope's writing there is a running argument with an unseen antagonist offering a different opinion and revealing an alternative point of view. Trollope establishes the reality of his person less through his opinions than by means of continuing reference to sweaty shirts, greasy meals, and mud that made an Irish bog seem like granite in retrospect. These are the realities of Trollope the traveler; the rest is opinion; here he is defensive, rushing into argument and protestation. It is this vociferous defense that always permits another opinion to be heard.

The problem of the West Indies was the existence of an emancipated black population controlled by a group of English settlers clinging to outmoded Anglo-Saxon traditions. In Trollope's view the latter seemed far stranger in this tropical society than the blacks. After a week he stated that he had become blind to color and appearance:

> The eye soon becomes accustomed to the black skin and the thick lip, and the ear to the broken patois which is the nearest approach to English which the ordinary negro ever makes. When one has been a week among them, the novelty is all gone. It is only by an exercise of memory and intellect that one is enabled to think of them as a strange race. (p. 57)

Even after a lifetime abroad, many English found it quite impossible to attain the altered vision that came so easily to Trollope. Color for Trollope was a superficiality; what interested him was whether the black was working efficiently in this society. Every black was scrutinized as though he were a recalcitrant postman having his walk tested by Anthony Trollope the surveyor.

In the West Indies Trollope was disconcerted to see his philosophy and method thrown to the winds by a country so generous in climate and produce that man could live comfortably without work. If he was not impressed by the Englishman's capacity for work in this climate he was disturbed by an environment that seemed designed to exempt the black from "the general lot of Adam's children." His indignation rises to a crescendo of denunciation as the negro is deemed infantile, incapable of right reason and generally below the mental capacity of the Englishman. At this point another voice is heard arguing against the Gradgrind of work and authority, discipline and order:

> And who can blame the black man? He is free to work, or free to let it alone. He can live without work and roll in the sun, and suck oranges and eat breadfruit; ay, and ride a horse perhaps, and wear a white waistcoat and plaited shirt on Sundays. Why should he care for the busher?[12] I will not dig cane-holes for half a crown a day; and why should I expect him to do so? I can live without it; so can he. (p. 67)

And this argument carries as much weight as the vehement censure of the black's inherent laziness. Against the picture of the black sucking oranges in the sun Trollope sets another image—the English worker abroad. The evidence is presented fairly and the reader may draw his own conclusion as to the relative merits of the two:

> The first thing that met my view on stepping out of the truck was a solitary Englishman seated on a half-sawn log of wood. Those who remember Hood's Whims and Oddities may bear in mind a heart-rending picture of the last man. Only that the times do not agree, I should have said that this poor fellow must have sat for the picture. He was undeniably an English laborer. No man of any other nation would have had that face, or worn those clothes, or kicked his feet about in that same awkward, melancholy humor. He was, he said, in charge of the saw-mill, having been induced to come out into that country for three years. According to him, it was a wretched, miserable place. "No man," he said, "ever found himself in worse diggings." He earned a dollar and a half a day,

[12] The overseer.

and with that he could hardly buy shoes and have his clothes washed. "Why did he not go home?" I asked. "Oh, he had come for three years, and he'd stay his three years out—if so be he didn't die." The saw-mill was not paying, he said; and never would pay. (p. 257)

Trollope's solution was a compromise that would not permit the dominance of one race but would encourage harmonious relationship of the two by miscegenation. The West Indies were to be neither black nor white, but brown: "a race that shall be no more ashamed of the name of negro than we are of the name of Saxon" (pp. 65-66). Trollope accepted an indisputable social fact—the English were a minority, the blacks, the majority, and any working partnership would have to acknowledge this. There was antagonism between the races: the sugar planter yearned for the days of slavery and a regular labor force, the black saw no need to work for a pittance, and both resented the "coloreds." Trollope applauded the social drive and ascendancy of the latter even as he smiled at their imitation of English legislative forms. His conclusion was blunt:

> The fact is, that in Jamaica, at the present day, the colored people do stand on strong ground, and that they do not so stand with the goodwill of the aristocracy of the country. They have forced their way up, and now loudly protest that they intend to keep it. I think that they will keep it, and that on the whole it will be well for us Anglo-Saxons to have created a race capable of living and working in the climate without inconvenience. (pp. 97-98)

Trollope was essentially pragmatic, assessing the worth of a society by its capacity to survive and succeed. When he examined the aborigine of Australia and the Maori of New Zealand he saw two races that seemed on the verge of extinction, and he concluded that the sooner they vanished the better it would be for society as a whole: "of the Australian black man we may certainly say that he has to go. That he should perish without unnecessary suffering should be the aim of all who are concerned in the matter."[13] Thus all the efforts of philanthropists and missionaries were futile and sentimental gestures retarding natural social change. He reserved particular scorn for the missionary who felt that a saved soul was worth the expenditure of time and money that could be more profitably spent in creating industry and jobs.

A man's dignity resided in his ability to work and, through his work, contribute to the general well-being of society. In his study of South Africa, written after the annexation of the Transvaal in 1877, Trollope arrived at a radically different solution to the problem of mixed races. When Trollope landed in South Africa, the black was working in an unregulated labor market and his wages were determined by demand, not by government regulation or any trades union. It was immediately apparent to Trollope that the black was not only competing with the emigrant Englishman, he was surpassing him. Trollope had only contempt for "sturdy English beggars" who refused to work alongside the black on equal terms. When he suggested to two such fellows that they should look for work on the railroad, they replied:

> "They had tried the railway, and had been offered 2s. 6d. a day. They were not going to work along side of niggers for 2s. 6d., which would only supply them with grub! Did we want real Englishmen to do that?
> We told them that certainly we did want real Englishmen to earn their grub honestly and not to beg it. . . ."[14]

Trollope was delighted when he discovered a black man, a cooper, earning three hundred pounds a year and spending some of his money on a carriage to drive around with his wife on Sunday.

It is clear that Trollope was capable of advising a different social solution for every country that he visited. In Australia and New Zealand he recommended the speedy, if painless, eradication of the native minority. In South Africa he came

[13] *Australia*, P. D. Edwards and R. B. Joyce, Queensland, 1967, p. 113.
[14] *South Africa*, 2 vols., London, 1878, vol. 1, p. 146.

to a quite different conclusion that should put to rest forever the accepted image of a blinkered Trollope stumping around the world enunciating crambos and clichés:

> South Africa is a country of black men,—and not of white men. It has been so; it is so; and it will continue to be so. In this respect it is altogether unlike Australia, unlike the Canadas, and unlike New Zealand. And, as it is unlike them, so should it be to us a matter of much purer gratification than are those successful Colonies. There we have gone with our ploughs and with our brandy, with all the good and with all the evil which our civilization has produced, and throughout the lands the native races have perished by their contact with us. They have withered by commune with us as the weaker weedy grasses of Nature's first planting wither and die wherever come the hardier plants, which science added to nature has produced. . . . In South Africa it is not so. The tribes which before our coming were wont to destroy themselves in civil wars have doubled their population since we have turned their assegais to ploughshares. Thousands, ten thousands of them, are working for wages. . . . The Kafir and the Zulu are free men, and understand altogether the privileges of their freedom. In one town of 18,000 inhabitants, 10,000 of them are now receiving 10s. a week each man, in addition to their diet . . . it must at the same time tell us that South Africa is a black country and not a white one;—that the important person in South Africa is the Kafir and the Zulu, the Bechuana and the Hottentot;—not the Dutchman or the Englishman. (vol. 2, pp. 332-333)

The implications of this passage speak to the present day with a troubling honesty and common sense.

The picture of Trollope that emerges is not particularly attractive, but is very different from the traditional one. He was often outrageously wrong in his judgments, dismissing races and institutions to oblivion as though they were dilatory clerks. When he examined a society he measured it by standards that were better suited to determining a postman's walk in Wales. However, if his verdict was often questionable, his mode of enquiry was commendable. Trollope always read widely before he visited a country and then took pains to collect as many facts as possible, facts that were then tested in the process of examining everyone he met. His first question of a man was generally how much he was paid and how long he worked for his wages. From this information he would often produce an opinion that was at variance with his own feelings. Unlike his mother he noted discomforts but did not permit them to affect his judgments. For example, Edward Gibbon Wakefield wanted to see the English class structure transferred to Australia and New Zealand. Trollope argued that Australian society was not, and never should attempt to be, a reflection of British traditions. Moreover, the new Australian had the right to order his society as he pleased without regard for the interests of England:

> Every man who goes out thither has a right to demand that his political status shall be used so as best to contribute to his own happiness, and that it shall not be manipulated to the advantage of others, except in so far as he is part and parcel with those others. (p. 60)

The only social allegiance the Australian owed was to that particular society in which he had chosen to live and work.

This did not mean that Trollope personally regarded the Australian community as more admirable than English society. On the contrary, he thought that the English gentleman was not at all suitable for emigration. His proper place was in his own society where servants were deferential and the classes were clearly defined. Within the compass of one page Trollope could state that the Australian was as objectionably abrasive in manner as the American, and then note that all criticism of this kind was irrelevant to the main issue. The only real subject of concern was the well-being of a society and its members. He accepted that Australia or America would never suit him as a home and acknowledged frankly that he did not feel comfortable in either country, but he urged those prepared to work to emigrate where class distinctions did not impose material barriers to progress.

Trollope never sought the cause of national calamities. He considered this to be the work of the historian—as a civil servant he was concerned with present conditions and their possibility for improvement. Thus, in providing the reader with a background to the annexation of the Transvaal, Trollope resolutely abjures an historical inquest and proceeds to recommend a number a texts for the reader who seeks such information. As in South Africa, so in Ireland, Trollope held the English guilty of injustice but he would not permit this to become a license for speculation. At an early stage of his career the civil servant learns that guilt cannot be translated or rendered in statistical tables. Indeed, Trollope spoke of the Famine as though it had acted like a surgeon's knife upon the sickness that was Ireland:

> The blow instantly affected the remedy. A tribe of pauper landlords had grown up by slow degrees who, by their poverty, their numbers, their rapacity, and their idleness, had eaten up and laid waste the fairest parts of the country. Then came the potato rot, bringing after it pestilence, famine, and the Encumbered Estates Court; and lo! in three years, the air was cleared, the cloud had passed away, and Ireland was again prosperous. (*West Indies*, p. 219)

Nothing could be more simplistic than this rendering of the event but it was typical of Trollope when called upon to analyze a problem that did not conform with the requirements of a report. Calamities of any kind were like acts of God, balky intrusions in the course of human life that must be accepted, not subjected to retrospective interpretation. In the Irish novels the hungry and oppressed speak on their own behalf and bear witness to their misery, but the travel books do not admit this kind of evidence. It is only in the novels, when fiction establishes its own reality within the formal bounds of the report, that a different kind of truth emerges, one that speaks less to contingent facts and more to a common humanity.

Society Examined

If Ireland was the shadow across Trollope's England, America was the touchstone for his own particular society of gentlefolk and class distinctions. As early as 1859, after his attempt to regulate postal services in the West Indies and negotiate a postal agreement with Grenada, Trollope wrote that the United States afforded "the best means of prophesying if I may say so, what the world will next be, and what men will next do." (*West Indies*, p. 380) His study of the country was the most extensive and ambitious report he was ever to undertake.

In 1862 the Republic was divided by civil war with victory seeming within reach of the confederate army. Trollope undertook to ascertain the causes of the war, predict its outcome, and set the whole conflict within the context of society. The work has always been wretchedly edited and issued in truncated form; nevertheless it is remarkable for Trollope's ability to marshal coherently an astonishing amount of material. It is always a pleasure to read the first edition of *North America* in an American library and find the pages carefully and approvingly annotated by a reader long dead.[15]

The two volumes met with a cold reception in England. The reason for this can be found in Trollope's insistence that his sympathies were wholeheartedly with the North even though he could understand the action taken by the South. It has become a popular historical myth that the English working class, and Lancashire in particular, were passionately against slavery.[16] Trollope, on the other hand, wrote bluntly that "It is no doubt the fact that the sympathies of England are with

---

[15] Trollope's work did not meet with the hostile reception in the United States that he anticipated in the last chapter. It was criticized in part, approved on the whole.

[16] Norman Longmate's *The Hungry Mills, the Story of the Lancashire Cotton Famine 1861-1865*, London, 1978, offers a different picture altogether. The heartfelt support of Lancashire for the abolitionists was a myth engendered by English nonconformist radicals who wanted to show that idealism would always triumph over selfish economic interests, by Marx who found Lancashire demonstrating the solidarity of the proletariat throughout the world, and by Lincoln who said that the English people had supported him even if Palmerston and Russell had favored his enemies.

the Southern States."[17] In *North America* he argued the case for and against secession with dogged fairness, following the same process of reasoned disputation that he had used so successfully in *West Indies*.

Never the best judge of his own work, Trollope regarded *North America* as "tedious and confused," yet it is never dull and its only confusion stems from a dual purpose: Trollope's intention was to describe the war and examine American society. The two were often disassociated and seemed to be separate issues. Trollope noted that there were large areas of America undisturbed by the conflict. To state this fairly and then describe armies on the move involved contrary aims and required an expository length that blurred Trollope's determination to predict the outcome of the war and the future state of American society. Far from pronouncing Olympian judgments in the manner of Froude, Trollope balanced his personal criticism by a judicial presentation of different aspects of the situation. There are the usual pejorative statements about the inferiority of the blacks, but they are immediately balanced by an account of his friend, the colored landlord in Washington, whose courtesy and kindness mitigated the curt incivility he found among so many white Americans in similar positions.[18] He deplored the rudeness and dishonesty of the frontier settler and concluded with a reasoned apology for such behavior in Biblical and Darwinian terms (vol. 1, ch. IX). In a report, or the travel book as Trollope conceived it, no relevant fact can be omitted. *North America*, with its wealth of anecdote and illustration, remains one of the most complete and discerning studies of the country at this time.

Trollope sought to give a measured and impartial account of society in all his travel books, deliberately eschewing the sensational in favor of the factual and representative. *West Indies* has always been the most popular because of its subject. Nonetheless, it is a very muted account of an area that was

---

[17] "The Present Condition of the Northern States of the American Union" in *Four Lectures*, ed. Morris L. Parrish, London, 1938, p. 33.

[18] Vol. 11, ch. IV. "No white American citizen, ocupying the position of landlord, would have condescended to such comfortable words."

a riot of freebooters, dictators, emigrant aristocrats, and other exotic specimens of society. Trollope brought back with him a collection of cuttings from local newspapers that show what a less disciplined and inhibited writer could have made of the subject. For example, the *Star and Herald* of Panama laconically recorded:

> On Tuesday night, a good deal of excitement was caused by the outrageous conduct of the Chief of Police, rendering it necessary to call out his own men and a military guard to arrest him, which however was not effected. One shot was fired by the Chief of Police during the affair, and two muskets discharged at him when he made his escape.[19]

Most novelists would have rejoiced in such material: Trollope excluded most of it and presented what remained in a temperate prose of alternating opinions.

The travel books are like a moving bridge between the formal report, objective, factual, and comprehensive, and the novels, where fiction establishes its own society in the world of known things. The definition between the novel and the travel book is never as fixed as that separating Trollope's reports from the rest of his writing. Fiction has its own logic and sets a course that is often at odds with its author's intention, but if Trollope could not always chart the direction he could keep his fiction close to shore and far from the open seas of fancy and romance. Certainly, for a writer who knew the world better than any novelist of his day, Trollope chose to examine a very small part of Anglo-Irish society in the novels. There are occasional excursions in search of a European background, but in the main Trollope looks at the gentry and its immediate branches. This nostalgic world of country squires and clergymen was where he chose to travel in those ordered and sequential daydreams. It was a society that he came to know from many different points of view, often American, occasionally Italian. It was subject to gradual

---

[19] *Star and Herald*, Panama, 30 April 1857.

change but not the radical dislocations of industry and organized labor recorded by so many novels written in the 1840's. Essentially, it was a small, ramified community sustained by customary laws and principles.

Unlike the world of the lawyer, Trollope's chosen society was not disturbed by acts of God or sudden conversions, spiritual or otherwise. Devoid of all metaphysical characteristics, it expressed the ideal of law without its practical application of translating the irrational into legal and comprehensible terms. In the novels, people act from known motives and progress to discernible goals. Even when mentally disturbed, their malady is the logical consequence of a defective personality in conjunction with abrading circumstances. When possible, Trollope avoided the circumstantial and accidental and if he could not, he apologized as though charged with a breach of court etiquette.

Trollope's society was unique: it existed only in England and could not be transplanted. When this was attempted in the West Indies, he found the result ludicrous and ineffectual. The societies he examined were embodied in certain types—the sharp-dealing and shooting man of the American frontier, the shrewd, calculating gold miner of Australia. Such men were incongruous in his own particular small world. Trollope could not deny luck a place in his scheme of things but he compresses it into a single personality. The Trollopian hero is a genial, good-humored young man who knows instinctively how to be popular, and in this society popularity can always be translated into success. We shall see how Trollope's fictional alter ego was related to the mature author who composed the *Autobiography*.

Chapter IV

Success and Personality: Autobiography and Biography

Trollope's *Autobiography* falls into two parts: there is the portrait of a clumsy, passionate child dragging his way through dusty lanes to school, unwanted there as at home. The child grows into an awkward young clerk who falls in love and is beset by creditors and stormy rages. These pages contain some of the most moving passages of childhood grief in literature. Then the autobiographical narrative ends and an account book begins setting out the method and means of acquiring success when you have no assets save industry and talent. It is a curiously unbalanced work, emotional and revealing in its early chapters, reserved and objective in the latter. In the first half, Trollope's family and Colonel Maberley exist as living people; in the second half a wife and two sons are dismissed in a few perfunctory lines and Trollope himself vanishes in a catalogued account of working methods, publishers, and general views on the novel-writing business. One part of the *Autobiography* is cast in the form of a confession, the other is the model of a post-office report, with quantity and speed becoming the criteria of success. But the whole divided work is haunted by the creation of the child's dreaming and the grown man's fiction—the gentleman, fair-haired, not brilliant, but kind, courageous, and good, and because of these qualities always popular with men and women. Popularity is the outward expression of virtue. Unpopularity points to a defect in character.

Of course, it has always been possible to look back and see

oneself in childhood as a distinct and different person. Childhood ends, early or late as the case may be, but there is always a time when age renders it not with the immediacy of experience, but as memory. Autobiography, unlike every other literary form, is bound to the individual life, and, since no one has recorded his own death, a frontier is established beyond which the autobiographer cannot pass except in imagination. Trollope appreciated this and left instructions for his *Autobiography* to be published after his death with a greeting to the reader from the other side of the grave. The realization of that moment when the child becomes an adult is a genuine *rite de passage*—certainly it is possible to see one's childhood as a completed life. The difficulty is to know oneself as an adult in quite the same way that the child is known. It is possible to rely on the views of friends—the writer can come to the reader with references like Henry Taylor presenting the admiring testimonials of his friends in high places.[1] Trollope, whose only popularity had come from his fiction, chose to deny the very nature of fiction in the shape of a civil servant grinding out novels as though a letter box were endlessly spewing its contents into the postman's bag. The essence of creativity is made dependent upon waking before dawn, filling a set number of pages, and learning to write in any form of public transport. The effect is unconvincing and a little ridiculous when set beside the evidence to the contrary within and outside the work.

As a civil servant Trollope had been respected, he was never popular. Even at a meet he was the myopic, noisy Mr. Pollock:

> "By George, there's Pollock!" said Maxwell, as he rode into the field by the church. "I'll bet half a crown that he's come down from London this morning, that he was up all night last night, and that he tells us so three times before the hounds go out of the paddock." Mr. Pollock

---

[1] *Autobiography of Henry Taylor* 1800-1875, 2 vols. (London, 1885). Henry Taylor enjoyed an enormous reputation in his own day. Trollope regarded him as one of the major poets of the age, to be ranked with Tennyson. Taylor's *Autobiography* becomes a dull catalogue of his literary excellences in the words of his friends.

was the heavy-weight sporting literary gentleman.
(*Can You Forgive Her?* vol. 2, ch. 16)

Trollope was always capable of seeing himself among his characters, floundering in the mud at a hunt meeting or vainly interrogating the doughty postmistress of Allington, Mrs. Crump (*The Small House at Allington*). His close friends were few and forbearing. Like many popular writers Trollope felt his own identity obscured and made trivial by the reality of his fiction, and it made him shout and thump the table more vociferously than ever.[2] Indeed, in the *Autobiography* he boasted that he had killed Bishop Proudie's wife in response to the complaints about her made by two elderly clergymen in his club. This is an author's declaration of absolute authority over his characters. Unfortunately, the evidence of *The Last Chronicle of Barset* does not confirm Trollope's statement. Mrs. Proudie dies when her game is played out and there is no longer any reason to live. Her husband has been driven to speak of suicide, or at least of resigning the diocese. All her plans are in ruins, her power has dwindled to ashes. And so she dies of a heart attack and is found standing upright, clasping a bedpost. There could be no more fitting end than her demise at the scene of her greatest victories over the bishop.

As he grew older, Trollope became noisier, as though trying to shout down and bluster against the multitude of voices he had created. Trollope knew those voices were always listened to with more affection and attention than his own.

The only lasting joy in Trollope's childhood was his faculty for traveling in a world of imagination where reality took on a kindlier and more consoling configuration. As we have seen, his work at the Post Office had taught him to discipline his dreams into an ordered sequence. This same discipline of mind expelled the image of himself as a child from his daydreams and his fiction. Yet it was always the pain of childhood that fired the imagination of so many of his contemporaries: Dick-

---

[2] Trollope's death by stroke, the result of a gale of laughter, is movingly described by Sadleir in *Trollope A Commentary* (London, 1945), p. 351.

ens recalling the blacking factory in *David Copperfield*, Charlotte Brontë evoking the anguish of her days at Cowan Bridge School in the Lowood of *Jane Eyre*. Trollope had suffered as much as they and remembered every flogging and bitterness of his childhood, but he never permitted children to enter his world of fiction except as stray pawns in the game of marriage and property. Every member of his fictional society must at some point be capable of rational thought and be competent to make decisions, even if they are the wrong ones. In his fiction, as in his daydreams, Trollope had chosen a persona, a man as far removed from his own appearance and cast of mind as the housewife's vision of herself as an international celebrity. This persona was an amiable, kind, clever, and popular young man whose nature ensures success in life. Trollope knew he could never be this young gentleman, but he could claim to own him, much as Magwitch felt he owned Pip in *Great Expectations*. By suppressing the creative and imaginative throughout the account of his writing in the *Autobiography* Trollope tried to make the novels seem of the same order as the reports. In emphasizing his authority over the novels he made himself a parody of the official surveyor—the bullying inspector priding himself on walking farther and faster than any postman or, in this case, of writing more than any other novelist.

The boy whose mind ran to despair and self-destruction is changed into a cardboard automaton writing novels to order like a shoemaker cobbling boots. But the reader cannot forget the child and is set to wondering what became of him. Again and again Trollope emphasizes his remarkable writing speed, then speaks of characters more real than actual people drawing him into their company. The pages fly from his pen; then he pauses to admit that he composes at least four drafts.[3] He writes of his hunting and his travels, his public lectures and his political aspirations as though these were the only serious concerns of his life. Writing was used to fill the hours before

---

[3] Trollope wrote in his *Autobiography*: "It has been my practice to read everything four times at least—thrice in manuscript and once in print" (ch. X).

dawn and those occasions in railway carriages when he brought out a portable desk to defend himself from the conversational sallies of fellow passengers. However, in *Thackeray* he wrote of himself as though he were a man whose every waking hour was spent in a world of fiction:

> To think of a story is much harder work than to write it. The author can sit down with the pen in his hand for a given time, and produce a certain number of words. That is comparatively easy, and if he have a conscience in regard to his task, work will be done regularly. But to think it over as you lie in bed, or walk about, or sit cosily over your fire, to turn it all in your thoughts, and make the things fit;—that requires elbow grease of the mind. (*Thackeray*, p. 123)

This is hardly a man writing to order like the shoemaker at his last, but a mind possessed by a reality of its own creating.

The latter part of the *Autobiography* echoes with voices heard from the chapters of childhood and youth. The child and the persona remain to question the account of Trollope's success. In his study of Thackeray, Trollope wrote of the necessity for adequate proportions in a story, of sufficient preparation for a conclusion. This is the failing of the *Autobiography*. In the latter sections there is no resolution of the child's grief and none of that special satisfaction of autobiography—the unmediated voice speaking truthfully. Instead there is deliberate concealment. What he does attempt is an effort to make the success of his career compensate for the pain of childhood. It is not very convincing. The child may not have worn rags as a man, or known poverty, but the child's yearning for popularity was never fulfilled by the man in his own right, only by his fiction. When Trollope tested his popular standing by seeking election for the seat of Beverley in 1868 he was humiliated and disabused. In his opinion, parliament and political life were the goals of any rational man—but they were goals denied the man without friends and following. Sir Thomas Underwood, out of office in *Ralph the Heir* knew that "there are various ways in which a lame dog may be helped over a stile,—if only the lame dog be popular among dogs" (ch. 1).

The child had longed for success and known despair when every road seemed closed to him. In the *Autobiography* Trollope beats the drum of his success as a novelist and proves that success to the tune of £68,939.17.5 paid out by publishers.[4] The child doubted whether he could ever be regarded as a gentleman with his school fees unpaid and not a penny in his pocket. He watched his schoolmates go on to university and train for professions with the ranks of a gentleman assured them. So he takes a number of pages to prove that the higher ranks of the civil service could be filled only by gentlemen like himself, and uses this argument against the detested merit promotion. However, in *Marion Fay*, the postal clerk George Roden is discovered to have a title, albeit an Italian one, and is speedily moved from St. Martin's-le-Grand to the more distinguished purlieus of the Foreign Office. The Foreign Office always employed gentlemen, the Post Office occasionally. Trollope feels on safer ground defending the professional status of the novelist and placing him in the ranks of barristers, clergymen, doctors, and engineers, who all "endeavour to fill their bellies and clothe backs . . . by the exercise of their abilities and their crafts." (*Autobiography*, Ch. 6). Only when he feels a degree of security as a gentleman can he look to popularity and success:

> I have certainly always had also before my eyes the charms of reputation. Over and above the money view of the question, I wished from the beginning to be something more than a clerk in the Post Office. To be known as somebody,—to be Anthony Trollope if it be no more,—is to me much. (ch. VI)

And here was the problem. Trollope had earned the money, but whose was the success? Who was really popular? Anthony Trollope or Phineas Finn?

[4] The final chapter of the *Autobiography* itemizes the sums received for each novel. At the time of his death *Can You Forgive Her?* had earned most: £3525.

Success and Personality

The Trollope of the *Autobiography* equates money with success and glories in every penny earned. He rides to hounds from a sense of duty and notes each instance when his rank as a gentleman is confirmed. These, of course, are only the outward trappings of the gentleman, and just as Trollope occasionally doubted his success as a novelist and tried to publish anonymously to see if the gold were still gold without a seal upon it, so too he wondered if he were quite the gentleman of his daydreams.[5] He lacked the appearance to begin with, and he was devoid of that sweetness of nature and unselfconscious charm that defines an Arthur Fletcher. Trollope knew this and felt that he was the kind of gentleman who had continually to present his credentials. It was so different for Harry Annesley.

Appearance counted for a great part of the gentleman's success, but appearance without personality produced a Burgo Fitzgerald or an Adolphus Crosbie. Personality was a term used with more definition and import in Trollope's day than it is with us today, when it denotes any quality that sets one person apart from another. In the course of writing about his father, Alfred North Whitehead used the word with considerable precision:

> He was a man with local interests and influence; apart from an understanding of such provincial figures, the social and political history of England in the nineteenth century cannot be comprehended. England was governed by the influence of personality: this does not mean "intellect." My father was not intellectual, but he possessed personality.[6]

---

[5] *Nina Balatka*, 1866, was published anonymously. James Pope Hennessy writes:
  Its author had begun to feel that his sales might now have become dependent on his mere name rather than on the quality of his books; so he wanted to launch *Nina Balatka* on its own merits and without any adventitious aid. *Anthony Trollope* (London, 1971), p. 243.

[6] Alfred North Whitehead, "Autobiographical Notes," in *Essays in Science and Philosophy* (New York, 1948), p. 7. Whitehead wrote of his father, Vicar of St. Peter's Parish in East Kent: "When the Baptist minister in the parish

Essentially, personality was the ability to please and influence others. It was the very source and wellspring of success. But popularity in Trollope's definition is always derived from moral excellence. Burgo Fitzgerald is admired but he is not popular; that Apollo, Adolphus Crosbie, has never been able to win friends although he is clever and astonishingly handsome.

The concept of the gentleman as a moral ideal and not a mere social classification was undoubtedly one of the great achievements of the nineteenth-century imagination. Decorum and propriety in the Johnsonian sense had to be precisely balanced in a man if he were to be a real gentleman. When a man of birth and property behaved outrageously he did not cease to be a gentleman: he became a cad and could never be deemed a true gentleman. Trollope accepted this but added something more to it. If he were possessed of all these qualities a gentleman was assured of the popularity denied a man of lesser worth. It is enough to read that Mark Robarts in *Framley Parsonage* is popular to appreciate that he will surmount all difficulties and gain his chosen end. Yet Victorian England, like every other age before and since, abounded in popular men who had no claim to any particular moral virtue. Trollope refused to acknowledge this self-evident fact and proceeded to write biography in accord with his belief.

Unlike the boy of the *Autobiography*, Palmerston had been the prince of Harrow, a credit in the classroom and captain on the cricket field. Schoolmasters praised him. His professor in Edinburgh, Dugald Stewart, wrote that he had never seen "a more faultless character at his time of life, or one possessed of a more amiable disposition" (*Palmerston*, p. 10). Trollope prefaces Stewart's encomium with his own observation that "he was by no means a man of genius, possessed of not more than ordinary gifts of talent" (p. 9). Here the difficulty begins, for if Palmerston was popular, there was no gainsaying that he was more popular with women than with men. Even as an

---

was dying, it was my father who read the Bible to him. Such was England in those days, guided by local men with strong mutual antagonisms and intimate community of feeling" (p. 8).

octogenarian, Palmerston's sexual escapades could occasion scandal. So, Trollope engages in some arch equivocation:

> The world has heard of no trouble into which he got about women. He became so popular with the world generally that the world was afraid to be censorious or to enquire into him with prying eyes. The world called him "Cupid" when he was young, and the world said nothing more severe than that.

This is special pleading, but Trollope knows he must hedge over what may be generally known and what can be proven. With the rhetorical reiteration of "the world" as public opinion, it begins to sound like the case of the man who has been frequently charged but never found guilty: a man whose innocence is the product of good pleading, not good character.

In fact, Palmerston was an incorrigible and unrepentant rake whose amorous adventures astounded three generations. Besides, in diplomacy he was often a bully whose gunboat diplomacy and jingoism alarmed the rest of Europe. More often than not he was saved by good luck rather than prudent counsel. Yet Trollope insisted on applying the moral equation that he had developed in the novels: men like Palmerston are lucky because their moral virtues ensure their popularity and success. In Trollope's final lines, Palmerston's life was exemplary: "I do not know the life of any man who has shown such a career of unchequered good fortune and jocund happiness,—or more unblemished honesty and truer courage" (p. 199).

Throughout his life Trollope maintained that he had no interest in philosophy, that facts and facts alone concerned him. "I regard as futile," he wrote in *Cicero*,

> the attempts which are made to rewrite history on the base of moral convictions and philosophical conclusion. History very often has been, and no doubt often again will be, rewritten, with good effect and in the service of truth, on the finding of new facts. Records have been brought to light which have hitherto been buried, and testimonies are compared with testimonies which have

not before been seen together. But to imagine that a man may have been good who has lain under the ban of all the historians, all the poets, and all the tellers of anecdotes, and then to declare such goodness simply in accordance with the dictates of a generous heart or a contradictory spirit, is to disturb rather than to assist history. (*The Life of Cicero*, vol. 1, p. 208)

And with such a rhetorical pronouncement—always useful in a court of law when there is an insufficiency of evidence—Trollope refuses to admit any discussion of Catiline's motives. Once popular opinion has judged a man it is the historian's duty to confirm that opinion, not seek to redress or deny it.

Just as with Palmerston, Trollope is concerned that Cicero should be a moral exemplar. Indeed, he so manipulates the evidence that he can state with confidence that Cicero in his day epitomized all the best qualities of an English gentleman. Transformations of this order require a great deal of sweeping and shuffling, long periods in which the reader is hectored and harangued, but Trollope never falters. His intention is plain: "I have endeavored, as I have gone on with my work, to compare him to an Englishman of the present day" (vol. 2, p. 224). The *Punch* cartoon that showed Trollope admiring the bust of Cicero crowned with a jaunty topper characterizes the theme and intention of the work.

It is not anachronistic to draw parallels between the society of Cicero's day and that of England in the last century. Nineteenth-century biographers never ceased to refer to these similarities, and the tradition continues.[7] But no one went quite so far, nor in quite the same direction, as Trollope when he

---

[7] For example, in his excellent *Cicero* (Oxford, 1971), David Stockton observes:
The society into which Marcus Tullius Cicero was born at the end of the second century would have appeared familiar enough to an English eye a few generations ago. Italy was very much a land of country towns, each dominated by a handful of local families who together made up what might be called "the gentry" or "the quality." These families ran the towns and the adjacent countryside, quarrelled over the ordering of local affairs, married off their sons to each other's daughters" (p. 1).

portrayed Cicero as an Englishman in an alien context. Extraordinary arguments were necessary for Trollope to maintain his thesis that a gentleman inevitably derives his popularity from the moral excellence of his personality. The problem, quite simply, was that Cicero's political career was a failure. After the year 63 Cicero committed one error after another. His brief period of glory in the Senate fired his ambition and he sought for power beyond his capacity and station. He had no wide political support and he did not possess the connections to support him in times of trouble. Some would even go so far as to state that Cicero lacked the intellectual capacity and the courage for a political role. Trollope cannot ignore this evidence so he falls back on an argument that he has developed throughout his observations of different societies. If Cicero had failed it was because of the nature of his society—he was a moral man in an immoral time and the times eventually defeated him. The appeal to extenuating circumstances is casuistical, but it has its origin in legal procedure. Trollope is not the first to plead that his client went astray because he fell into bad company.

In traveling abroad, Trollope examined foreign society on its own terms. If the Englishman did not flourish in Australia then the Englishman was advised to stay at home where he belonged. Cicero was a different matter altogether. The Victorians, like previous generations, tended to read themselves into the life of Cicero. Tacitus was out of favor among Victorians who deplored his cynicism; however, Cicero seemed to embody some of the best principles of politics and law. Nonetheless, even Trollope's contemporaries were startled by this portrait of Cicero as a dedicated civil servant prepared to give up his life for the good of the state.

All Trollope's biographies follow the same pattern. If a man succeeds it is because he is popular. If a man of moral excellence fails it is because of deficiencies in society. Caesar succeeds because he works harder than any man of his day: Thackeray does not reach the extent of his intellectual and creative capacity because of laziness. And Cicero fails because he is an English gentleman forced into the company of bloody-minded and factious politicians. What may seem specious and simplistic points to Trollope's profound conviction that a just society existed by reason of gentlemen. It is this bond between gentlemen that brings the Reverend Mr. Crawley and Archdeacon Grantly together at the conclusion of *The Last Chronicle of Barset* " 'We stand,' said he, 'on the only perfect level on which such men can meet each other. We are both gentlemen' " (ch. 83). This "perfect level" is the golden mean of society, the balance between decorum in a social sense and propriety as a moral dimension.

In this society it requires intelligence of a high order in a woman to discern the true gentleman from those who are accorded that rank. Moreover, it is within a woman's power to make a gentleman in "the fullest sense of the word," that is, a man committed to public service. Alice Vavasor is naturally forgiven her three engagements in *Can You Forgive Her?* because she forces John Grey from a selfish life of seclusion in Cambridgeshire into a political career. Women are slaves to convention, as Mrs. Roden states in *Marion Fay*, knowing that it is not women who have ordained their own servitude. But even slaves have a limited authority over their own lives. They have the right to choose a husband. Glencora knew that she could have refused to marry Plantagenet Palliser even if she could not have married Burgo Fitzgerald until she came of age. Lily Dale chose Crosbie for her lover without thought and consideration. The test of a woman as a rational and moral being occurs when she names the true gentleman as her future husband. Miss Dunstable's good sense is evident when she selects Dr. Thorne from among all the admirers of her great fortune.

Because Trollope accords all honor to those who are popular and can use that popularity to serve and guide others, he is alive to all aspects of failure. Success appears in one person in the novels: it is embodied in a fair-haired, aquiline-nosed gentleman like George Roden or Arthur Fletcher. Even the Irish Phineas Finn is given golden hair and a suitable nose. It is occasionally possible to dispense with appearance as with Colonel Stubbs in *Ayala's Angel* but the popularity of the gentleman is a constant. He marries well and becomes a kind and useful member of society. There are many who cannot accomplish this harmonious relationship between character and community. True, failure may rest with the community, as in the case of Cicero. More often it comes from a flawed personality. Occasionally the world may be mistaken and what seems failure in life will be acclaimed as success after death. Trollope cites the posthumous renown of Cicero as proof of this unusual occurrence.

In the novels the balance between success and failure can be assessed more equitably than when dealing with historical facts. Cicero required special pleading, but of Mr. Harding we are told: "He had never been forward enough in anything to become the acknowledged possessor of popularity. But, now that he was gone, men and women told each other how good he had been" (*The Last Chronicle of Barset*, ch. 81). A reputation for goodness extending beyond the grave is not quite compensation enough for a lack of popularity in life, but it merits some praise.

Nobody can exist without society in Trollope's novels. Those who fail are condemned to solitude: they take their own lives or are driven into exile, and exile and death carry the same penalty. Success and failure are always resolved in social rather than in individual terms. The measure of existence is human in Trollope and extends no farther back than living memory and no farther forward than the hope of children. Any dialogue between man and God becomes impossible in a world that does not admit religion except as a social convention functioning well or badly according to those who support it. But even though heaven and hell exist only in catch-phrases and conventional exclamations, there is an abiding faith at work that seeks the creation of a just society. Trollope describes a world of convention and law, a world that derives its forms from human nature and its authority from the social will. To express this pragmatic, rational society in all its diversity required a special language: one derived from law and attempting, in Archbold's phrase, "to persuade, not to impress."

Chapter V

Society and the Language of Law

Trollope was not a lawyer but he had been trained in legal modes of argument and the presentation of evidence. The Freeling report, derived from Archbold, provides the structure of his novels, and Archbold's requirements for a language devoid of unnecessary ornament and designed "to persuade, not to impress," regulates Trollope's famous "non-style." It is significant that although critics have carped at Trollope's repetitions and clichés, lawyers have found his writing consistently satisfying. Certainly, it could be argued that until recent years more lawyers, beginning with Maitland, than literary critics have commended Trollope. After judicially examining the claims of other literary contenders, F. Lyman Windolph ruled in 1956 that "the novels of Trollope will be read and enjoyed longer than those of either Dickens or Thackeray."[1] Lengthy briefs have been written on various aspects of the legal situations in the novels, culminating in the ferocious correspondence between Henry S. Drinker and Sir Francis Newbolt. Drinker responded to Newbolt's criticism of *Orley Farm*,

> In the enclosed memorandum, I have endeavored to show that Trollope was not guilty of a number of the most serious inaccuracies of which you accuse him, and that in your zeal to win your case you have unconsciously allowed yourself to indulge in inaccuracies which, weighted by your relative training and expectation for exactness

[1] *Reflections of the Law in Literature*, Philadelphia, 1956, p. 12.

in legal matters, are comparable to those of which you accuse the author.²

Newbolt's refusal to accept the challenge was noted by Drinker with great pleasure.

At issue was *Orley Farm*, a novel set out in accordance with the requirements of a declaration and involving a forged will. Drinker and Newbolt argued over Trollope's knowledge of the law, but the novelist demonstrated that the resolution of the case depended not on legal wit and acumen but on the contending lawyers' inability to ask the right question at the proper time. Two witnesses had survived from the signing of a document that Lady Mason maintained was a will leaving Orley Farm to her son. All the finest legal talent of England had been summoned to the trial, with Sir Charles Leatherham for the prosecution and Mr. Chaffanbrass for the defense. At the conclusion, Lady Mason, although guilty, is acquitted because the prosecuting lawyers have failed to ask one specific question of Bridget Bolster, a witness to the signing of the document in question. Over supper in Great St. Helen's, Moulder, the commercial traveller, is conducting his own interrogation of the two witnesses, John Kenneby and Bridget Bolster, when Bridget volunteers the crucial information:

> "But the paper as we signed," said Bridget, "wasn't the old gentleman's will,—no more than this is," and she lifted up her apron. . . . "Wasn't the old gentleman's will!" said Moulder, turning on poor Bridget in his anger with a growl. "But I say it was the old gentleman's will. You never dared say as much as that in court." "I wasn't asked," said Bridget. (ch. 77)

This point was overlooked by Drinker and Newbolt too, but it illustrates neatly Trollope's conviction that lawyers could provide only partial truths whereas he had the power to reveal the whole truth to the reader.

Throughout his novels the form of the declaration provides

---

² Henry S. Drinker to Sir Francis Newbolt, Dec. 5, 129. MSS. Biddle Law Library, Univ. of Pennsylvania, AD3-3780.

the narrative structure. There is a commencement stating the form of action (the legal mode suited to resolving the specific "cause" or case). It defines the nature of the dispute and the parties to the action. It is followed by a statement setting out the cause of action (the facts or events that must be shown to be true for the form of action to succeed) and a conclusion that shows the resolution of the initial cause (how the dispute is to be settled). The morphology of the declaration still held the capacity to incorporate the charge against the defendant and plaintiff's probable case and the defendant's charge to be sustained by the evidence of witnesses. Trollope both revives and modifies the mode. The dialogue is always given in the form of evidence by characters that Blackstone would have designated "the witnesses or followers of the plaintiff" (Blackstone, *Commentaries*, 111, p. 295).

With only two exceptions, Trollope's theme is always that of a transaction involving money and marriage.[3] Money and property are active presences, capable of functioning like personalities in the work: for example, the diamond necklace of Lizzie Eustace that turns out to be paraphernalia in the convoluted legal opinion of Mr. Dove.[4] In this case, Trollope shows the law constructing a more absurd fiction than any contrived by a novelist, and he plays the same game in a number of novels, matching his own veracity and perception against the lawyer's. It is Mr. Scarborough's particular delight to set the whole law of entail on its head by means of two marriage certificates. *Mr. Scarborough's Family* is a study of the ways in which a dying man can flout the law, yet gain nothing more in the end than an understanding of his unworthy sons and the pleasure of acquiring this knowledge at the expense of lawyers and debt-collectors. According to Trol-

[3] The two exceptions are *La Vendée* and *The Fixed Period*.
[4] In the preface to *The Eustace Diamonds*, Oxford, 1973, Michael Sadleir notes that Charles Merewether, Trollope's legal friend, was responsible for Mr. Dove's opinion that Lizzie's necklace was not an heirloom but paraphernalia. In this instance the legal opinion is made to seem of the same fictional order of absurdity as Lizzie's tearful account of how the jewels were given to her by a loving husband.

lope, the law establishes a society that bears only passing resemblance to reality but retains the power to impose this fictitious version of reality upon people. At least Mr. Scarborough knows that he has been able to oppose the law and see his will prevail, even if he cannot change the nature of his two most unsatisfactory sons in the process. Of course, it must not be forgotten at any point that in Trollope versus the law the plaintiff is a layman (in this case an informed and legally minded civil servant) with his own conception of the law.

Thomas Eisele is correct in observing that "Each profession fancies itself—this is not a fanciful fancy—to have discovered a new level of reality, or a new reality. This will seem—indeed will be—the discovery of a new world."[5] Trollope, furnished with weapons from a legal armory, wrote to establish his own reality set midway between the world of known things and the society of law. Above all else, his world was based upon the identification of the reasonable man and the rational correlation between character and event. He was always uneasy when confronted with calamities or any incident not predicated by character, so he strenuously avoids the conventional Victorian scene of revelation at a deathbed. Marion Fay's death is recorded in a few conventional phrases and Hampstead's vision of her at the grave is more an indication of a troubled mind than any actuality. In Trollope's world, people die as they lived. In *He Knew He Was Right*, Louis Trevelyan does not forgive Emily at the end, although she chooses to imagine he has, and Sir Roger Scatcherd in *Dr. Thorne* dies from the brandy he has managed to hide under his pillow. While appearing to describe a death, Trollope immediately ascribes to it a moral and legal status. It is not Marion Fay's death that has import but its effect upon the mind and future of Hampstead: as an event, it has no significance except as social influence. This quality of description and ascription is a characteristic of legal writing, and Trollope employs it continuously.

[5] "The Legal Imagination and Language: A Philosophical Criticism," *Univ. of Colorado Law Review*, 47 (Spring 1976), 379.

Whereas the lawyer seeks to regulate the flux of events, Trollope asserts the existence of a rational natural order and is disturbed by unexpected calamity or coincidence. His language is the precise reflection of his society, but the lawyer is beset with a fundamental paradox: "the more technically and logically satisfactory the statements within a set of rules, the more those rules must fail to express what the situation thus regulated really holds."[6] The failure to make the punishment fit the crime reflects the lawyer's inability to express a rule that correctly embodies experience. The lawyer is given his material, Trollope creates his: therein lies the essential difference between the two. But if the law can admit paradox Trollope is bound to his rational premise. Dickens may kill his characters off at will, Charlotte Brontë can discover long-lost cousins on any strange doorstep, but Trollope's world functions to a different rationale, and sudden death and coincidence are incongruities. For example, in *Ralph the Heir*, Squire Newton is killed while foxhunting when he has almost succeeded in buying out the legitimate heir on behalf of his natural son (ch. 48). Throughout the chapter Trollope voices a chorus warning the reader that Squire Newton is "too loud" in his triumph over the legitimate Ralph Newton. The repetition implies that some moral or personal negligence is involved, with the Squire's death seeming a logical consequence. A contrivance is tricked out to seem a natural occurrence by means of an appeal to an imaginary rule, a case of liability with proof of negligence on the part of the Squire. The result, like most instances of fabricated law, is meretricious. At the conclusion of the chapter the bastard Ralph Newton is set adrift on the world but Trollope's manipulation in this case resembles the sleight of hand of a dishonest lawyer.

Appeal to an imaginary rule is one means Trollope employs to gloss over the problems of chance and coincidence; he is more effective when using the diversionary tactics of legal

[6] James B. White, *The Legal Imagination,* Toronto, 1973, p. 240. The best illustration of this principle can be found in *The Fixed Period*, particularly John Neverbend's account of the "fixed period" in the first chapter. Right reason and sound law fail when they attempt to regulate human nature.

rhetoric. In *The Small House at Allington*, it is necessary that young Johnny Eames, the hobbledehoy who so resembles the young Trollope, should acquire the means to live as a gentleman. Plums do not fall into men's mouths in Trollope's world, although many spend their lives waiting for such a fortuitous happening. Thus Eames does not inherit money from a long-lost uncle, but he does manage to save Lord de Guest from an enraged bull. This *Taurus ex machina* is the novelist's stock-in-trade, but Trollope tries to make it credible and inoffensive by shifting the reader's viewpoint. It is a device that parallels the barrister's change in demeanor when desiring to divert a jury's attention from damaging evidence.

Thus, with diversion as the intention, considerable importance is attached to the nature of the bull throughout the scene. It is a quiet animal, a veritable lamb among bovines. We are told at considerable length that Lord de Guest has long been accustomed to treat it like a farmyard pet. On this occasion, however, he blows his nose with a red pocket handkerchief and the bull charges. It is also made known that Johnny Eames has always chosen to walk home past the bull's paddock and the possibility therefore of his presence at that particular spot when the bull attacks is fortuitous but not improbable. Then the perspective alters and Trollope deliberately minimizes the excitement of the two men fending off the beast by concentrating upon the emotions of the bull. Nothing could be more alien to Trollope's method and mode of thought than to attribute human passions to an animal, but this bull is made the protagonist of the scene, the subject for philosophical commentary as follows: "When the animal saw with what unfairness he was treated, and that the number of his foes was doubled, while no assistance had lent itself on his side, he stood for a while, disgusted by the injustice of humanity." The men manage to make their escape and the bull is dignified with a short homily:

> He had knocked his head against the stout timber, which was strong enough to oppose him, but was dismayed by the brambles which he might have trodden under foot

without an effort. How many of us are like the bull, turning away conquered by opposition which should be as nothing to us, and breaking our feet, and worse still, our hearts, against rocks of adamant. (*The Small House at Allington*, vol. 2, ch. 1)

The effect is comic, a study in the alteration of traditional roles and customary rhetorical emphasis, but the comedy in this instance diverts attention from a coincidence. Johnny Eames has gained his patron, and the philosophical bull and the red handkerchief successfully disguise a mechanical contrivance. The scene ends with a flurry of trivialities over dress and dinner, and the reader is satisfied that what he has witnessed is reality, not fabrication. Just as the lawyer seeks a resolution to a problem that is not merely sound in law but demonstrably just, Trollope scrupulously avoids all the devices of the sensation novelists to sustain interest—when he cannot avoid a charging bull he employs a number of rhetorical forms to regulate the excitement. In his study of the West Indies he had eschewed the flamboyant and exotic to concentrate the reader's attention on the social and economic structure of the area: particular incidents were used only if they served to corroborate or deny a stated thesis. And in *Barchester Towers* he pauses to inform the reader that Mr. Slope will not marry Eleanor Bold and that Mrs. Proudie will become the unconsecrated but actual bishop of Barchester.

There is neither novelty nor remarkable invention in Trollope's plots. Indeed it is possible to categorize them under certain headings and, if this is so, it then becomes necessary to find the reason for Trollope's ability to sustain interest in stories that are predictable by design and authorial intent.[7] As

---

[7] Ruth apRoberts neatly summarizes a typical encounter on this subject: John Dustin ("Thematic Alternation in Trollope," *PMLA*, 1962) proposes a classification of the novels according to theme: in type A, a heroine must make a choice of suitors and an inheritance is involved; in type B, a hero makes an error of moral judgment and must find his way out of difficulties. Types A and B alternate in Trollope's career so long as he writes "mechanically;" type C breaks the pattern with variety and profundity and the "darkness" that Cockshut sees in the late novels.

James White states: "the process of telling a story generates a pressure towards the inexpressible, the inexplicable . . . whatever one's original intentions the story creates a meaning of its own as it goes along."[8] Trollope was continually aware of this power, knowing that he could be absorbed by his novels as he was in his daydreams. The most effective method of controlling his characters was to confine them within the transactional structure he borrowed from the legal declaration and official report. But prisoners have been known to escape from the stoutest prison and characters surmount the most rigid linguistic form. Mrs. Proudie does not die in consequence of an arbitrary decision from the novelist as judge, and the charming Miss Mackenzie is described by Trollope as a "very unattractive old maid, who was overwhelmed by money troubles" (*Autobiography*, ch. 10). Yet no description could be less apt when her attractions are related in the course of the novel. Trollope chose to believe that he could manipulate his characters much as the barrister hopes to direct the course of a cross-examination, but all too often the characters eluded his authority, and Miss Mackenzie blossoms forth as the beauty in freckled muslin at the charity bazaar.

It was natural enough for Trollope to distrust narrative since it gave characters a life beyond his control. Even his persona, the fair-haired and popular young gentleman, could shake him off and embark on a life of his own just as the tractable child suddenly becomes an independent adult, disowning all duty and obligation to parent and home. Throughout the novels there is a dialectic between the necessity for narrative and the authority of expository characterization, the

---

William Cadbury takes issue with Dustin in "Shape and Theme: Determinants of Trollope's Forms," *PMLA*, 1963. He himself puts the novels in pairs according to shape, then in different pairs according to theme, and then in different sets according to type—epic, romance, or picaresque. . . . ("Anthony Trollope," in *Victorian Fiction: A Second Guide to Research*, ed. George H. Ford, New York, 1978, pp. 148-149) Of course, there is similarity of content in Trollope's novels but the sustaining similarity is in form. I live in hope that I may add a complicating variant to this engaging discussion.

[8] *The Legal Imagination*, p. 863.

balance always residing with the latter. Trollope made a virtue of his inability to construct ingenious plots:

> I have never troubled myself much about the construction of plots, and am not now insisting specially on thoroughness in a branch of work in which I myself have not been very thorough. I am not sure that the construction of a perfected plot has been at any period within my power. But the novelist has other aims than the elucidation of his plot. He desires to make his readers so intimately acquainted with his characters that the creations of his brain should be to them speaking, moving, living, human creatures. (*Autobiography*, ch. 12)

Because Trollope regarded the elucidation of character as the novelist's main duty, he singled out Thackeray as the greatest of all English novelists.

> His knowledge of human nature was supreme, and his characters stand out as human beings, with a force and a truth which has not, I think, been within the reach of any other English novelist in the period. (*Autobiography*, ch. 13)

When the lawyer speaks of "knowing" his client, he uses that term in much the same way as the novelist does when he describes a character of his own creation. Francis Wellman went so far as to claim that if his knowledge of a witness was thorough he could confidently predict the outcome of a cross-examination and the subsequent verdict. Wellman despised histrionics in the courtroom and the tendency of some legal orators "to grasp the thunderbolt."[9] He relied on examination and exposition to carry an argument. Trollope, the civil servant, brought the same techniques to the writing of his novels.

Trollope had been trained in the writing of reports based on Archbold's requirements for information that was "certain, positive and true." The resolution of an action is always by means of reasoned argument involving different opinions. In his travel books a snatch of dialogue, a dramatic incident will

---

[9] *The Art of Cross-Examination*, New York, 1948, p. 1.

be set against a passage of expository prose presenting a contrary view. In the novels, Trollope engages his characters in dialogue that functions as a form of examination. No one took greater pleasure in cross-examining a startled postmaster than Trollope, and he soon overcame a certain diffidence when called upon to question the complaining gentry. Interrogation to elucidate fact had become part of his daily life and yet no one more keenly resented being made the subject of examination. As a witness he was as much intent on revealing his interrogator's ignorance as on demonstrating his own superior knowledge.[10] Thus, in the novels, Trollope engages his characters in dialogue that functions as a form of cross-examination. Characters do not simply talk in Trollope; there is no attempt to permit dialogue a freedom divorced from literal meaning. Instead, there is question and response with a definite purpose in mind. It is not possible to define a character by a particular ideolect as in Dickens: Trollope's characters, with few exceptions, use the same vocabulary in the same patterned cadence.[11] The identification of characters within

---

[10] Trollope's recall of fact under examination was remarkable, but his resentment and discomfiture at being questioned is always apparent. Thus in 1855 when examined by Viscount Monck on postal arrangements in Ireland:

[Trollope] I do not think any other officer has local knowledge of the whole district except myself; I have local knowledge over the whole area.

What important towns are there upon the line between Limerick and the junction and Waterford—Clonmel is the most important. Do not you pass through Tipperary?—I do not think Tipperary an important town; I have omitted other towns similar to Tipperary; I call those important that return members to Parliament.

Then, of course, you would call Portarlington an important town; you do not think the importance of towns is to be measured by their commercial importance?—It is very hard to distinguish which are important towns and which are not, but I will undertake to say that no one who knows the country will say that I have not given the more important towns. . . . (*Report from the Select Committee on Postal Arrangements* [Waterford, etc.]; House of Commons, 31 July 1855, Evidence 16 July 1855, p. 128)

[11] When middle-class people or the gentry speak. As John W. Clark notes in *The Language and Style of Anthony Trollope*, London, 1975, Trollope makes frequent use of dialect, ranging from English provincial to American.

a passage of dialogue seldom requires a mention of particular names; rather, identification is established by argument. The cause of each character is known, and through the argument advanced to support that cause the character is made known to the reader.

The reader is always a witness to the testimony of the characters' speech, or permitted to read letters, but evidence without examination offers only partial truth. It is not enough to testify, it is also necessary to interpret the evidence from every possible standpoint, often setting the characters' statements against the advocacy of narrative comment. Characters question each other, and the narrator as advocate can then examine and cross-examine the characters in a process of judicial analysis that draws upon precedents derived from society and shared experience. Explanation and evaluation constantly oscillate with the result that the evidence presented is frequently contradictory. Is Alice Vavasor a jilt in *Can You Forgive Her?*, is the reader right to condemn her for emotional vagaries, and should her own declarations of unworthiness be accepted? Or should one rather consider the change wrought in that erstwhile recluse, John Grey?

> The husband had very fully discussed with his wife that matter of his parliamentary ambition, and found in her a very ready listener. Having made up his mind to do this thing, he was resolved to do it thoroughly, and was becoming almost as full of politics, almost as much devoted to sugar, as Mr. Palliser himself. He at any rate could not complain that his wife would not interest herself in his pursuits. (ch. 80)

How can we speak, or even consider the notion of forgiveness, when we are given a woman who has created a useful member of society and provided herself with the political life she has always desired? Alice Vavasor is successful, and success is always to be commended in Trollope's world. The final judgment is that of the reader, who is called upon to relive the character in the mind of a reasonable man, and, unlike the law, Trollope is quite prepared to admit the reasonable woman.[12]

It is because Trollope recognizes the power of narrative that his feelings toward it are so ambivalent, because he appreciates its capacity to undermine the dominance of character. So he deals awkwardly with concurrent events or shifts in time, "taking the reader back" to certain incidents and engaging in elaborate apologies for the need to recall past incidents. He cannot master the synchronized surge of events that characterizes so many of the novels of Dumas or Dickens. Instead he subordinates narrative to analytic exposition.

To witness, to understand after the manner of a judge asking a jury to decide what a reasonable man would have done in similar circumstances is Trollope's art. Certainly the reader is given evidence that allows him to sit in judgment upon the judge himself. Thus, in *John Caldigate*: "Judge Bramber could not as yet quite make up his mind. It is hoped that the reader has made up his, but the reader knows somewhat more than the judge knew" (vol. 2, ch. 27). The reader is called upon to relive a story in terms of character, not event. All the relevant evidence is made available (far more than would be admitted in a court of law)—the witnesses have been heard and examined as to motive and intent; the reader's duty is to identify himself with the character in such a way that his actions can be realized not as animated abstractions, but as reasoned and felt experience. It is Trollope's intention to induce a moral and social commitment on the part of the reader by convincing him of the reasonableness of the action. Is Lily Dale to be pitied because of her love for Crosbie and should she then be commended for refusing Johnny Eames? Or is she engaging in an elaborate defense against the public admission of failure just as Emily Wharton in *The Prime Minister* shuts herself off from society in widow's weeds of impenetrable

---

[12] Which is more than the law has done in creating this remarkable fiction. Ronald K. L. Collins traces the concept of "the reasonable man" in "Language, History, and the Legal Process: A Profile of the 'Reasonable Man,'" *Rutgers, Camden Law Jour.*, 8 (Winter 1977), 311-323.

gloom? These are the questions that are continually put to the reader, who must come to a conclusion through a process of rational and sensitive evaluation.

The cure of souls is the duty of the priest; the lawyer may choose to regard himself as the temporal part of "one of the great civilizing forces in human society."[13] Trollope appropriated the functions of both priest and lawyer, defending his novels as secular sermons that required not an affirmation of faith or acceptance of a verdict, but merely a reasoned agreement. Throughout the *Autobiography* he defined his profession in these terms: "I have ever thought of myself as a preacher of sermons, and my pulpit as one which I could make both salutary and agreeable to my audience" (ch. 8). Trollope viewed the religious sermon as occasionally useful, often fatuous, and always boring. The sermons described in the novels either inflame the minds of the impressionable or serve as a metaphor for eternity. The novelist's purpose was quite otherwise. The passage of the *Autobiography* in which he develops this concept continues:

> But the novelist, if he have a conscience, must preach his sermons with the same purpose as the clergyman, and must have his own system of ethics. If he can do this efficiently, if he can make virtue alluring and vice ugly, while he charms his reader instead of wearying him, then I think that Mr. Carlyle need not call him distressed, nor talk of that long ear of fiction, nor question whether he be or not the most foolish of existing mortals. (ch. 12)

Trollope insisted on his right to promulgate his vision of the social order. It employed the practices of lawyers, and the very language of the law to undermine the legal assumption that law was the bond of society in a disordered and depraved world. The novelist's social ethic postulated the rationality of free choice in an ordered (and particularly English) universe where the individual was not at the mercy of chance and

[13] "Law as Institutional Fact," *The Law Quarterly Review*, 90, No. 357 (Jan. 1974). "Brute facts" and "institutional facts" are explained in philosophical terms in J. Searle's *Speech Acts*, Cambridge, 1966, pp. 50-52.

contingency. To Trollope social justice was the meting out of rewards and punishments as the consequence of right or wrong decisions. The law, as he depicted it, was often an impediment to this process. He regarded himself as a preacher but his sermons were models for conduct in a rational society. Lawyers and priests were unreliable guides and Trollope cheerfully assumed the revised duties of both. Post office surveyor and popular novelist were elevated to a more responsible social sphere.

Trollope's society and the choices available within it were based upon the relationship between the individual and the institutional identity of a person. In law this may be defined by reference to Neil MacCormick's terms of "brute facts" and "institutional facts."[14] Character without any regard for chance or providence, determines the individual in Trollope's opinion, but the individual has then to establish an institutional role that expresses the personality and serves the public need. The model for Trollope is always the gentleman who chooses to become a member of parliament, devoting his energy and mind to the service of others. For this reason popularity assumes its dominant importance, for without popularity, a man cannot influence and help others. Palliser's failure results from his inability to live comfortably with his fellow men: Phineas Finn's success is founded on a multitude of friendships. Trollope knew and preached that the greatest sinners are not the failures of the world but those

> who promise themselves the triumph, and then never struggle at all. The task is never abandoned; but days go by and weeks;—and then months and years,—and nothing is done. The dream of youth becomes the doubt of middle life, and then the despair of age. (*Ralph the Heir*, ch. 40)

The Felix Carburys and George Hotspurs are failures, but only in a social and institutional sense. They do not fail as individuals because they have no higher vision of themselves

---

[14] Dennis Lloyd, *The Idea of Law*, Harmondsworth, 1977, Preface.

than pleasure and creature comfort gained at the expense of others. Sir Thomas Underwood had a dream of parliamentary power and composing a biography of Sir Francis Bacon that would do honor to the great chancellor. But it comes to nothing and he endures the greatest suffering of all, which is the recognition of one's personal responsibility for failure in life. Alone in his chambers he listens to a wavering and discordant flute from a back attic in Southhampton Gardens, and it speaks to his mind of hopes lost and a once promising life given up to sullen indolence:

> There comes upon us all as we grow up in years, hours in which it is impossible to keep down the conviction that everything is vanity, that the life past has been vain from folly, and the life to come must be vain from impotence. (*Ralph the Heir*, ch. 51)

Trollope's society abounds with rogues who are active enough and want the right things for the wrong reasons. A Ferdinand Lopez and a George Vavasor desire parliamentary office, but only that they may better serve themselves. Such men are committed by society to death and exile. To fail is one thing, but to attempt success by cheating is a social crime not easily forgiven. Still, the suffering of these men is not so acute as that of a Harry Hotspur or a Thomas Underwood who know that the reason for their failure is not because of schemes gone awry, but the result of a deficiency of character and will. This was Trollope's own particular anguish, for no one had yearned more for popularity and success and fought for it more honestly. To be successful was the avowed ambition of the *Autobiography*, that record of high aspiration and partial fulfillment. In *Marian Fay*, Sir Boreas of the Post Office puts it more simply: "Of course what we all want in life is success" (vol. 3, ch. 6). And George Roden learns that he must accept a compromise between his radical individualism and his institutional self if he wants to move from the Post Office to the Foreign Office and live at peace with his wife's family and friends.

Trollope's heartfelt ambition to sit in the House of Commons was the source of his greatest disappointment. The collapse of his political hopes at Beverley made him recognize that failure was as much the common lot of man as death: "It is sad to say it, and sad to think it, but failure is the ordinary lot of man."[15]

The goal was splendid, but so few could attain it. Nonetheless, every human being had to engage in the struggle to define himself as an individual and in society. It was more difficult for women since their ability to act was restricted, but they too could fulfill the dual role required of everyone. Only a handful could hope to stand beside the Phineas Finns and George Rodens of this world, so there had to be an infinite gradation of compromise or reasoned antagonism between personal identity and institutional role. In *On the Subjection of Women,* Mill argued that given electoral power women could reform men and society. In Trollope's world it is often a woman who makes a man aware of his institutional identity and then sustains him in that role.

Political office is the goal but need not be the only measure of success: Luke Rowan in *Rachel Ray* chooses to become a good brewer and the fine beer of Baslehurst, rivaling the local Devonshire cider, is testimony to his own degree of success. It is even possible for a man with sufficient honest energy and intelligence to become a gentleman. Sir William Patterson, the Solicitor-General in *Lady Anna,* predicts that Daniel Thwaite, the tailor, will one day sit in parliament and be known as Sir Daniel. It is society that has the final authority to assess a man's success, just as "the world" would hear no ill of Palmerston. Mr. Harding was regarded by himself and his colleagues as a failure, but after his death society recognized his merits. A man may judge himself in solitude, but the final verdict is brought in by the jury of his friends and associates. In the novels judgment resides with the reader as the embodiment of society.

Thus the hunting scenes in the novels are not set pieces—

---

[15] "The Town Incumbent," *Clergymen of the Church of England,* London, 1866, p. 74.

much though Trollope enjoyed writing them. They are the testing-places for popularity and success: popularity in that rules must be observed in the company of others, success in that courage and intelligence are required to abide by those rules and still strive to be first at the kill. The hunt is the microcosm of Trollope's world, delicately balanced between authority and free will but presided over by a spirit of immutable justice in the form of the M.F.H. It is, of course, quintessentially English to regard sport seriously and religion as a joke.[16] And politics are like sport, the warm reception to the Barchester novels and the cold response to a work like *The Prime Minister* can be explained by the ripple of anticipatory mirth when a clergyman appears in print or on stage and the seriousness accorded political life.

Trollope employed sporting imagery continuously: Plantagenet Palliser had never played games and therefore could not understand that a cabinet should be managed like a cricket eleven. And nothing reveals the squalid perfidy of the Countess de Courcy so clearly as her reduction of "the noblest game" to terms of vulgar matchmaking:

> It was part of the game which was as natural to her as fielding is to a cricketer. One cannot have it all winnings at any game. Whether Crosbie should eventually become her son-in-law or not it came to her naturally, as a part of her duty in life, to bowl down the stumps of that young lady at Allington. If Miss Dale knew the game well and could protect her own wicket, let her do so. (*The Small House at Allington*, ch. 18)

Every reader knows that the duty of a good cricketer is not necessarily to win, but to play well, meaning unselfishly. Trollope accepted cricket as the public expression of Saxon manliness but he preferred the sport he knew, hunting. Football

[16] Religion was a source of social division; sport gave the illusion of contest without serious consequences. Witness the elevation of cricket to its quasi-religious status in the nineteenth century. I have discussed this in "A Straight Bat and a Modest Mind," *The Victorian Newsletter*, No. 49, Spring 1976, pp. 9-18.

was condemned out of hand because of its "irregularity and lawlessness" (*British Sports and Pastimes*, p. 2). Sport showed the individual how to work with authority: it was a training-ground for the more complex games of life.

It is necessary not only to reach agreement between the individual and the institutional self, but to establish an accord between a man and his familial identity. William Whittlestaff in *An Old Man's Love* "had not been a fortunate man, as fortune is generally counted in the world. He had not succeeded in what he had attempted" (ch. 16). After a life of quiet disappointments he desires to marry his ward Mary Laurie, and he sees himself as lover and husband. But there is a younger man and an older love in the presence of John Gordon. Reluctantly, Mr. Whittlestaff has to relinquish his familial role of prospective husband and accept that of a surrogate father. People cannot live comfortably with each other in Trollope's world unless their relationships (with all the rights and duties dependent upon those social and personal contracts) are precisely defined. The action of the novels is always concerned with refining these mutualities.

The compromise between the personal and familial self is more painful for Roger Carbury in *The Way We Live Now*, involving delicate modulations of pride and identification. It is not simply that Roger loves his cousin Hetta—his deepest concern is for the stewardship of Carbury Manor. He knows that Hetta would care for the property with his own sense of devotion, but Hetta loves his best friend, Paul Montague. In order to remain as effective custodian of Carbury Manor, Roger must redefine his relationship to Hetta, to Paul, and to the property. Again, the language both is descriptive and ascribes a definite legal status to the action. To Hetta, Roger speaks in conclusory terms:

> "I look forward to your presence and Paul's presence at Carbury as the source of all my future happiness. I will make him welcome as though he were my brother, and you as though you were my daughter. . . . let this be your home,—so that you should learn really to care about and

> love the place. It will be your home really, you know, some of these days. You will have to be Squire of Carbury yourself when I am gone, till you have a son old enough to fill that exalted position." With all his love to her and his goodwill to them both, he could not bring himself to say that Paul Montague should be Squire of Carbury. (vol. 2, ch. 99)

In this passage cousin and lover have become father; friend has been transformed into brother; and a young woman is made Squire of Carbury. The issue at stake here is only in part the fulfillment of love: its proper concern is the property and its maintenance. By means of shifting relationships the future of Carbury Manor is assured, and all the parties to the transaction have been forced to change roles, some more profitably than others.

In a man, the compromise that takes from the individual self and gives to the familial role is always accompanied by a sense of loss. This is the general sensation of marriage, when a man knows that his freedom to act has been limited, that he has chosen a familial role accompanied by duties and obligations. Some men feel like sacrificial cattle, prepared for financial immolation on the altar like Adolphus Crosbie, but even a Jonathan Stubbs in *Ayala's Angel* is aware of the weight of the matrimonial contract:

> There is always, on such occasions, a feeling of weakness, as though the man had been subdued, brought at length into a cage and tamed, so as to be made fit for domestic purposes, and deprived of his ancient freedom amongst the woods; whereas the girl feels herself to be the triumphant conqueror, who has successfully performed this great act of taming. (ch. 114)

In only a very few, and these are the favored young gentlemen, is the harmonious triad of personal, familial, and institutional identity achieved. Phineas Finn not only achieves his ambition to serve his country as a member of Her Majesty's government, but he marries for both love and money, enjoying the company of an intelligent woman whose charms and income increase with age. His popularity extends from country house to city club, from the hunting field to the House of Commons. Finn refuses to compromise, and surrenders neither principle nor personal integrity in his quest for success. Even the Arthur Fletchers and the George Rodens make some concessions in accomplishing the successful triad: Arthur Fletcher must accept a widow for his wife, George Roden has to give up some of his Radical sentiments and accustom himself to being known as the Duca di Crinola amongst his wife's relations.

For women, the compromises are lifelong, requiring the subjugation of rational will and the adaptation of love to a form of adoration. It is because of the complexity and the pain of transferring intellect to emotion and then to a species of worship that Trollope delineates women with such perception and pity. They are victims, like children, and must learn to adapt themselves to the narrow confines permitted by society. Justice exists in this society—but little equality. Men live by rules that confer powers, women by rules that impose duties.[17] Women may serve, but they cannot work, and yet no one venerated work more than Trollope, not even Carlyle.[18] Women can write, like Lady Carbury, or paint, like Ayala. Even the management of an Austrian banking house by Marie Goesler is intimated, never defined, and Marie Goesler is after

---

[17] This is an appropriation of one of the most prominent theses in contemporary legal philosophy. My apologies to H.L.A. Hart, *The Concept of Law*, Oxford, 1961 and to J. Raz, *The Concept of a Legal System*, Oxford, 1970.

[18] In *South Africa*, Trollope regarded missionaries as being of the same order of social inefficiency as slave-owners. *South Africa* concludes with Trollope's stated conviction that work would civilize the Kafir more effectively than would the Bible or the lash: unfortunately Trollope was writing of a more equitable society than now exists:

The Kafir can make his own contract for his own labour the same as a white man;—can leave his job of work or take it as independently as the white workman;—but not more so. Encouraged by this treatment he is travelling hither and thither in quest of work, and is quickly learning that order and those wants which together make the only sure road to civilization. (vol. 2, p. 338)

all a foreigner.[19] In *South Africa*, Trollope asserted that the right to work and regular wages would civilize the Kafir more effectively than would psalm-singing and Sunday prayers. He had no faith in religion as a reforming influence and regarded missionaries as well-meaning but ineffectual. Women, on the other hand, were denied work and made dependent upon men for their "wages" and the disposition of their inheritances. Marriage provided a measure of emotional and economic security, but that security was paid for with obedience.

Trollope, as we have seen, once wrote to a young postman advising him "to teach yourself not to regard the service with dissatisfaction." Women had to teach themselves to accept marriage with the same effort of will fortified by a sense of religious dedication. Women were called upon to worship their husbands because so few merited rational admiration. In Trollope's world, no man commits himself to God with the selfless devotion that a woman gives to a man. The ensuing conflict between reason and faith resembles the moral dilemma when human law is seen as the emanation of divine justice. The women who marry either adopt a quiet cynicism, or rebel like Louis Trevelyan's wife in *He Knew He Was Right*. There can never be the freedom for women that men enjoy and Trollope lets them testify to their dissatisfaction, anger, and grief. Mary Twentyman, holding her baby and watching the hunt and her husband ride past, longing to be with them but bound to the home, is Trollope's image of the happily married woman.

Few men are religious in Trollope's world, most women become so when they declare their love. It is the connotation of love as worship that makes marriage a moral as well as an economic virtue. Recognizing the gentleman and then marrying him marked the transition from the individual to the familial and institutional self in a woman, and it required intelligence, fortitude, and an awareness that the future would never be so pleasant as the present. Ayala Dormer knew this

---

[19] In "The Telegraph Girl" Trollope shows a post-office telegraphist barely able to live on her wages. Single women were, of course, expected to live with relatives until they married, as Lucy does.

instinctively and wished that courtship could last a little longer. In *Mr. Scarborough's Family*, Florence and her husband, Harry Annesley, are on an Alpine honeymoon when he chooses to question her confidence in his good nature. Florence's reply is reasoned and temperate:

> One has to risk dangers in the world, but one makes the risk as little as possible. I know they won't give me a pony that will tumble down. And I know that I've told you to look to see that they don't. You chose the pony, but I had to choose you. I don't know very much about ponies, but I do know something about a lover;—and I know that I have got one that will suit me. (ch. 114)

Harry Annesley is content in the company of a woman who is richer and more intelligent than he can ever hope to be, and sensible enough to keep the precise terms of the marriage contract to herself.

Social acceptance marked the transition from the individual to the familial self in woman; thus, every responsible young woman made marriage conditional upon acceptance by the man's family. Lucy Robarts refused Lord Lufton's offer until she was accepted by his mother; Grace Crawley insisted that marriage was impossible until it was sanctioned by Major Grantly's father, the Archdeacon. Isabel Boncassen was quite prepared to declare her love for Silverbridge on certain conditions:

> You ask if I love you. You are entitled to know the truth. From the sole of your foot to the crown of your head I love you as I think a man would wish to be loved by the girl he loves. You have come across my life and have swallowed me up, and made me all your own. But I will not marry you to be rejected by your people. No; nor shall there be a kiss between us till I know that it will not be so. (*The Duke's Children*, ch. 52)

Despite the persuasiveness of such a wholehearted affirmation of love, the real import of the passage rests with one conditional sentence—and that sentence is powerful enough to ensure that Isabel will one day become the Duchess of Omnium and Gatherum.

Occasionally the familial self can become institutional—as Alice Vavasor constructs her future life as the wife of a politician—but the confines of womanhood make public life a second-hand affair at best. No woman learns this more painfully than Lady Glencora, and voices her chagrin more eloquently: "They should have made me Prime Minister, and have let him be Chancellor of the Exchequer. I begin to see the ways of Government now. I could have done all the dirty work" (*The Prime Minister*, ch. 56). If a woman does manage to assume the institutional role of a man she becomes a social anomaly and abomination like Mrs. Proudie. A woman can make a public life for herself only through the career of the man she marries. Woman's right is the right to reform and restore a man to his proper place in society. Since marriage is the key, no woman can be blamed for changing her mind when selecting a husband. And for a woman to marry satisfactorily a social contract has to be observed. One without the other predicates failure, and failure in Trollope's world is always a bitter experience, particularly for a woman, who negotiates with fewer assets than a man.

The society Trollope describes is transactional by definition and concerned with the contracts of money and marriage. The language is conditional and restrictive in its avoidance of any original image and metaphor. Trollope quoted Palmerston's aphorism: "Half the wrong conclusions at which mankind arrive are reached by the abuse of metaphors" (*Lord Palmerston*, p. 64). The metaphors Trollope employed had been in use for so long that any gloss of originality had long since vanished: lives fall into pleasant lines, but plums do not necessarily fall into men's mouths. It is not so much the avoidance of metaphorical language as an insistence on meaning at the expense of all linguistic ornament. Trollope has never provided fertile ground for the "new critics," who have spurned him as trite, prolix, and obvious. It has never been customary to praise Trollope for his prose. Nevertheless, Trollope's use of language is as considered and deliberate as the lawyer's when he comes to draw up a brief. And we have Ronald Sokol's assurance that "There is no inherent reason why a brief must be dull."[20] The rationale for Trollope's "non-style" is the rhetoric of legal persuasion, and its purpose is to inform in the hope of convincing. Where Trollope feels the particular need to convince is in the character of individuals, and not in their interaction, for there it is the reader who must play the "reasonable man."

Lawyers often deplore the need for technical formulae as they plunge deeper into jungles of impenetrable prose where mysteries of legal legerdemain are celebrated. Legal writing at its best must make use of technical terms, and John Clarke notes that when Trollope uses them he does so correctly.[21] However, effective legal writing always recalls Archbold's injunction that "general terms will suffice" and his asseveration that the style of his own work "will be found plain, simple and unadorned." Legal writers are seldom consulted on matters of style but Dennis Lloyd today stands as a literary model. Indeed, Thomas Eisele has written:

> Nowhere have I found an adequate appreciation or acknowledgment of the extent to which the words of legal language are the same. Nowhere have I found a recognition of the fact that much of the power which the language of the law has for us comes from the power of ordinary language, some of whose terms it has borrowed and now shares. Some words of the law are drawn straight from ordinary language. The basis of legal language in ordinary language (not only in ordinary words, but also in ordinary speech and grammatical patterns) is what in the first instance makes the language of the law recognizably a language.[22]

The essential difference between legal and literary writing is that one seeks the specificity of meaning whereas the other

---

[20] *Language and Litigation*, Charlottesville, 1967, p. 13.

[21] *The Language and Style of Anthony Trollope*, p. 136.

[22] James B. White, "The Legal Imagination and Language: A Philosophical Criticism," p. 371.

may choose to delight and inform by whatever means it pleases.

Legal language, as Margaret Bryant observed, places considerable emphasis on "form words," and their considered usage will often define the difference between legal prose and ordinary language.[23] Few writers have made greater use of "form words" than Trollope, particularly in dialogue. Trollope sets the scene for dialogue and then withdraws. Knowing the characters, understanding the nature of the argument makes the "said haughtily" and "replied angrily" of traditional prose dialogue unnecessary. Trollope's dialogues are testimony and are given as such. Thus Oswald to his sister Laura, speaking of her husband and her misery that is really the remorse of having refused Phineas Finn:

> "He does not beat me, if you mean that." "Is he cruel to you? Does he use harsh language?" "He never said a word in his life either to me, or, as I believe, to any other human being, that he would think himself bound to regret." "What is it then?" "He simply chooses to have his own way, and his way cannot be my way. He is hard, and dry, and just, and dispassionate, and he wishes me to be the same. That is all." (*Phineas Finn*, ch. 55)

What follows is expository in the form of the direct examination of Laura's true feelings. No lawyer could undertake this, but Trollope goes beyond legal advocacy to determine the character's real intention.

It is in these passages of exposition that he will occasionally engage in social banter and philosophical digression, practices not unfamiliar to the barrister who knows his judge and his court. But the digressions are purposive in Trollope, establishing analogical relationships between the characters, the narrative advocate, and the reader who is then permitted to draw conclusions that are often at variance with the narrative

---

[23] In *English in the Law Courts*, New York, 1962, Margaret M. Bryant discusses such form words as "about," "around," "but," and "that," noting the difficulties they pose when used imprecisely by lawyers. Trollope's style is dictated by the deliberate use of form words.

pleading. For example, throughout *The Belton Estate*, Mrs. Askerton is described as a woman of sin, an adulteress who left a brutal husband to live with Colonel Askerton. Both Clara Amedroz's declared lovers make it their business to find out Mrs. Askerton's past and warn Clara of the dangers of associating with such a woman. Naturally, it is Captain Aylmer and his mother, Lady Aylmer, who make the issue a condition of marriage. Now, despite the narrative advocacy referring the reader to the world's opinion of adultery and adulteresses in particular, Mrs. Askerton becomes the symbol of Clara's independence. She has always resented her dependence on others. As she declares to Captain Aylmer:

> . . . I should do just as you do if I had the power. But women—women, that is, of my age—we are such slaves! We are forced to give an obedience for which we can see no cause, and for which we can understand no necessity. (ch. 7)

Thus when Clara's two lovers and her friends denounce the questionable friendship, she deliberately makes Mrs. Askerton her declaration of freedom. The narrative advocacy has described Mrs. Askerton's shortcomings in full; now it examines Clara's own feelings, and the exposition is followed directly by Mrs. Askerton's examination of Clara in a series of questions:

> Clara's mind was the more active at the moment for she was resolving that in this episode of her life she would accept no lesson whatever from Lady Aylmer's teaching;—nor any lesson whatever from the teaching of any Aylmer in existence. And so for the world's rules, she would fit herself to them as best she could; but no such fitting should drive her to the unwomanly cruelty of deserting this woman whom she had known and loved,—and whom she now loved with a fervour which she had never before felt towards her.
> "You have heard it all now," said Mrs. Askerton at last. "And is it not better so?" "Ah;—I do not know.

How should I know?" "Do you not know?" And as she spoke, Clara pressed her arm still closer. "Do you not know yet?" Then, turning herself half round, she clasped the other woman full in her arms, and kissed her forehead and her lips. "Do you not know yet?" "But you will go away, and people will tell you that you are wrong." "What people?" said Clara, thinking as she spoke of the whole family at Aylmer Park. "Your husband will tell you so." "I have no husband,—as yet,—to order me what to think or what not to think." (ch. 18)

It is a passionate episode in which the love of two women signifies liberation from the "world's rules" and the authority of men. The dialogue, however, is cast in the customary examinational mode. The form words, "as yet," in the last sentence are crucial, conveying Clara's decision, and also her awareness that this freedom is temporary and may exist only in such passing moments of compassion and understanding between women. Clara will marry, as she intimates, but she will negotiate for the best terms she can possibly get: a life and a new home at Belton with a husband amenable to her wishes. She also accepts that in marriage she will be subject to the will of a husband who may not even remain awake long enough to answer her spoken thought.

Captain Aylmer has arrived at Belton with his new wife, Lady Emily, and Clara wonders:

"I cannot conceive why any man should marry such a woman as that. Not but what she's a very good woman, I dare say; only what can a man get by it? To be sure there's the title, if that's worth anything." But Will Belton was never good for much conversation at this hour, and was too fast asleep to make any rejoinder to the last remark. (ch. 32)

The novel ends with Clara's certainly having the last words as she evaluates the marriage of her old lover—but the response to her reasoned comments is the silence of her husband. Again, in Clara's words it is the form words that are of most significance, the "not," the "only," and "if." They effectively express Clara's dubiety at the contract of marriage and what is tendered by the consenting parties.[24]

Trollope designed his metaphors, like his sporting images, to put the reader at his ease—the courteous and conciliatory passwords that bespeak a common ground. And they are also the means of keeping his characters within the bounds of shared sympathy and understanding. The moral purpose of Trollope's writing is to make us aware of the checks and restraints on human conduct and the means by which we can live decently, and even honorably, in a society founded on a sense of common weakness and imperfection. At all times we are made aware that his characters live by rules of society and nature known to us all. The special attributes of some characters are traditionally designated by name: the Quiverfuls and Fillgraves of Barsetshire. But this nomenclature is reserved for minor characters. Major characters bear names and titles that may or may not reflect character and social rank. What Trollope seeks is our identification with his characters of either sex or any rank. And he accomplishes this with metaphors of common reference. Thus, at the point of emotional crisis in Lady Glencora's life when she dances with Burgo at Lady Monk's party and he pleads with her to run away with him, Trollope writes:

> The waltzers went on till they were stopped by want of breath. "I am so much out of practice," said Lady Glencora: "I didn't think—I should have been able—to dance at all." Then she put up her face, and slightly opened her mouth, and stretched her nostrils,—as ladies do as well as horses when the running has been severe and they want air. (*Can You Forgive Her?* ch. 50)

In case the reader imagines himself in the realm of high romance, he is speedily and genially brought down to earth with

---

[24] Juliet McMaster writes on Trollope's use of the form word "now" in *Trollope's Palliser Novels*, New York, 1978; "The opening 'now' is characteristic too: it asserts again the stance of explainer to eager audience" (pp. 207-208).

the reminder that women, like horses, can run out of wind.

The comedy is seldom in visual episodes, although it is difficult to forget the magnificent broadside of Signora Neroni's sofa against Mrs. Proudie's flounces—or forgive the dismal episode of the misplaced mustard plaster in "Christmas at Thompson Hall"—one of the required Christmas pieces that Trollope abhorred. The most effective comedy resides in the recurring disjunction between the spoken word and the unvoiced intention. *Kept in the Dark* is concerned with two passionate, obstinate, and rather silly lovers who contrive to bring a marriage to near-disaster because the wife has kept a past engagement in the dark. But when the two are reconciled it is to a chorus of self-incrimination, each claiming to be more at fault than the other, and a different kind of darkness descends upon them. The novel turns upon the repetition of the phrase, "kept in the dark," and the cliché is used to display every conceivable folly of marital understanding. The comedy is bleak indeed as we are reminded how often in marriage the most ruthless battles are fought over trifles like "being kept in the dark," because of an implicit understanding that the darkness at the heart of the marriage should never be stated.

What is said and what is meant are not always in accord. Together they constitute legal irony at its best, a continuing duel between purpose and statement as in Ferdinand Lopez's desperate profession of love to Lady Eustace, promising her a life of bliss in Guatemala. The words of the frantic lover soar into poetry, but Lizzie remembers another suitor who murmured poetry to her and knows that prosody is no substitute for hard cash:

"Lizzie Eustace, will you go with me, to that land of the sun,
  Where the rage of the vulture, the love of the turtle,
  Now melt into sorrow, now madden to crime?
Will you dare to escape with me from the cold conventionalities, from the miserable thraldom of this country bound in swaddling clothes? Lizzie Eustace, if you will

say the word I will take you to that land of glorious happiness.

But Lizzie Eustace had £4000 a year and a balance at her banker's. "Mr. Lopez," she said.

"What answer have you to make me?"

"Mr. Lopez, I think you must be a fool." (*The Prime Minister*, ch. 54)

Trollope enjoyed poetry but in his society of contracts and agreements it was generally the refuge of the deceiving mind.

Words are like coins in Trollope's world, they must ring soundly on the counter of meaning and never lose their value or change into flowers. Trollope, like the good barrister, made language the servant of meaning: "The language used should be as ready and as efficient a conductor of the mind of the writer to the mind of the reader as is the electric spark which passes from one battery to another battery" (*Autobiography*, ch. 12). Each novel describes one or more transactions concerning money and marriage, and the language is a faithful rendering of the agreements made or broken. There is no writer who can use the smallest currency of language and extract such worth from it.

We are made to observe a system of equity by which we can judge society, the law, and the world of known things by means of his own sense of justice. His language is derived from a legal source but the purpose of that language is to define truth by means of fiction. It is not so far from the practice of law as Trollope would have us believe.

Chapter VI

The Macdermots of Ballycloran

Each of Trollope's novels takes one of three structural forms derived from the legal declaration. First, there is the single transaction involving an individual's efforts to reconcile money and marriage so that the personal, the familial, and the institutional desires may be fulfilled. It can be Miss Mackenzie striving to find herself a husband who will give her the institutional role she wants without alienating her family, or it can be Sir Harry Hotspur sacrificing his daughter's life to family pride. A second structural form takes the single transaction and develops it analogically by means of similar cases in different classes of society. Thus, in *Can You Forgive Her?*, Alice's quest for success in life is argued out in Mrs. Greenow's preference for the "rocks and valleys" of Captain Bellfield to the bread and cheese of Mr. Cheesacre, and, in the highest ranks of society, Lady Glencora's choice of her husband and institutional success over the personal fulfillment she could hope to find with her lover, Burgo Fitzgerald. Finally, a third form of the novel extends the analogical argument through related social classes into a wider frame and we have Barsetshire and the world of political life where the simple transaction is translated into a complex series of agreements and contractual relationships. The structure is extended, but its source can always be traced back to Archbold's declaration with its initial definition of the cause of the action, its development, and its resolution. Within this context Trollope contends with the law on one hand, and the customary forms of fiction on the other, developing and refining his own vision of social truth.

There are exceptions to these rules. The most obvious is *La Vendée*, an historical novel written in the family tradition that rattles and clatters with standard tropes. Adolphe is speaking in the long fustian tradition when he proposes to Agatha and "curled his upper lip, and showed his teeth in a very ferocious manner" (ch. 8). And there are unfortunate echoes of Scott when Annot Stein falls into the mock-Scotch that had become the customary speech for all foreign peasants in English novels: " 'If I can't get a husband without finding one, indeed, I'm sure I'll not fash myself with seeking . . .' " (ch. 6). It is this work that most resembles the convoluted prose of Frances Trollope's novels.[1] It was clear that he could write "bow-wow" bombast as fluently as his brother and trick it out in historical costume, but it was contrary to his natural voice. This emerges in the middle of the novel with the interpretation of Robespierre as a man destroyed by his faith in reason and his refusal to accept human fallibility:

> He believed in nothing but himself, and the reasoning faculty with which he felt himself to be endowed. He

[1] Trollope's Barsetshire novels owe very little in the way of characterization to his mother's *The Vicar of Wrexhill*, London, 1840. The style of *La Vendée*, is clearly set in the same marzipan mold. For example, Victorine in *La Vendée* walks a rhetorical maze to make a very simple point:
> but there will be others also, whose valour will claim a token of admiration from the gratitude of their countrywomen; we will all do this for Henri and our other brave defenders; but if I know his character, the gratitude of many will not make him happy without the favour of one, and she will be the lady of his love; the remembrance of whose smiles will bear him scatheless through the din of battle. (ch. 5)

The inversions in this passage, the use of subordinate clauses resemble Frances Trollope's long periods in *The Vicar of Wrexhill*:
> Helen blushed deeply at the unexpected ardour of this address from a very tall, handsome, fashionable-looking personage, whose face she certainly would not have recognized had she met him accidentally: but a happy smile accompanied the blush, and he had no reason to regret the politic freedom of his first salutation, which had thus enabled him to pass over an infinity of gradations towards the intimacy he coveted, at one single step placing him at once on the footing of a familiar friend. (ch. 9)

In *An Autobiography* Trollope advised aspiring writers to emulate the clarity and the short sentences of Macaulay.

thought himself perfect in his own nature, and wishing to make others perfect as he was, he fell into the lowest abyss of crime and misery in which a poor human creature ever wallowed. (ch. 22)

The heroic and the historical were alien to Trollope's temperament, and after *La Vendée* he returned to the form that had served him so well in his first novel, *The Macdermots of Ballycloran*.

The Macdermots of Ballycloran, which appeared in 1847 to a tepid response from the reviewers, is Trollope's first example of the single transaction. The ostensible cause of the action is the disposition of the property of Ballycloran, just as later novels in this form were to employ a disputed property or inheritance (Llanfeare in *Cousin Henry*, Hiram's Hospital in *The Warden*, the Ball inheritance in *Miss Mackenzie*), and then resolve the matter by means of marriage. The English always find it difficult to read Irish novels, and even more difficult to write them. Trollope was more successful than most with an affection for Ireland as the country that had rescued him from poverty and failure. He was alive to the irony that he had found prosperity in a country that gave the majority of its people no choice between adversity and emigration. While voicing his gratitude, he never forgot that he was an Englishman, a servant of a government regarded by many Irish as a foreign tyranny. When Trollope wrote of Ireland outside the novels he was quite prepared to defend English authority and argue for its continued presence in the country. In the novels, even though the narrator may speak for continued Engish rule, the characters testify on their own behalf and demand a different order and another Ireland.[2] Facts cannot be concealed, the evidence must be given in full, every relevant witness permitted to have his say: this is the mode by which evidence is presented in a fair report. Just as Trollope hectors us with his own opinion of the blacks in the

---

[2] Trollope's letters on the Irish Famine were published in *The Examiner* by John Forster in 1848 and the early part of 1849. They are full of praise for English efforts to relieve the distress.

West Indies and then permits them to speak on their own behalf, so he belabors the Irish while they confound his statements with the expression of their own experience.

By the 1850s the starving Irish of history had been all too comfortably set at a distance by means of comic reduction. It was impossible to take seriously a people that was so innately funny. The Irish were jolly buffoons at their best and bigoted thugs at their worst. The jolly type had a long tradition in fiction and had been immortalized by Charles Lever in *Charles O'Malley* (1841). For contemporary readers O'Malley seemed the embodiment of the Irish spirit—it was left to a later generation to see the pain and the guilt in Lever's boisterous characterization. Any writer who chose to depict Irish life had to find his way to the truth through a bog of misconception and preconceived ideas with the purblind English reading public as a guide. Trollope had read the Irish novels, he was aware of English attitudes and shared many of them, but he could also affirm with honesty that he had seen more of Ireland than most Irishmen.

Throughout his life and in all his writing, Trollope maintained that the Famine had been of lasting benefit to the country—and he has always been castigated for this opinion.[3] Unlike most people he did not see the Famine as the bridge from a halcyon past to an impoverished present. He knew Ireland before the potato blight, and *The Macdermots of Ballycloran* recorded that society in all its hopeless misery. Because the Famine had struck like a plague Trollope could see no reason to praise what it had destroyed. Contemporary historians are more inclined to accept Trollope's icy judgment over the myth of a prosperous country ruined by an act of God designed in England.[4]

---

[3] Ruth apRoberts writes: "*Castle Richmond* will remain distasteful to many readers for Trollope's apparent view of the famine as a warrant of God's mercy...." *Victorian Fiction: A Second Guide to Research*, ed. George H. Ford, New York, 1978, p. 159.

[4] In *The Modernisation of Irish Society 1848-1918*, Dublin, 1973, Joseph Lee argues for an improved economy after the Famine with commercial farming replacing subsistence agriculture and a general increase in the size of farms. While placing the blame for the Famine squarely with England,

Trollope's work begins and ends with the tragedy of Ireland. The Ribbonmen of *The Macdermots of Ballycloran* are blood relations to the murdering gangs of *The Land-Leaguers*. This is a society so flawed by poverty, violence, and treachery that a man may well be hanged for his virtues and rewarded for his vice. Just as Trollope argued that Cicero had been destroyed by a society inimical to honesty, truth, and justice, Thady Macdermot goes to the gallows because he has tried to protect his sister, his property, and his tenants. By instinct he is a gentleman, but in *The Macdermots of Ballycloran* Trollope declares without equivocation that no gentleman could survive in Irish society as an Irishman. Therefore, in a later novel, Phineas Finn is brought to England, where a rational society accords him success in marriage and political life. All that Thady can see ahead of him is the gallows. Despairingly, he tells Father John that his soul is sick within him and his only hope to "sthrike one blow for the country, and then, if I war hung or shot, or murthered any way, devil a care" (ch. 5).

In its essential structure *The Macdermots of Ballycloran* is a report accounting for the ruin of a house that is a "picture of misery, of useless expenditure, unfinished pretense, and premature decay" (ch. 1). The house is the outward form of the Irish gentry and of Thady, whose life is a wretched scrounging for rents that his tenants cannot afford to pay.

Lawrence J. McCaffrey in *Ireland from Colony to Nation State*, New Jersey, 1979, writes:
> Under the provisions of the Encumbered Estates Acts, five thousand purchasers bought one-seventh of Irish landed property over a ten year period. Until recently, Irish historians described these new landlords as insensitive seekers of profit without concern for Ireland or her people. This description is myth. Very few of the new landlords were British capitalists. Ninety-five percent of them were Irish, including a large number of Catholics, often the younger sons of landlords, lawyers, and shopkeepers who had made money during the famine (pp. 74-75).

This is the society that Trollope describes in *The Kellys and the O'Kellys* that is ostensibly set in the early 1840s. Martin Kelly is typical of the new landlords, buying property with money made from trade and commerce. The son of the local shopkeeper, he makes a late marriage to the wealthy Anty Lynch—the late marriage was a characteristic of post-Famine Ireland.

Once the jerry-built imitation of a gentleman's residence, the house is now a ruin of "rotting joists and beams, some fallen, some falling, the rest ready to fall, like the skeleton of a felon left to rot on an open gibbet" (ch. 1). It is also the condition of Ireland, a society in which poverty feeds on misery and hunger sits at every hearth. Treachery and betrayal walk between friends and everybody can be taken for a price. Not even in *The Way We Live Now* did Trollope present so drear a vision of the human condition. Ireland convinced Trollope that the good life was not of the spirit, but in the creature comforts of food and snug houses, warm fires, and good friends, and whoever denied the latter to preach the disdain of worldly good was a hypocrite and a fool. It is the lack of worldly goods that denies Thady his right to be a man and a gentleman.

There is an attempt to use the device of the "tale told," reminiscent of Scott, since the story of Ballycloran is initially narrated by the guard of the Boyle coach. But this traditional narrator is dispensed with in a few lines and we have the mode of exposition and examination that Trollope was to maintain throughout the novels. He can already be seen presiding over a court in which he prosecutes and defends, in which the parties to the action question each other and occasionally speak at variance with the understanding of the advocate and of each other. No attempt is made to create suspense through unexpected turns in the plot—the end is foretold and it moves to that end with the anguish and pity of great tragedy. Trollope could see only one future for Irish society before the Famine, and that was death.

In its first published form in 1847 the novel was in three volumes; later, in 1860, Trollope removed three chapters, improving the work immeasurably.[5] The second version is neither digressive nor discursive. It is obvious now that the

---

[5] R. C. Terry argues for Father John as the moral center of *The Macdermots of Ballycloran* in *Anthony Trollope: The Artist in Hiding*, Totowa, 1977, p. 188. The three chapters removed by Trollope are discussed by Terry in "Three Lost Chapters of Anthony Trollope's First Novel," *Nineteenth Century Fiction*, XXVII, June 1972, pp. 71-80.

last volume was going to be shorter than the first two so Trollope sent Father John off to Dublin on a journey to his brother-in-law, the butter-man, from whom he borrows the twenty pounds needed for Thady's defense. The trip on the Boyle coach is the occasion for some raucous "Irish" comedy, with a red-nosed buxom matron accusing the flustered priest of trying to put his arm around her. Certainly, the Dublin butter-man owes more to Gerald Griffin than was Trollope's original intention. The final chapter of the first version, with its sentimental resolution of loose ends, vitiates the stark rendering of the hanging in the silent town of Carrick where every shop is shuttered and no one walks the streets. It is less than necessary in the original last chapter to be told that Father John came to look upon Thady as a martyr.[6]

Thady Macdermot is the heir to Ballycloran, its ruined house, its miserable tenants, and its mortgaged land. His father, senile at fifty, sits over the fire sucking whiskey and water; his sister Feemy has become the mistress of the local English excise officer, Myles Ussher, who cannot be persuaded to make her his wife. Like Thady, there are no choices for Feemy, whose mind is filled with the heroines from melodramatic novels and who yearns passionately to be one of them. There is no place for love in Thady's life and with one exception he receives none. He is the only hero in all Trollope's novels who is neither loved by a woman nor falls in love. Across his heart there is one word inscribed, and that is "rents": without them he cannot pay the mortgage on his house; with them his tenants must starve. Not only is Thady

---

[6] The main objection to the last chapter is that it vitiates the power of the penultimate with its resonant account of a town in mourning. The writing of the last chapter weakens by overstatement. Thus of Father John:

He rarely mentions Thady's name; but sometimes as he sits over his own fire of a winter evening with one single friend, he will do so, and when once he begins, no other subject will be mentioned that night—he has utterly forgotten all his faults, and all his follies—he speaks of him as a martyr to the villainy of his enemies—as a man whose life and death were such as could only inspire love and pity; but as one who to a certainty would receive in the glories of heaven full compensation for the miseries of his human execution (p. 436).

emasculated by his plight, but every hope he has for the respectability of his family is destroyed by poverty. The only men who will stand by him and call him friend are the Joe Reynoldses and Corney Dolans, outlaws who want to enlist him in a conspiracy to murder. The only person who loves Thady is Father John. In this relationshop the Protestant Trollope offers a remarkable statement concerning the role of the Roman Catholic Church in Ireland. The latter exists as the natural expression of Irish society whereas the Church of England is alien and remote from the people. Since every institution is judged by its utility there can be no place for a Protestant church in a congregation of Roman Catholics.

In *The Macdermots of Ballycloran* Trollope enunciates themes and principles that recur in all his fiction. The two great sins of poverty and isolation govern the society of Ireland and are manifest in the violence and treachery of everyday life. In Trollope's world there is nothing more pitiful than a man alone. To be deprived of society is to be less than human, a creature without law since law cannot exist without society. The man who wilfully condemns himself to isolation is shameful and merits the oblivion of exile in Bordeaux or a small German town—but there are some who are forced into isolation through no fault of their own. Phineas Finn is thrust into prison for a crime he did not commit and endures the horror of solitude. But the most pitiable of all is Thady, driven from his home and into a society that he abhors. When isolation is combined with a loss of class, abject misery is assured. In "The Spotted Dog" Trollope related the story of a certain Julius Mackenzie, who professed his radical sentiments by marrying a woman of the working class, and ended in the gutter with her. Thady clings to the few remaining tatters of his class and his family's respectability. He struggles to retain his rank as a gentleman and is demented with grief when he sees the only society that will accept him at Aughacashel.

Every attempt Thady makes to defend his family is misunderstood and read as treachery by his father. Myles Ussher, the excise officer, is killed because Thady tries to defend his sister from seeming rape, but Feemy herself is then the first to call her brother a murderer: "I hate you—you're a murdherer; you've murdhered him because you knew I loved him . . ." (ch. 21). When he explains to his father that Myles was dragging Feemy away with him, old Larry Macdermot sits mute and staring, then he too finds the strength to denounce his son:

> "Murdher," at last said the old man, laughing; "who doubts but that it was murdher? in course they'll call it murdher. Well, he was the only frind you'd left me, and now that you've murdhered him, you may go now; you may go now—but mind I tell you, they'll be sure to hang you." (ch. 21)

For Trollope, it is possible for a rational man to prophesy his own fate, and Thady's prediction of death by hanging becomes fact.

In the romantic landscape of Glorvina, moonlit and misty, Thady stumbles and runs past Drumleesh to Corney Dolan's cabin. In Trollope, landscape always reflects the human condition, and now moonlight is dangerous because it makes a fleeing man visible, and mist chills aching joints. The solitary journey is a constant in his fiction, but none is more powerfully evoked than this ascent into the picturesque mountains that precisely define a contrary social descent into a nether world of savage poverty. It is the same landscape that confronts Herbert Fitzgerald in *Castle Richmond* when he tramps across the famine-stricken country to say farewell to Clara. Fitzgerald is going into exile in England, but for Thady there is nothing but aching despair and the growing awareness that he has crossed a frontier of blood into a country that now has the right to claim him as a citizen. At Corney Dolan's cabin he is on the threshold of the society that he has long feared and adjured. This is the Ireland that generates terror and violence, and its perimeters are revealed in the form of a naked child and an imbecilic old man.

The vision of Thady's new society begins with the child at Corney Dolan's:

> The child now got up and opened the door, and let him into the single room which the cabin contained. There were still a few embers of turf alight on the hearth, but not sufficient to have enabled Thady to see anything had not the moon shone brightly in through the door. There was but one bed in the place—at the end of the cabin farthest from the door, standing between the hearth and the wall, and in this the old woman was lying. The child, about eight years, had jumped out of bed, stark naked, and now in this condition was endeavouring with a bit of stick to poke the hot embers together, so as to give out a better heat and light.   (ch. 22)

At Aughacashel an old man sits by the turf like the image of what Thady will one day become if he manages to escape the gallows. These are some of the most telling passages in all Trollope's writing, an examination of a man's feelings and inexpressible grief. This is the mood of Raskolnikov in *Crime and Punishment*, swept between conscience and fear, life and a longing for an end of pain and the finality of death. But for Raskolnikov there is the redemption of love, for Thady there is only the solitude of the mountain and the greater loneliness in the company of the old man:

> There he sat on the bed, quite imperturbable; he had not spoken ten words since Thady got up, and seemed quite satisfied in sitting there enjoying the warmth of the fire, and having nothing to do. How Thady envied his quiescence! Then he began to reflect what had been this man's life; had he always been content to sit thus tranquil, and find his comfort in idleness? At last he got almost alarmed at this old man; why did he not speak to him? why did he sit there so quiet, doing nothing—saying nothing—looking at nothing—and apparently thinking of nothing? it was as sitting with a dead body or a ghost—that sitting there with that lifeless but yet breathing creature.   (ch. 23)

Thady knows, watching the old man, that death in life is far preferable to a living death. He escapes once again to Father John's cottage and the end on the gallows.

Poverty sustains the violence in every aspect of Irish life. It is born with the naked child in Corney Dolan's cabin and then spreads out like mist to infect the gentry and the governing class. The steeplechase with its death of a fine horse brutally ridden by George Brown is the analogy for Dillon and Fitzpatrick's drunken pursuit of Stark that finishes as the latter is carried home with a broken face. Every man carries a stick, and Keegan belabors Thady just as Thady later knocks down Ussher and kills him. Magistrates duel and tenant farmers plot murder. Violence becomes a social code, regulated by a standard of rewards and punishments. The maiming of Hyacinth Keegan is carried out as methodically and laconically as though it were a regular occurrence like stripping the roof from a defaulting tenant's cabin. Keegan has begun to move at ease around Drumleesh when he is accosted along a little lane by the bog. He is knocked from his horse and the authority of the oppressed is enforced:

> The blow and the fall completely stunned him, and when he came to himself he was lying on the road; the man who had stopped his horse was kneeling on his chest; a man, whose face was blackened, was holding down his two feet, and a third, whose face had also been blackened, was kneeling on the road beside him with a small axe in his hand. Keegan's courage utterly failed him when he saw the sharp instrument in the ruffian's grasp; he began to promise largely if they would let him escape—forgiveness—money—land—anything—everything for his life. Neither of them, however, answered him, and before the first sentence he uttered was well out of his mouth, the instrument fell on his leg, just above the ankle, with all the man's force; the first blow only cut his trousers and his boot, and bruised him sorely—for his boots protected him; the second cut the flesh, and grated against the bone; in vain he struggled violently, and with all the force of

a man struggling for his life; a third, and a fourth, and a fifth descended, crushing the bone, dividing the marrow, and ultimately severing the foot from the leg. (ch. 25)

The clinical enumeration of the blows in this passage, the ordering of flesh and clothes, life and property, as things of equal value, establish the commonplace nature of the event. This is the justice of the people when the law is represented by men like Myles Ussher and the local landowning magistrates.[7] The counterpart to the rudimentary punishment at the bogside is the murder of Thady at the hands of the law in Carrick. Reynolds and Dolan are merciless as they hack off Keegan's foot, leaving him to drag himself to the nearest cabin. The law is more tortuous but equally pitiless as it finds Thady guilty of murder and hangs him as a warning to local dissidents.

Throughout the latter part of the novel the law maintains its own fiction against the truth of the novelist in the debate that distinguishes Trollope's mode of enquiry. The facts of Ussher's death are known, but when they cannot be proved from the testimony of Feemy, the jury brings in a verdict of guilty. Larry Macdermot reviles his son to the end, Feemy dies whispering the name of Myles Ussher, and Thady becomes a martyr for a cause he adhorred. Trollope's truth is invariably ironic because it must contend with legal fiction and the romantic fiction of popular thought. The truth in the work does not reside in narrative exposition, authorial statement, or the evidence of the witnesses (who may be partial when not actually lying), but in the reader's judgment of all that he has heard and assessed. Even Father John, the model of fair-minded social responsibility, is liable to rash statement and

---

[7] M. R. Beames in "Rural Conflict in Pre-Famine Ireland: Peasant Assassinations in Tipperary 1837-1847," *Past and Present*, No. 81, November 1978, pp. 75-92, describes the assassinations in this period as the work of "a landholding peasantry rather than a rural proletariat" (p. 85). Keegan was typical of the kind of men who were killed or maimed. And, just as Keegan is attacked in February, Beames states: "The assassinations occurred most frequently in the winter months from October to January" (*ibid.*).

has to be checked by Mrs. McKeon when he protests that he can never forgive Feemy for her lack of charity to her brother. Mrs. McKeon, of course, knows more of Feemy's desperate situation than Father John and realizes when Myles is killed that Feemy has lost the father of her unborn child. The continuing references to shared knowledge of the world serve to make the reader search his own experience. The more belligerent the authorial voice, the prompter the reader is to respond with agreement or dissent. The reasonable man in Trollope is found seldom in a single character, and never in the narrator, but he is always expected in the reader.

Although Trollope approved of the English control of Ireland there is disturbing evidence against it presented in the novels. Thady is executed by a corrupt society just as Cicero was put to death by his. Both are seen as victims of their own virtue. Certainly, English law is not the agency of peace in Ireland, a function which belongs more rightly to Father John, who mediates every social dispute. The arms of English authority in Ireland were coercion and espionage and Trollope inveighed against the use of informers in this novel:

> Let the police use such open means as they have—and, God knows, in Ireland they should be effective enough; but I cannot but think the system of secret informers—to which those in positions of inferior authority too often have recourse—has greatly increased crime in many districts of Ireland. I by no means intend to assert that this system is patronised or even recognized by Government. (ch. 11)

This passage is immediately followed by the account of a government official's secretly acknowledging his spies in a small Irish town, and the incident is set in the wider context of a society that is defined by "schaming."

Deceit and scheming constitute Mrs. Kelly's favorite invectives in *The Kellys and the O'Kellys*, but they are made to seem the very substance of Trollope's Irish society. McGovery feigning sleep across a table at his own wedding breakfast in *The Macdermots of Ballycloran* so that he can overhear Brady and the boys with Thady. Feemy pulling in her laces to conceal her pregnancy, the conniving of Keegan and Pat Brady—the arch *agent-provocateur*. In every work the source of authority is English and situations find their resolution in London. This authority is lauded by Trollope in his essays—the novels seldom regard it so benignly. The "government" in *The Macdermots of Ballycloran* is embodied finally in a court where justice is more formal, but of the same order as the Ribbonmen mutilating Keegan. In *The Kellys and the O'Kellys*, England is where Barry Lynch learned to become an imitation gentleman, where Irish fortunes are lost by Kilcullen, and Irish fortunes made with a Derby winner and an unexpected inheritance. The blackmailers of *Castle Richmond* are English and they set about the ruination of a fine Irish family.[8] Irish girls cannot expect to find husbands in English officers, only seducers, and this is the theme of *An Eye For An Eye* and the fate of Feemy Macdermot. Finally, it is to England that an Irish gentleman like Phineas Finn must go to make his fortune.

Trollope regarded cruelty as part of human nature that had to find expression—preferably in a foxhunt, less happily on a battleground or in a court of law. Violence was a manifestation of cruelty and an element of society that could not be condemned out of hand. Blackguards were to be found in the most respectable company. Johnny Eames is certainly not reproved at Allington when he knocks down Crosbie, and, in *The Way We Live Now,* John Crumb becomes a local hero and also makes a friend of the police when he pummels Sir Frank Carbury. This violence was permissible and even admirable because it showed the natural leaders in a rational society acting spontaneously in the cause of justice. It is like Mr. Armstrong in *The Kellys and the O'Kellys* enforcing a justice on Barry Lynch that was not within the power of a

---

[8] Irish critics have been more sympathetic toward Trollope's Irish novels than Americans. There is a perceptive study of *Castle Richmond* by the American Hugh Kennedy in *Eire*, Dublin, 1972, entitled "Love and Famine, Family and Country in Trollope's *Castle Richmond*." Kennedy emphasizes the importance of the Molletts, betraying each other and blackmailing the Fitzgeralds.

court of law. Nobody in Trollope's English society is thrashed who does not deserve a good hiding; even those who fall foul of muggers are the less worthy members of the community.[9] This is not the case in Ireland. Young Florian in *The Land-Leaguers* is shot because the choice he must make is between concealing evidence and thereby aiding a crime, or speaking the truth and ensuring his own death. It is impossible for a virtuous man to succeed in a society where poverty is the common lot and survival depends on deceit. Those who flourish are schemers within the bounds of decency like Martin Kelly or the grand O'Kelly, Lord Ballindine. The cause of Ireland's poverty and the vices it engenders are never clearly defined by Trollope in his letters to *The Examiner*, and the narrative advocacy is oblique and often contradictory in the novels. But the starving peasants of *Castle Richmond* hold out skeleton hands for the Indian corn provided by the English government, and in *The Macdermots of Ballycloran*, Thady's last words are a reproach to the dead Englishman, Myles Ussher, and all that he represents in Ireland: "Oh! why, Father John, could he not let us alone? We were poor, but we were not worse; but there's an end of us now altogether, and perhaps it's for the betther as it is" (ch. 33).

The revised version of *The Macdermots of Ballycloran* concludes with the real strength of Irish Society revealed in Carrick. Father John has called on everyone to keep to his house when Thady is hanged: Dolan, Reynolds, and "the boys" enforce his request.

> Not one human form appeared before the gaol that morning. Not even a passenger crossed over the bridge from half-past seven till after eight, as from thence one might just catch a glimpse of the front of the prison. At the end of the bridge stood three or four men guarding the street, and cautioning those who came, that they could not pass by; and as their behests were quietly obeyed the police did not interfere with them. (ch. 33)

[9] Consider the murder of Bonteen by Mr. Emilius, in *Phineas Redux*: a bad man was never killed by a worse.

These are the men who will eventually take control because a government tolerates the naked child and the starving old man, and their justice will be a bogside mayhem. They are not a Carlylean mob, an outraged proletariat, but an organized community functioning in the context of Irish society. Yet in his letters Trollope wrote of the incapacity of the Irish for organization and pronounced their revolutions to be no more than large brawls. The evidence of the silent town is proof to the contrary.

Nobody is civilized by sermons, Trollope argued as he traveled the world, only by work and fair wages. To covet money was sinful but to disregard it was folly. If Thady Macdermot had possessed the means of a Martin Kelly he could have withstood Keegan and "the boys," just as Kelly could defend himself against Barry Lynch. But Thady was as poor as his tenants and therefore defenseless against the world. This was Ireland before the Famine, and even though his succeeding novels, with the exception of *The Land-Leaguers*, described a pre-Famine society, the prospect was more cheerful because Trollope was convinced that death and emigration to America and England had effectively resolved the minute apportioning of land and the worst of the rack-renting.

The Famine did not leave Trollope unmoved. It confirmed his belief in the goodness of material things properly used—and this belief provides the moral ethic for all his fiction. Prayers and preaching were no compensation for food and shelter, and all the religion in the world could not clothe a naked child. As Trollope came to fashion his just society, he set the proportions between greed and comfort, defining the good life as one lived among friends in agreeable surroundings. Money was essential, but it had to be gained honestly and used wisely for one's own benefit and that of society. This was a call not for general philanthropy but for stewardship—and the parable of the talents defines Trollope's regard for the material things of this world. To submit to poverty, or to inflict it on others was the most grievous sin. If Thady had merely sought to enrich himself and his family, his plight would not be so tragic, but he cares for his tenants, never stripping their roofs and evicting them from their land.[10] But such is the nature of Irish society that all his efforts to do good are rewarded with evil. Like the trial at Carrick that is a travesty of justice, Irish society mocks the concept of a good life.

Ireland is not a society that can be defined by law. When H.L.A. Hart wrote of social morality he described a regulated system of life:

> Among such rules obviously required for social life are those forbidding, or at least restricting, the free use of violence, rules requiring certain forms of honesty and truthfulness in dealing with others, and rules forbidding the destruction of tangible things or their seizure from others. If conformity with these most elementary rules were not thought a matter of course among any group of individuals, living in close proximity to each other, we should be doubtful of the description of the group as a society, and certain that it could not endure for long.[11]

What Hart describes is the antithesis of Trollope's Ireland under English control. The end is inevitable, but in the course of reaching that end a man like Thady Macdermot can expect no more from society than the gallows.

Behind the personal tragedy of Thady and the brooding problems of Irish society in general lay the novel's basic structure of the property transaction involving Ballycloran itself. Two other novels which unify larger themes by the same single underlying thread are *The Warden* and *Cousin Henry*. In the former the issues of personal conscience presented by the institutionalized form of the Church of England repose upon the property of Hiram's Hospital: in the latter the guilty manipulation of the English law of inheritance revolves about the estate of Llanfeare.

---

[10] R. C. Terry points to the differences in the food of the gentry at the races and the scrap of bacon provided for Thady at Aughacashel. *Anthony Trollope The Artist in Hiding*: Totowa, 1977, pp. 186-187.

[11] H.L.A. Hart, *The Concept of Law*, Oxford, 1978, p. 167.

Chapter VII

The Single Transaction—
Conscience and Society: *The Warden*

Since Trollope's English society was essentially just, good men did not perish or fail to receive the rewards of their virtue. The same could not be said of the church. It was not possible for Thady Macdermot to love or be loved, to protect his family or to live as a gentleman in Irish society. Mr. Harding, the Warden of Hiram's Hospital in Barchester, was a man content within himself, loved by his family—particularly his daughter Eleanor, but quite unable to reconcile his personal happiness with the institutional role demanded of him by the church. In the Warden's case the fictional transaction of the novel is not so straightforward as Thady's inevitable progress to the gallows. Is it possible that Mr. Harding could survive without the church, and is his ostensible failure the triumph of the person over the institution? It is agreed that poverty should be abjured and the world's goods sought, but can the price for them be too high in terms of conscience? Are there occasions when poverty is preferable to wealth, even simple comfort? Before comment is offered on the resolution suggested by Trollope to these questions there is need to consider how the novelist adapted his legalist pose to the general issues of institutionalized religion.

Reginald Hine has written engagingly in defense of lawyers, who, he says, are seldom, if ever, religious. Like most legal apologies his statement calls for a reduction of culpability and affirms by implication the rectitude of his own religious misgivings. If doubt is the price to be paid for common sense, logic, and caution, then the lawyer does not feel he has been shortchanged. Enthusiasm, whether spiritual or temporal, is often an expensive emotion in a court of law. Hine leaves us in no doubt that he lives comfortably with his shortcomings:

> By common repute we lawyers are an irreligious race. Once, indeed, I heard a client declare that we deserved to be "exiled from the eternal providence." And the reasons are manifest. In the first place our spiritual and moral sensibilities are apt to grow blunt under the wear and tear of daily practice. Day in and day out—making the worse appear the better reason—we are defending men and women who have been breaking every letter of the Decalogue. They that be whole need not a physician; those that are saints consult no solicitor. Virtue, we know "lives up three flights of stairs," but we do not look for affluent clients there . . . It was not without due cause that lawyers were classed with Pharisees in Holy Writ. They do not support a church. They prefer to be supported by it—to enjoy by the formal connection a certain respectability of status.[1]

Trollope had learned to reason like a lawyer and his rhetoric was legal, but he always considered that his fiction surpassed the law in veracity and reality. There are very few novels in which he does not contrast a legal situation with his own fictional and more equitable version. In religion he was a practicing Anglican who enjoyed "a certain respectability of status" from his membership in a church that more often resembled a club than a religious community. He accepted the church as a social institution that it would do more harm to abolish than to retain. The words so often inscribed on eighteenth-century bells suit Trollope admirably: "No enthusiasm, and Prosperity to the Church of England." A gentleman should go to church occasionally, but he need not make a habit of it. Religion was a private concern that only bigots or

[1] Reginald L. Hine, *Confessions of an Un-Common Attorney*, London, 1946, pp. 245-247.

hypocrites flaunted publicly. As a potential source of social dissent it was unmannerly to discuss it openly. These sentiments are rendered with considerable insight when Lizzie Eustace first makes the acquaintance of her would-be mother-in-law, Lady Fawn:

> She had heard of that sermon read every Sunday evening at Fawn Court, and she believed that Lady Fawn was peculiarly religious. "There," she said, stretching out her hand backwards and clasping the book which lay upon the small table—"there; that shall be my guide. That will teach me how to do my duty by my noble husband."
>
> Lady Fawn in some surprise took the book from Lizzie's hand, and found that it was the Bible. "You certainly can't do better, my dear, than read your Bible," said Lady Fawn,—but there was more of censure than of eulogy in the tone of her voice. She put the Bible down very quietly, and asked Lady Eustace when it would suit her to come down to Fawn Court. (*The Eustace Diamonds*, ch. 9)

No good Anglican needed to refer to the Bible in public: it was rather like calling attention to the fact that one's face had just been washed.

At their best, Trollope's churchmen are English gentlemen who think and behave in a socially responsible fashion: Mr. Armstrong putting Barry Lynch to flight in *The Kellys and the O'Kellys*; then, in *Is He Popenjoy?* Dean Lovelace knocking the Marquis of Brotherton into the fireplace when his daughter's name has been defamed; or Dr. Wortle, in *Dr. Wortle's School*, protecting a young couple from ostracism. These are churchmen who behave exactly as a gentleman should, showing concern for society in the knowledge that if people lived honorably their souls would not require special attention. Unfortunately, the church was not a replica of contemporary society, and Trollope implies that its initial foundation was an imposition on weak minds that had been sanctified by tradition and long observance. Nonetheless, if a church was acknowledged by the majority of people then it was entitled to protection and preservation in much the same way that an historical monument should not be defaced or demolished. If, on the other hand, a church was maintained for the few at the expense of the many, like the Church of England in Ireland, it deserved to be thrown to the winds. Trollope wrote in "The Irish Beneficed Clergyman" that "of all men the Irish beneficed clergyman is the most illiberal, the most bigoted, the most unforgiving, the most sincere, and the most enthusiastic."[2] And since the novels provide a system of equity to alleviate judgments like this, we are given the Anglican Mr. Armstrong who is, point for point, the exact opposite of every stated characteristic attributed to his brethren in Ireland.

The trouble for Trollope was that it was difficult for him to defend the Church of England except in terms of custom and tradition since he was convinced that its teaching, like the law, could be acquired without the special ministrations of a parson. It was absurd that a gentleman should be told how to conduct his affairs by the local vicar. If the vicar were a gentleman and a friend then, of course, it was a different matter altogether. The only office that really magnified a man was that won by popular acclaim, and bishops were not elected. Moreover, although the church resembled society it functioned by the worst forms of toadying and self-seeking. Senator Gotobed's strictures in *The American Senator* were not unfounded. The church embodied the social past with all its prejudices and inequalities faithfully maintained, frequently practicing the contrary of what it preached in the matters of poverty and humility, and always persecuting those who insisted on a literal interpretation of the Gospel.

Despite the apparent and disarming simplicity of its plot, *The Warden* is one of the most elaborate defenses of failure that Trollope wrote. And because Trollope, unlike Hine's typical lawyer, does not feel bound to make the worse appear the better reason, but gives all reasons equal value, the conclusion rests with the judgment of the reader. It is enough to examine the evidence and see how deftly statement and rebuttal are presented so that a small man's conscience becomes

[2] "The Irish Beneficed Clergyman," in *Clergymen of the Church of England*, London, 1866, p. 115.

of greater account than newspapers, attorney generals armed with all the authority of the law, popular pundits, and the hierarchy of the church. It is possible for a test case to be based on a seeming trifle, but it must first be necessary for that trifle to be seen as an exemplum that can serve as precedent. Trollope accomplishes this by using every form of legal rhetoric, and then making that rhetoric put the law and public opinion to flight.

James Kincaid has argued that *The Warden* and *Barchester Towers* are "about Mr. Harding and his enemies. They seek to tell us all about the two sides and the conduct of the battle, and they seek to convince us that Mr. Harding wins by losing."[3] This martial explanation considerably simplifies the action of the novel and resolves it by recourse to the genre of comedy, much as the archdeacon would settle the whole matter by referral to the law and Sir Abraham Haphazard's opinion in particular. What may seem a friend of a man's institutional self may be the enemy of his personal integrity, and the enemy of the person may quite confound a man's familial role. Of one thing only is there certainty—if a man has friends, even though they have seemed enemies, then he will survive and prosper. Nobody in this world who has good friends can fail.

The Warden celebrates the friendship of old men that is more tender and unselfish than the love of young people, more serious because less passionate. It is the triumph of age over youth, simplicity over guile, and weakness over strength. In its theme, *The Warden* of 1855 is the male counterpart to Elizabeth Gaskell's joyful evocation of female old age, *Cranford* (1853). The friendship of a group of elderly women creates an idyllic community in Cranford, a small Utopia where age has no fear and youth does not threaten. *The Warden* shares *Cranford's* spirit but it is neither pastoral nor idyll; rather it shows a fallible man contesting social institutions that can, in the case of the church, both perpetuate indolence and inefficiency and persecute virtue and resolution. Because

[3] James R. Kincaid, *The Novels of Anthony Trollope*, Oxford, 1977, p. 97.

so many of Mr. Harding's failings are those of his church, he can remain within its fold. Had he been consumed with a reforming passion, his life would have been less comfortable. Implicit in *The Warden* is the feudal conservatism of the church that will tolerate a curate starving on a pittance and accept the opulence of an archdeacon. The insistence on rank, privilege, and panoply is orchestrated to the full in *Barchester Towers*, where Miss Thorne's garden party is the anachronistic social comment on the church. Because Mr. Harding never questions his church, but only his conscience, he will never be cast out to fend for himself.

Typically, the work begins in the form of a declaration, setting out the cause of the action and the parties to that action. At issue is Hiram's Hospital and its warden with his eight hundred pounds a year, residence included. As precentor of Barchester Cathedral, in charge of all the music of the church, Mr. Harding receives a mere eighty pounds. In the light of his salary, the church can hardly be deemed a patron of the arts. The ostensible question throughout is whether Mr. Harding, as warden, deserves so much money for so little work. Certainly, eleven of the twelve bedesmen do not think so and are only too eager to dispossess the warden and lay claim to a hundred pounds a year—the amount they have been told is rightfully theirs from Hiram's will. John Bold and his friend, Tom Towers of the *Jupiter*, are complacently convinced that Hiram's Hospital is a monstrous instance of the church robbing the poor. The most simplistic resolution of the problem comes from the law in the form of Sir Abraham Haphazard who says, in effect, that since the parties to the action have not been correctly named then the action cannot proceed.

Mr. Harding has never been a very energetic or a very thoughtful man. His personal, his familial, and institutional life have been a melodious idyll. One daughter married to the archdeacon, who is the bishop's son, has provided him with a comfortable sinecure. The daughter left at home adores him and is quite prepared to battle the world on his behalf. This domestic accord is surely what we would all wish for, and where is the carping spirit to insist that every comfort in life should be earned? Mr. Harding's greatest love is his music and the violoncello that he plays, with or without instrument. There is no evidence that he is a particularly fine musician, or that his efforts are admired by his brethen. Indeed, when he joins in a small group, the guests retire promptly to whist. The twelve old bedesmen are a captive audience and only one, the faithful Bunce, appears to enjoy the plaintive strains. If this is pastoral, then it is of Mr. Harding's creation and those who share it with him are motivated less by musical taste than economic necessity. It is not that Mr. Harding fails in the end, but that he is so clearly a failure from the beginning. The crime of which he stands convicted is not that of taking money under false pretenses, but indolence. The archdeacon's lawyers have no illusions about the duties incumbent upon the warden: " 'Eight hundred a year!' said Mr. Cox. 'And nothing whatever to do!' said Mr. Cumming . . ." (ch. 19). The question put to the reasonable reader is whether he would not gladly accept such an income for so little work—if it could be managed without social censure.

Trollope berated the West Indies blacks for their laziness and then asked whether any sensible person would not sooner live without work. If Mr. Harding has been indolent, this indolence is what we all secretly desire even though we may preach the virtues of industry and toil. There is little question that Mr. Harding will remain one of Trollope's most liked characters because he evokes a common sympathy. Thus, when his thoughts are examined with the honesty and sympathy denied the professional lawyer, he speaks to all of us who have never quite been able to persuade anyone to gratify our personal predilections for leisure with a handsome income:

> All manner of past delights came before his mind, which at the time he had enjoyed without considering them; his easy days, his absence of all kind of hard work, his pleasant shady home, those twelve old neighbours whose welfare till now had been the source of so much pleasant

> care, the excellence of his children, the friendship of the dear old bishop, the solemn grandeur of those vaulted aisles, through which he loved to hear his own voice pealing; and then that friend of friends, that choice ally that had never deserted him, that eloquent companion that would always, when asked, discourse such pleasant music, that violoncello of his—ah, how happy he had been! but it was over now; his easy days and absence of work had been the crime which brought on him his tribulation. (ch. 10)

These are words that speak to our hearts, and if a lawyer could once produce such a response in a jury then Mr. Harding would be confirmed in his office forever.

However, there are more than two parties to the action and the shade of Mr. Harding's pleasant home obscures the lives of others within the church. After Cox and Cumming have marveled at a man who would refuse eight hundred pounds a year for doing nothing, there is mention of Mr. Quiverful of Puddingdale with his twelve children (later to be fourteen), and an income of four hundred a year. These are the less happy corners of the church that Trollope was to explore in the course of the Barsetshire novels. In *The Warden*, clerical poverty is no more than a disturbing twinge of conscience. The somber opulence of Archdeacon Grantly's residence is set against the modest comforts of Hiram's Hospital and the unmentioned but imaginable squalor of the Quiverfuls. John Bold was not tilting at windmills when he determined to proceed against the inequities of the Church of England.

Trollope sets out to win his case for Mr. Harding but he is not prepared to gloss over the man's weakness and his less than impressive intellect. The warden has always been a man of excessive sensibility, one whose feelings are of delicate refinement because they have never been abraded by the world. The church, like Mr. Harding, is in the world but not necessarily of it. In many ways it is indefensible as a rational institution, but it does serve as a refuge for a man like Mr. Harding. And here the reader is asked to resolve whether the church is justified because it provides an income for Mr. Harding, or whether he should be sent off to earn an honest living after he has resigned. The opinion of the community is given and we are told:

> The mercantile part of the community, the mayor and corporation, and council, also most of the ladies, were loud in his praise. Nothing could be more noble, nothing more generous, nothing more upright. But the gentry were of a different way of thinking,—especially the lawyers and the clergymen. They said such conduct was weak and undignified; that Mr. Harding evinced a lamentable want of esprit de corps, as well as courage; and that such an abdication must do much harm, and could do but little good. (ch. 20)

The commendation and criticism is itself questionable since feeling has so clearly obscured the main issue. The cause of the action is the propriety of the Hospital and whether it is being maintained in accord with Hiram's will. Surely then it is the welfare of the twelve old men that should be considered? Unfortunately, eleven of them have satisfactorily removed themselves from our sympathy by their rapacity. Yet they are the trust of Hiram's will and the responsibility of those who must administer it. If this is so, then can Mr. Harding be applauded so resoundingly for placing his conscience before his duty to these old men? Can every problem in life be resigned because it is suddenly made the subject of criticism? If there is tragedy in *The Warden* then it is not Mr. Harding's, but that of old Bunce, who has loved and defended the warden. The parting of these two men makes the heart ache:

> It was in vain that the late warden endeavoured to comfort the heart of the old bedesman. Poor old Bunce felt that his days of comfort were gone. The hospital had been to him a happy home, but it could be no longer. He had had honour there, and friendship; he had recognized his master, and been recognized; all his wants, both of soul and body, had been supplied, and he had been a happy man. He wept grievously as he parted from his friend, and the tears of an old man are bitter. (ch. 20)

The angle of vision is altered at this point and we are led to wonder if any act is good that causes so much grief to others. Mr. Harding is free to satisfy his conscience as he sees fit. He is free to go or stay, but there is no freedom of choice for Bunce.

Hiram's Hospital falls into decay, the bedesmen are left without a warden, and Mr. Harding returns only to console the dying. Their misery has been in part of their own making but they would have gone to their graves more comfortably had Mr. Harding remained at his post. Friendship had once made them happy and contented men until they were told they had a legal right to a hundred pounds a year from Hiram's Bounty. This illuminates another question within the work concerning the price to be paid for comfort. Initially, the harmonious relationship among Mr. Harding's three identities is based upon an unthinking acceptance of the good things of this world. His lot had fallen into pleasant lines and he never asked why this should be so. When his honesty is impugned he cannot find a compromise that will reduce his income and still leave him as warden of the Hospital and guardian of the old men. Instead he resigns. This is really the easy way out, and it is the one that most of us would take.

As can be seen, there are difficulties in making Mr. Harding appear so sympathetic. In the first place, Trollope forces us to recognize that the warden's faults are our own, that his life has been what most of us would choose, and that his failings have been condoned if not approved, by the church. The means by which he accomplishes this approval are primarily expository and descriptive: there is less dialogue in *The Warden* than in most of Trollope's novels. Moreover, the simplicity of Mr. Harding's utterance is set against a rhetoric that continually moves into the parodic recall of literature. Pope is evoked as the archdeacon deals his cards, Shakespeare and Sophocles when Eleanor demands that John Bold drop his suit against her father, Carlyle and Dickens as public conscience and popular feeling, and the Bible throughout. It is not simply the institutions of church and state that are ranged against the warden, but language itself. The music of the violoncello struggles to be heard over the clamor of argument, symbol of the private self at odds with the public. And Mr. Harding must learn to refashion the lost accord between the personal and institutional selves.

Trollope sounds one constant note throughout *The Warden* that recurs in all his fiction. The bonding force of society is not religion or love, but friendship. Love is a passion not subject to reason and it can therefore deflect a man from his rational purpose. John Bold, because of love, must humiliate himself before the archdeacon (and worse, his children) and Tom Towers of the *Jupiter*. All his dreams of becoming a professional reformer are gone with a kiss, and he chews the head of his cane with chagrin after the archdeacon has crowed over him. Love is comic, a crescendo of misunderstandings when Eleanor weeps her way into hysterics and gains both John Bold's promise of marriage as well as his agreement to withdraw from the case. As with the warden's resignation there is a questionable note to Bold's romantic refusal to press suit against Hiram's Hospital. His action is exactly what we would expect from the popular fiction that always proclaims the supremacy of love—a principle as far removed from reality, in Trollope's opinion, as is the law's interpretation. As usual, Trollope takes issue with both law and popular fiction, preferring a thesis that requires the active collaboration of the reader.

It is never denied that Hiram's Hospital, and others like it, is in need of reform. Bold selected a target ripe for investigation and then abandoned it for love. We can sympathize with this action even as we do with the warden when he resigns. Both men go to London and find it a vale of humiliation as they try, each in his own way, to reason with public opinion and the law. Neither can produce a solution to the problem that will bring comfort to old Bunce. Everything in the novel may be challenged and questioned save one thing alone, and that is friendship. Wherever he goes, no matter what he does, Mr. Harding is supported by friends. In London, we are told, he could have stayed with friends but he does not want to make his ordeal less painful so he wanders along from Westminster Abbey to chop house and coffee shop. But friends are within call, and closer friends still in Barchester. None is dearer to him than the bishop, and none has more power to help him.

In the warden, the bishop can recognize himself. They are men cut from the same cloth, gentle, inoffensive, and ineffectual. Few moments in literature are more reassuring than when the two old men are plotting to defeat their respective son and son-in-law, the archdeacon. It is obviously a problem, however, to find a well-paid position in the church that actually requires some recognized duties. The bishop is bewildered when Mr. Harding insists that his income should be justified by some real work:

> His first proposition to Mr. Harding was, that they should live together at the palace. He, the bishop, positively assured Mr. Harding that he wanted another resident chaplain;—not a young, working chaplain, but a steady, middle-aged chaplain; one who would dine and drink a glass of wine with him, talk about the archdeacon, and poke the fire. The bishop did not positively name all these duties, but he gave Mr. Harding to understand that such would be the nature of the service required. (ch. 20)

Conscience and pocket are satisfied when the bishop bestows upon Mr. Harding the smallest parish in Barchester, the church of St. Cuthbert with a "clear income of seventy-five pounds a year." But after we have been charmed with the church of St. Cuthbert perched over a gateway of the Cathedral Close, there is an odd and slightly disturbing note. Nothing could seem more appropriate to Mr. Harding's needs than St. Cuthbert, where "on the front seat of those devoted to the poor is always to be seen our old friend Mr. Bunce, decently arrayed in his bedesman's gown" (ch. 21). If Mr. Bunce is indeed our friend, then should we not be as much concerned with his happiness as we are with Mr. Harding's?

The attempts to reform Hiram's Hospital, and the efforts to retain it as a church sinecure, end in failure. Nothing is accomplished and the house and garden fall into ruin. The reasons are plain and are derived from the initial recourse to law. Trollope states those reasons with considerable force: "It was very clear that to Sir Abraham, the justice of the old men's claim or the justice of Mr. Harding's defense were ideas that had never presented themselves" (ch. 8). Because the law intervened at the outset all hope of reconciliation and compromise was lost. Sir Abraham Haphazard could see only a friend in his client and regarded all opposed to him as enemies. This duality defeats the contractual nature of a stable society, creating arbitrary divisions where it is always possible to find agreement. Public opinion, too, flies to opposite camps and declares war. Only friendship binds men as different as old Bunce, the bishop, and Mr. Harding together with bonds that nothing can break. It is Trollope's conviction that nothing in this world save death can destroy friendship. Certainly, Mr. Harding's friends remain true to him and, such is his nature that even his proclaimed enemies have become friends. The joy of old age is to know the friendship of Mr. Harding who "is never left alone, even should he wish to be so."

Though *The Warden* seems so tender and luminous it has discordances that are central to the work. The law cleaves the significant evidence, distorting it in the process. Popular fiction would dwell on the happy romance of Eleanor and John Bold, but Trollope looks to the disjunctions between conscience and duty, personal happiness, and the well-being of others. Defining these problems is the irrational allocation of wealth and income within the church. In *The Warden*, we are told to the last shilling what a clergyman earns. Trollope never ceased to inveigh against this sanctioned poverty. Shadowing the narrative is the outline of a Post Office report that could be generally described as an investigation into anomalies and injustices concerning the administration of the Church of England. The conclusion of that report is not in the church's favor even though we may approve of the men who serve it with varying degrees of efficiency and zeal.

Shortly before his death, on his journey to Iceland, Trollope savagely recorded that the Presbyterian minister at St. Kilda was paid eighty pounds a year and noted that such a pittance could only produce a "deterioration in the energy and intellectual capacity of the clergyman selected for the purpose."[4] Poverty destroyed the mind before the body, reducing men to unscrupulous and self-seeking creatures who would cut any corner to make an extra shilling. Mr. Harding is never reduced to this condition but we are told of Quiverful, a likely applicant for the position of warden despite the storm of public outcry about Hiram's Hospital. Quiverful cannot afford delicate feelings or a refined conscience. As the archdeacon knows: "A man with twelve children would do much to double his income" (ch. 19).

Clerical poverty becomes a dominant theme in the Barsetshire novels, and we are given a man like Mr. Crawley who is driven to madness by the needs of his family. And the enquiry is extended to the wives and children of these men who lose all pride as they plead for the means to put food on their tables. This is the reality behind the opulence of the archdeacon's home that we are only permitted to glimpse in *The Warden*. No man should have poverty thrust upon him as a condition of his service. If the Presbyterians wanted a minister at St. Kilda they should pay him a living wage. And Mr. Harding should not be given pocket money for arranging all the music of the cathedral and ten times that amount for watching over twelve old men.

If the church had not insisted that those who served it should be gentlemen, Trollope would not have raged so eloquently. The key to his understanding of a just society was the regard given a gentleman. The church accepted Trollope's principle, and everywhere practiced against it, condemning scholars to hovels and rewarding well-born fools with fat livings. These arguments and accusations are continued in *Barchester Towers*, and in this work Mr. Harding makes the same decision to refuse office that he does in *The Warden*. But because the issues are clearer there is no ambiguity in his

---

[4] *How the "Mastiffs" Went to Iceland*, London, 1878, p. 2.

action. It is one thing to resign the wardenship of Hiram's Hospital; it is another altogether to refuse to be dean. As Trollope wrote: "A Dean has been described as a church dignitary who, as regards his position in the church, has little to do and a good deal to get."[5]

[5] "The Archdeacon," in *Clergymen of the Church of England*, London, 1866, p. 42.

Chapter VIII

The Single Transaction—
Guilt and Society: *Cousin Henry*

Thady Macdermot is condemned to failure and death by the irrational nature of Irish society. Mr. Harding finds an uneasy compromise between his own failings and those of the church, but Henry Jones of *Cousin Henry* (1879) is a man who fails because of lack of resolution and meanness of mind. He typifies those who bring about their own ruin by reason of greed, dishonesty, and cowardice. At the heart of their failure is the inability, or the refusal, to see things as they are. They are first convicted of being unreasonable before they are found guilty of graver errors. And the analogue for Henry, the weak, womanish craven, is the young gentleman, courageous, resourceful, popular, and sympathetic, who inherits the estate and happens to be a young woman, Isabel Brodrick.

At the outset the transaction is stated—who will succeed to the property of Llanfeare when there is no direct heir? Isabel Brodrick, Indefer Jones's niece, has long been regarded as the heir: she is competent and well liked by the tenants and servants. But there is a cousin, Henry Jones, who bears the family name—this despite the fact that the setting is Wales where if the name is not Evans or Owen then most assuredly it is Jones. Henry Jones is disliked by everyone, but he is male and old Indefer feels bound in conscience to the principles of entail and primogeniture. Conscience is the prompting to the individual self whereas duty speaks primarily to the institutional self. Mr. Apjohn, the family lawyer, indicates the difference when he makes reference to the occasion when he

The Single Transaction 2

advised Indefer Jones not to change his will: "Mr. Indefer Jones remarked that it was not my business to lecture him on a matter in which his conscience was concerned. In this he was undoubtedly right; but still I thought I had done no more than my duty, and could only be sorry that he was angry with me" (ch. 6). Because Indefer Jones has confused conscience and duty, he fills his nephew with false hopes and then leaves the young man consumed with a sense of injustice when he makes a new will leaving Llanfeare to Isabel.

If there is to be harmony and social accord, then conscience and duty must be complementary. Mr. Harding fulfilled one at the expense of the other by satisfying his own desire for honesty and privacy and neglecting the dependent old men of the hospital. Isabel Brodrick, by comparison, is determined to subordinate her conscience to her sense of duty. When Indefer tells her, as the future heiress, that she may not marry William Owen, a minor canon and grandson of an innkeeper, Isabel dutifully obeys despite her love for the young man. When she is penniless and Owen eager to resume his suit, Isabel refuses him because of her poverty. She puts her social responsibilities before her personal happiness, and so is made to seem the moral equivalent of the gentleman. Indeed, Trollope describes her in terms that he more often uses with reference to a man:

> In appearance she was one calculated to attract attention,—somewhat tall, well set on her limbs, active, and of good figure; her brow was broad and fine, her grey eyes were bright and full of intelligence, her nose and mouth were well formed, and there was not a mean feature in her face. (ch. 2)

Like all the admired young gentlemen of Trollope's just society, Isabel is unaware of her charm and popularity, thinking herself to be "rough, unattractive and unpopular."

She embodies the moral strength of society; her cousin Henry, its weakness. And following traditional usage, Trollope defines strength as male and frailty as female—a definition that is immediately denied by the evidence of the characters. Henry is abused by Mr. Apjohn for whining like a woman and reproaches himself for behaving in a womanish fashion. Yet a dominant theme in the work is the power of woman. With a combination of courage, foresight, and prudence, Isabel is able to accomplish the triadic unity of personal, familial, and institutional success. Of course, to admit an exception to every rule, to allow contradictory statements and countering arguments is the very essence of Trollope's method and art. His legalistic cast of mind is most obvious in this ability to see the multiplicity of human actions in society and the various and often inconsistent ways of interpreting those actions.

The language throughout *Cousin Henry* is a compendium of legal terms. In the course of the novel a word is first defined precisely in law and then given a moral connotation. The will of Indefer Jones is the counterpoise to Henry's lack of will. A word is thus first defined precisely in law and then given a moral connotation that serves as an ironic counterpoint to the original meaning. The significance of rights, obligations, duty, instrument, and judgment are provided with a legal sense according to Trollope, and then translated into a wider context. For example, Mrs. Brodrick is enraged when her stepdaughter returns home and bluntly refuses to accept four thousand pounds from her cousin, or to marry William Owen. Isabel's reasons are explicable in the light of her own concept of duty: she will not take money from a man she believes to have robbed her of the estate, and she will not endure a marriage of poverty. The latter she explains less from a personal sense than from a recognition that her children would be the real victims of such a marriage. In Trollope's world there is no virtue in poverty. But if Isabel's duty impels her to refuse both money and marriage, Mrs. Brodrick insists that she has an obligation to accept one or the other, preferably both, in order to fulfill a contract with her father in which she promised never to be a burden to him. The argument between the two women, seeking for an admission of acknowledged duty, is phrased in legal terms. Isabel pleads eloquently, scrutinizing each point as her stepmother makes it and then putting in a plea of confession and avoidance regarding an error on her uncle's part. Mrs. Brodrick begins by referring to Isabel's father and his rational expectation:

> "He had reason to expect, ample reason, that you would never cost him a shilling. He had been told a hundred times that you would be provided for by your uncle. Do you not know that it was so?" "I do. I told him so myself when I was last here before Uncle Indefer's death." "And yet you will do nothing to relieve him? You will refuse this money, though it is your own, when you could be married to Mr. Owen tomorrow?" Then she paused, waiting to find what might be the effect of her eloquence. "I do not acknowledge papa's right or yours to press me to marry any man." "But I suppose you acknowledge your right to be as good as your word? Here is the money; you have only got to take it." "What you mean is that I ought to acknowledge my obligation to be as good as my word. I do. I told my father that I would not be a burden to him, and I am bound to keep to that. He will have understood that at the present moment I am breaking my promise through a mistake of Uncle Indefer's which I could not have anticipated." (ch. 12)

The form of this argument, the emphasis upon the authority implicit in certain words, is legal reasoning at its best. These are not two people playing at being lawyers, but women who accept the contractual nature of society and who try to live in compliance with justice.

Mrs. Brodrick is not a bad woman, a wicked stepmother intent on feeding her own children at the expense of her husband's first-born. Rather, she endures genteel poverty, and her days are a fretful concern with new shoes, mending, and generally trying to make ends meet. She is the embodiment of what Isabel intends to avoid in her own life. When Mrs. Brodrick accuses her of being a burden, Isabel not only accepts the accusation but gives it greater clarity and definition: "Of course I am a burden. Every human being who eats and wears clothes and earns nothing is a burden" (ch. 16). The toughness of Isabel's thinking is based upon experience. Most children grow up unthinkingly within a marriage—Isabel was witness to one from its inception to its drably domestic conclusion. She loves William Owen passionately but she will not endure the kind of poverty with him that suffocates love in a crowded nursery or at a bare table. She has always regarded her stepmother as a marital warning: she has also known the joyful independence derived from the property of Llanfeare rather than as the wife of William Owen.

Poverty is not unendurable if it can be born alone. Isabel is quite prepared to work as a maid, but she will not inflict her poverty on others. Her ability to reason provides the source of her strength. She rejects cousin Henry's offer of marriage and refuses to lie when she does. Her reasoning results not from a hard head and a cold heart, but from passion controlled by intellect. Thus she is not afraid to tell William Owen that she loves him physically:

> There has never been a man whose touch has been pleasant to me;—but I could revel in yours. Kiss you? I could kiss your feet at this moment, and embrace your knees. Everything belonging to you is dear to me. The things you have touched have been made sacred to me. The Prayer-Book tells the young wife that she should love her husband till death shall part them. I think my love will go further than that." (ch. 12)

Not unnaturally, Owen is convinced that Isabel will be eager to marry him in poverty and bear his children in greater poverty for the sake of love. However, although she is moved by powerful feeling she is governed by reason. The chapter ends with two sentences, one of affirmation, and one of denial: "How infinitely better was he than any other being that ever crossed her path! But yet she was quite sure that she would not marry him."

Isabel's victory is complete when Mr. Apjohn discovers the will and she is acknowledged to be the owner of Llanfeare. To win back Owen, now reluctant to offer himself to the heiress, is no problem. She proposes to him and he accepts her without argument. "She, as a woman, could be stronger than he as a man" (ch. 13). The property is made secure under entail, William Owen becomes Jones, and prosperity is ensured. The servants rejoice with the tenants, for they are part of the property that cannot be disregarded. Land, as Mr. Apjohn points out, is both personal property and something to be shared contractually with others. When Indefer Jones made over Lianfeare to Henry Jones because he had a conscience on the matter, he was disregarding his duty to those who considered they had a contract with him that guaranteed them a good landlord. The contractual nature of society extends from individuals to groups, from a man and his wife to landlord and tenants:

> Suddenly to be told that they were servants to such a one as Cousin Henry,—servants to such a man without any contract or agreement on their part;—to be handed over like the chairs and tables to a disreputable clerk from London, whom in their hearts they regarded as very much inferior to themselves! And they, too, like Mr. Griffith and the tenants, had been taught to look for the future reign of Queen Isabel as a thing of course. In that there would have been an implied contract,—an understanding on their part that they had been consulted and had agreed to this destination of themselves. (ch. 14)

To ignore the contractual nature of society is a dereliction of duty that cannot be condoned by any appeal to the personal demands of conscience. Isabel had referred to her uncle's revised will as a "mistake," but to others it was cruel and wicked since it affected not only Indefer's niece, but so many others on the property. Because an "implied contract" had been broken, the tenants felt justified in tendering Henry neither deference nor respect. The jumble of cracked china and the cold mutton on his breakfast tray are the visible evidence of the housekeeper's feelings toward her new master.

Only one person resents Isabel's restoration to Llanfeare, and that is her stepmother. She does not feel comfortable with an heiress and would have far preferred Isabel to marry Owen with four thousand pounds. Like most of Trollope's women, Mrs. Brodrick cannot reconcile her personal and institutional indentities; indeed, for many the institutional and familial selves are conjoined. Isabel is an exception and she enjoys the fulfillment of Trollope's gentleman as she marries to her satisfaction and knows that she will always be regarded as the Squire of Llanfeare. Unfortunately, Mrs. Brodrick can only identify herself as a wife and the mother of children, and when one of those children, albeit a stepchild, becomes the greatest landlord in the area, her own role in life is diminished.

The balance between right and wrong reason is established by Isabel and Henry. Physically and mentally they are opposites: he is as weak as she is strong, and he is as irresolute as she is determined. If Henry Jones were no more than a conniving villain bent on defrauding his cousin there would be little tension to the story and no compulsion to follow every tortured thought in his mind. But Henry believes passionately that his right to Llanfeare is just and in accord with his uncle's wishes and the English tradition of primogeniture. He had been brought to Llanfeare as the heir, told and shown what he was to expect. He had even proposed to Isabel as his uncle requested, although he disliked her intensely. In return he had been cast over in what seemed to him like a dotard's act of caprice. Then, as though by divine providence, he had discovered the second will—and simply failed to admit any knowledge of it when the house was searched.

In consequence, he laboriously puts together an ingenious defense based upon his sense of injustice and the conviction that he had not committed an actual crime when he denied knowing of the will. Nonetheless, even though Henry regards himself as a cruelly misused innocent, he recognizes that withholding evidence is legal malfeasance and, in the eyes of society, he is no better than a perjurer and a thief. The belief that he is entitled to the estate by right is constantly assailed by the prompting of duty that commands him to hand over the will. From the beginning the will is made to seem of the same order as holy writ by Indefer's placing it in a volume of sermons, and its destruction a form of murder since a man may be said to live on in his property. Isabel knew her uncle's intention from his dying words: Henry has to live in the presence of his accusing uncle every day he remains at Llanfeare watching over the will.

Desperately Henry equivocates and pleads, making the contest one between himself and his dead uncle's will. But no man can live alone, and Henry finds that the opprobrium of servants and tenants is given a clarion voice in *The Carmarthen Herald*, which begins to publish a series of articles and letters questioning his claim to the estate, and accusing him of being that most alien and suspicious of creatures—a man without a friend. There is no one who will speak for him, and he is forced, reluctantly, to agree to prosecute for libel. Still, in his own mind he is guiltless, and if he has committed any sin then it is one of omission, not commission.[1]

> He had not destroyed the will. He had not even hidden it. He had only put a book into its own place, carrying out as he did so his innocent intention when he had first lifted the book. When these searchers had come, doing their work so idly, with such incurious futility, he had not concealed the book. He had left it there on its shelf beneath their hands. Who could say that he had been guilty? (ch. 13)

At this point Henry has not committed any crime for which he can be legally charged, and he knows it. Sins of omission, like acts of negligence, are awkward to define and difficult to indict. Lord Lloyd, explicating the question of liability for negligent acts, has stated:

> But what of *omissions*, that is *failures* to act? Are these to be classified as acts for this purpose? For instance, I see someone proceeding up a steep path which I know to be dangerous, but I fail to warn him of the danger. Or I am a strong swimmer and see a small child drowning in a pool of water but do nothing to save it. This marginal type of problem cannot be resolved simply by examining

---

[1] Dennis Lloyd, *The Idea of Law* (Middlesex, 1977), p. 268.

the logical or semantic implications of the word "act," or even by attempting to assess whether there is any decisive analogy between negligently driving a car or negligently failing to rescue a drowning child.[1]

And Lord Lloyd includes a note to the effect that "English law declines to impose any general duty to rescue or help a person in distress, but many other legal systems do recognize such a duty."[2]

Failing to produce the will is no crime; lying to Mr. Apjohn and the tenants about it is not an offense since nothing was said under oath. Henry is acutely aware of his strength in common law however weak his position may be morally.[3] But Trollope now shows society acting as the agent of natural law. The voices grow from whispers to shouts and then, almost by accident, he does commit a crime and is forced to contemplate a greater. The will must be proven in Carmarthen and Henry makes a false declaration, committing perjury. The local paper continues its accusations, he is jeered at by his tenants, and Apjohn, determined to have him questioned under oath, insists that he sue for libel. Still Henry cannot bring himself to reveal the will, or burn it and eat the ashes.

> When he thought of what it might be to be Squire of Llanfeare in perhaps five years' time, with the rents in his pocket, he became angry at his own feebleness. Let them ask him what questions they would, there could be no evidence against him. If he were to burn the will, there could certainly be no evidence against him. If the will were still hidden, they might, perhaps, extract that secret from him; but no lawyer would be strong enough to make him own that he had thrust the paper between the bars of the fire. (ch. 15)

[2] *Ibid.*, p. 354.
[3] Ruth apRoberts finds the donnée for *Cousin Henry* in Ciceronian ethics and writes: "It is to be noted that when he is at last found out, he can be proved guilty of no crime, legally, just as he is guilty of no overt positive sin, morally." *The Moral Trollope* (Ohio, 1971), p. 169. It should be remembered that Henry made a false declaration in Carmarthen when the will was probated. This could bring, at the least, a charge of perjury. Moreover, I cannot agree that his sin was so covert when a good part of Wales was aware of it.

It is not a stream of consciousness when Henry pleads his case in this fashion, but a disputation with a narrative advocate who challenges his reasoning, continually reminding him of the social consequences of his action and its definition in terms of law. He is reminded that his personal sense of innocence may well be regarded by others as a felony that can be punished with a prison sentence. Sound reason in Trollope's words is always in search of social solutions, whereas false reason is private and idiosyncratic. Therefore, although the narrative advocate may engage the defendant in debate, he also examines the validity of other evidence by means of shared social perceptions. The auctioneer at Carmarthen is quite certain that Henry will romp through the trial for libel and return to Llanfeare, laughing in his sleeve. The narrative advocate now makes clear that this statement may be false, and we should remember that what we are reading is a declaration and declarations do not contain unexpected information. They relate facts and belong irrevocably to the past. Novels may attempt to create suspense with unexpected endings, but not the novel as Trollope chose to write it. The final appeal in the passage is to the reader's reason:

> They little knew the torments which the man was enduring, or how unlikely it was that he should laugh in his sleeve at any one. We are too apt to forget when we think of the sins and faults of men how keen may be their conscience in spite of their sins. While they were thus talking of Cousin Henry, he was vainly endeavoring to console himself with the reflection that he had not committed any great crime, that there was still a road open to him for repentance, that if only he might be allowed to escape and repent in London, he would be too glad to resign Llanfeare and all its glories. The reader will hardly suppose that Cousin Henry will return after the trial to laugh in his sleeve in his own library in his own house. (ch. 17)

The inference here is that the reader does indeed know as much about Henry as the advocate and may hold a quite contrary opinion.

It is never religion that moves Henry. Every night he says the Lord's Prayer as though it were a symbol of his respectability, a token of his innocence. What racks his mind is the thought of justice. Should he destroy the will, he is confident that God could be appeased with a rubric of words, but society could not be placated so easily. Clearly, conscience is a poor guide to conduct but duty implies a public responsibility. Equally so, it is the certainty of detection and punishment that deters men from crime, not the threat of any supernatural judgment. Henry is fully aware of his "impotence in deceit" and recognizes it as the fruit of a dull mind rather than the result of excessive virtue. Far from being driven mad by his crime, he continues to scheme, threading excuses to delays, waiting for events to turn in his favor. Even duty assumes a personal and perverted form in his pleading: "There was rising in his heart so strong a feeling of hatred against those who were oppressing him that it seemed to him almost a duty to punish them by continued possession of the property" (ch. 20).

Doggedly, Henry argues his case against the will of society, refining his concepts of duty and obligation until he is, quite simply, a law to himself. However, he cannot extricate himself from society's laws:

> That not telling of the will had been burdensome to him only because of the danger of discovery. But to burn a will, and thereby clearly steal 1500£. a year from his cousin! To commit felony! To do that for which he might be confined at Dartmoor all his life, with his hair cut, and dirty prison clothes, and hard food, and work to do! He thought it would be well to have another day of life in which he had not done the deed. He therefore put the will back into the book and went to his bed. (ch. 20)

The thought of burning in hell for all eternity is like a child's nightmare, but Dartmoor is the horror of every waking hour.

The man who resolves the issue by finding the will is a country attorney, Mr. Apjohn. Legal writers have questioned Mr. Apjohn's voracious pursuit of the truth by means that are more appropriate to a detective than a lawyer. Nevertheless, it is because Mr. Apjohn is prepared to violate the confidential relationship with his client, Henry Jones, that he is able to force an admission from him that the will exists and that he knows where it is hidden. Desperate with fear at the thought of being questioned by Mr. Cheekey, the redoubtable Irish barrister who can wring the truth from the most intransigent witness, Henry determines to burn the will.

> And he thought that the deed when done would give him a new courage. The very danger to which he would have exposed himself would make him brave to avoid it. Having destroyed the will, and certain that no eye had seen him, conscious that his safety depended on his own reticence, he was sure he would keep his secret even before Mr. Cheekey. (ch. 20)

The next day, positive that his client is now frantic with terror, Mr. Apjohn and Isabel's father burst into Henry's bookroom, and the will is discovered.

Mr. Apjohn is the lawyer that Trollope would like us all to admire, charging down on quaking rogues, shaking the truth from them with a fusillade of questions, and bypassing the finer points of the law to grapple with the truth. He personifies justice and speaks for the secular ethic that sustains Trollope's world. In a well-ordered society there is a measure of predictability that allows people to regulate their lives with some sense of security. Chance, coincidence, and providential events must be eliminated wherever possible and every action should seem the result of social, rather than of personal intention. Thus, Mr. Apjohn sees to it that Llanfeare is entailed in order that there may no longer be any doubts as to its future disposition. If events are the consequence of rational decisions and implied contracts between people, and not the result of individual whim, then society will flourish and be content. Mr. Apjohn reminds Isabel of Henry's passionate, and understandable, feeling of injustice: ". . . you see what terrible misery may be ocasioned by not allowing those who are to come after you know to what it is they are to expect" (ch. 24).

Not only did Trollope eliminate suspense from his novels,

he insisted that the reader must be given the end with the beginning in compliance with the form of a declaration. Nothing should be permitted to divert the reader from the moral purpose of the fiction—the recognition of a rational, and therefore predictable, society, demonstrated by individuals of everyday character. If people could only be made to conform with the directions of his fiction then justice would prevail and a world of law proclaimed. Men would behave like Isabel Brodrick, realizing that if it were possible for a woman to be a gentleman, then it was not a rank beyond their own reach. Lawyers would learn to emulate Mr. Apjohn, who admits his failings and then puts them to work in the cause of truth:

> I own to all the litigious pugnacity of a lawyer. I live by such fighting and I like it. But a case in which I do not believe crushes me. To have an injustice to get the better of, and then to trample it well under foot,—that is the triumph that I desire. It does not often happen to a lawyer to have had such a chance as this, and I fancy that it could not have come in the way of a man who would have enjoyed it more than I do.   (ch. 24)

Trollope argued that although cruelty and violence were inherent, they could be sublimated, as Mr. Apjohn had shown. His concern with lawyers was founded in his conviction that they ought to be what in general they were not, the proper guardians of reason, those who should constantly remind others of their duty to make law a living precept, not a dead letter to be revived when a crime had been committed. Law should be the substance of rational life, according to Trollope, and lawyers should be its exemplars. Instead, he found them everywhere perverting justice and denying truth, the most insidious enemies of his fictional world. In several novels he was to challenge lawyers with his own legal system, and nowhere so eloquently as in *Orley Farm*. In *Orley Farm*, however, Trollope preferred to use a more complex structure, that of the multiple transaction.

Chapter IX

The Multiple Transaction—
Social Contracts—Law and Justice:
Orley Farm

The basic social contract, the one most idealized in concept and most abused in practice, is marriage. Just as marriage is the social compromise of love, law represents the flawed efforts of inadequate men to seek the truth and grant justice to all. Trollope found many lawyers to admire, from O'Malley in *The Macdermots of Ballycloran* to Mr. Apjohn in *Cousin Henry*, and many more to despise. Those he admired were unswerving in their quest for the truth and carried the cause of justice like a banner. What he deplored most was the lawyer who accompanied a guilty client to court, knowing his guilt, and there pleaded his innocence with all the forensic skill in his power. A witness could be subjected to mental torture in the process of cross-examination, verbally bludgeoned into false admissions, and then dismissed with his character in rags. In consequence, a guilty man might well be slipped through a legal loophole or whitewashed by a barrister's rhetoric, and then be dismissed from the court without rebuke or punishment. The complaint is not unfamiliar. The shame of being subjected to a false accusation in court still rankled with Trollope,[1] but he had also delighted in hectoring and badgering his postmasters. What he disliked and condemned most

[1] Op. cit., the incident when Trollope was cross-examined by Sir Isaac Butt and accused of having put a marked coin into the prisoner's pocket.

was what gave him enormous satisfaction, and both the pain and the pleasure are manifest in *Orley Farm*.

Trollope belligerently chose to misunderstand the system of advocacy whereby everyone is entitled to the best defense a lawyer can provide, whether or not he is guilty. It is hardly for the lawyer to determine the question of guilt, derogating the authority of judge and jury. However, *Orley Farm* is not a thundering denunciation of legal perfidy; rather, it explores the social compromises that may resolve problems more effectively than any judgment in law. Because ultimate justice is a compromise between society and law it is argued with the analogy of marriage: we are given crime and its resolution by social and legal justice, and love unrequited and love consummated by marriage. Neither marriage nor the justice of the court is seen as flawless; rather, they are subject to all the weaknesses of the involved parties and the degree of reason and good will they bring to those contracts. And, at the conclusion of the novel, Trollope is less certain that advocacy is partial and brutal than he was at the beginning. It is quite apparent that Felix Graham the idealist and legal reformer has been changed by the prospect of marriage. If a man learns to compromise in one direction, he will scarcely notice that his absolutist theories have crumbled to the level of other men's feet.

Throughout *Orley Farm* Trollope practices his own advocacy, arguing for and against the testimony of each witness, often finding himself at variance with the evidence, frequently permitting dubiety of utterance to be his own and not that of a character.[2] And the ending of the work complies neither

---

[2] For example, Trollope addressed a homily to the reader on the virtues of hard work and success earned late in life:

> There is no human bliss equal to twelve hours of work with only six hours in which to do it. And when the expected pay for that work is worse than doubtful, the inner satisfaction is so much the greater. . . . Success is the necessary misfortune of life, but it is only to the very unfortunate that it comes early. (ch. 49)

Now this is very plausible but it must be weighed against the success of Judge Staveley, who began his career as a young barrister, married a young woman without a great fortune, and was appointed to the bench in middle age. His

with the requirements of popular fiction nor with the verdict of the court. Rather, a compromise is reached between the two that does not ensure happiness but is demonstrably just. At all times we are told that Lady Mason is guilty of having forged the codicil to her husband's will. And the tension and excitement depends on the reaction of those around her to the imputed crime. The reader is given all the evidence: evidence concerning those immediately involved and those who are only tangentially affected. Crucial for the reader's understanding is the testimony and state of mind of the lawyers who undertake the case for disparate reasons. This is Trollope's system of equity, in which lawyers are subjected to the same scrutiny as witnesses. Nothing is withheld save the details of one instance where Lady Mason voices her religious doubts to Mrs. Orme.

The work is set out in accordance with the requirements of a declaration and extends through analogies and parallel marriages in the structure of the multiple transaction. The action involves a charge of perjury brought against Lady Mason of Orley Farm. At issue is the property that has now passed to her son, Lucius Mason. Twenty-two years before in the Probate Court, Joseph Mason of Groby Park, Sir Joseph Mason's eldest son, had contested the validity of a codicil to his father's will that left the farm to his infant stepbrother, Lucius. There were curious circumstances about the will, but the two witnesses gave evidence and Lady Mason testified, with the result that Joseph Mason's case was dismissed. For over twenty years Lady Mason lived at Orley Farm in quiet seclusion, enjoying the revenues of the estate and the respect of her neighbors. And for the same period Joseph Mason gloomed in the belief that Lady Mason had either forged the codicil and the signatures of the witnesses, or else exerted undue influence over his dying father.

At the commencement we are told that Lady Mason was

---

family is a delight to him, his work a source of satisfaction. A passage like this makes the reader look more closely at Judge Staveley and Mr. Furnival. The truth may then be found to reside more with the person than with the condition.

determined, like Rebekah, to save some small part of the estate for her baby son, Lucius. She had raged over her husband's injustice to Lucius and when he refused to leave Orley Farm to "the brat," she decided to follow the Biblical precedent of Rebekah. Lady Mason cannot accept Christian doctrine but she is able to accept a Judaic code of justice. The law and society may feel required to call her a felon: Joseph Mason longs to see his stepmother whipped through the streets and hanged to satisfy his sense of justice. Rebekah is the witness who speaks for another form of justice. Despite all the laws of primogeniture, is it right that the eldest son should take everything, leaving the younger with a pittance at his father's death? Rebekah did not think so, and by deception gained Isaac's blessing for her son Jacob. Far from being punished by God, Jacob lived to become the father of his people and was known as Israel. When Mrs. Orme, with her muddled Gospel tags, calls on Lady Mason to atone for her sin, the shadow of Rebekah is between them. The adult Lucius, with customary lack of apprehension and tact, comforts his mother in her sorrow with the assurance that although there is nothing for her in this world "there is another world before you,—if you can repent of your sin" (ch. 75). There is no Biblical account of Jacob's reproaching his mother for having secured his birthright by guile.

Orley Farm demonstrates one of Trollope's basic principles—religion is a dangerous guide for human conduct particularly when the Bible is used as literal reference. Religion is accountable and useful only when it becomes a tradition of social observance: the pat phrases of Mrs. Orme that she uses to express her own sense of compassion and social conservatism, or the Christmas attendance at church in Noningsby that has less significance than the family rituals of snapdragon and blind-man's-buff. Trollope is fond of telling the reader that God tempers the wind to the shorn lamb, but not all his lambs survive the rigors of the season.

Lady Mason sacrificed her life and reputation for her son, yet it is Lucius who precipitates her ruin by provoking the local attorney, Dockwrath. The latter ferrets out the information that leads to her being charged with having committed perjury at the previous trial. Lucius is an arrogant and impetuous young man who closely resembles his stepbrother in temperament and appearance. In *The Warden*, Archdeacon Grantly's abominable sons are as much a commentary on his own nature as they are evidence of their mother's calculating and mundane spirit. So, in *Orley Farm*, young Peregrine Orme shares his grandfather's quixotic and romantic character, and Sophia Furnival is her father to the last quizzing examination of a prospective lover. Madeline and Augustus Staveley are proof of the generosity and urbanity of their father, Judge Staveley, who believed that children "should be allowed, as far as was practicable, to do what they liked. . . . Children, he said, if properly trained would like those things which were good for them" (ch. 47).

The failure of a marriage and its bitter fruit in Lucius, an ungrateful son, is at the heart of the work. Lady Mason had committed one crime in her life, and that for her son, not herself. But the child become a man is neither comfort nor strength to her. He takes possession of Orley Farm and immediately begins to buy guano for a method of scientific farming that will feed the starving millions of the world. With more intelligence than common sense he demands the return of two fields that Dockwrath, the Hamworth attorney, has enjoyed at a peppercorn rental for twenty years. Within weeks Dockwrath has taken to Joseph Mason the evidence that will bring Lady Mason to trial.

From the beginning, Lady Mason is made to question whether her great sacrifice has been justified by her son. He is not a Jacob, the leader of his people, although he has plans for compiling a natural history of all the races when he is not actually farming. Lucius is her life, but she knows that her wishes mean rather less to him than the purchasing of pure guano in Liverpool. The moment he returns she is made to feel that Orley Farm is no longer her home but a place of temporary residence that can be taken from her as abruptly as Lucius demanded Dockwrath's fields. When she is accused of perjury her son insists that she leave her friends at the

Cleeve, go into seclusion, accept legal advice of his choice, and generally be commanded by him in all things. As he proposes to Sophia Furnival, who rightly suspects her father of having a romantic interest in Lady Mason, he laments the news that his mother is planning to marry Sir Peregrine Orme: "All the world are talking about it. Miss Furnival, you have never known what it is to blush for a parent" (ch. 55). And at the end, when he is told that she did indeed forge the codicil by Mrs. Orme and realizes that he must return Orley Farm to his stepbrother, he feels neither pity nor understanding for his mother. The only words he can find for her are those of reproach that she should have brought him to such disgrace. In his own way, Lucius is just as hard and inflexible as his stepbrother:

> "I will not ask you to forgive me," she said plaintively. "Mother," he answered, "were I to say that I forgave you my words would be a mockery. I have no right either to condemn or to forgive. I accept my position as it has been made for me, and will endeavour to do my duty." (ch. 75)

In the eyes of the public, Lady Mason is a heroine because she had successfully outwitted a selfish old man for the sake of her son. In the world's opinion it is not dishonest to steal for a child, and Rebekah should be applauded in any age. Even the lawyers admire Lady Mason's courage and understand her motive. Only Lucius is unrelenting. They go into exile to a small German town and there he leaves his mother and travels to Australia. This is the reward of Rebekah in the modern world. Lady Mason has lived by Biblical precept and, in her way, is a deeply religious woman who begs God for strength, just as Mrs. Orme prays to Christ for his forgiveness.[3] The tragedy and tension of *Orley Farm* is the anguished

---

[3] Lady Mason's prayers for strength puzzled some contemporary reviewers. The *Spectator* referred to the "needless religious falsehood" of Lady Mason's expressions when speaking to Mr. Furnival and Sir Peregrine Orme. It should be noted that Lady Mason trusts God and doubts Christ. *Spectator*, 11 October 1862, xxxiii, 1136-38, in *Anthony Trollope, The Critical Heritage*, ed. Donald Smalley (London, 1969), p. 149.

despair of Lady Mason when her son is told the truth and the work of her life decays around her in festering resentment. She can triumph over the law, but she cannot win her son's love or prevail against the social laws that maintain order in society.

For every relationship in *Orley Farm* that implies a contract—husband and wife, parent and child, lawyer and client—there is a reflecting analogue, and all in their turn are modified by the experience of the trial. At the outset, Lady Mason seems to have a model son who is compared with Mrs. Orme's ratcatching boy Peregrine. Lucius Mason is more intelligent, more resourceful, and considerably less a gentleman than Peregrine Orme. This is a question not so much of birth and breeding as of sympathy and understanding. Peregrine is foolish, but he has enough sense to appreciate his inadequacies. Moreover, he is sympathetic and can show friendship to a rival in love even though he would like to see that rival dead. It is Peregrine who sits with Lady Mason at her trial and awkwardly tries to comfort her. At the least, Peregrine can live with his fellow men—this is impossible for the solitary, Lucius Mason, always "looking down from the height of his superior intellect on the folly of those below him . . ." (ch. 73).

Lucius is a man alone and his isolation is made explicable for the reader in terms of a German education that never taught him to accept his failings and tolerate the weakness of others. Above all else, Lucius is devoid of humor, and when the hunt is proposed at Noningsby he excuses his inability to join the sport with the moral observation: " 'They have nothing to do but amuse themselves,' he said to himself; 'but I have a man's work before me, and a man's misfortunes. I will go home and face both' " (ch. 27). Felix Graham does not hunt either but he is ready to try his luck with the rest. Whereas Felix tries to live by his moral convictions, Lucius is guided by an abstract notion of duty that has no foundation in reality, and for this reason his language and his actions are frequently at variance. When not inarticulate, Peregrine Orme can make and mean two contradictory statements with the same breath, but Lucius Mason is never affected by a loss of words. Honesty is not necessarily contingent upon fluency or consistency. Aphorisms and elevated moral abstractions are the mode of Lucius' social discourse, yet when he confronts Dockwrath he blunders and falters like a guilty schoolboy. In order to captivate Sophia, he assures Mrs. Furnival that all women have intellects comparable with men: " 'they have minds equal to those of men,' said Lucius gallantly, 'and ought to be able to make for themselves careers as brilliant.' 'Women ought not to have any spheres,' said Mrs. Furnival" (ch. 11). Even as he says this, Lucius is calling upon his mother to be guided by him and remain at Orley Farm in a condition of maternal tutelage.

Marriage is the contract that ultimately tests the capacity to work with others. When successful, a marriage is the microcosm of an ordered society. Judge Staveley and his family at Noningsby are the model, and the reader is shown why husband and wife, children and grandchildren can live together in satisfaction and content. The judge is a man of understanding and great good humor who "always spoke of his wife as though she were an absolute part of himself" (ch. 65). Lady Staveley's sphere is Noningsby, where she produces eggs and butter that surpass any in the county. Far from being an appendage of her husband, Lady Staveley remains in charge of her farm when the judge goes to London on legal matters. And in London Judge Staveley can be found in bachelor's lodgings. She is well-meaning and socially ambitious for her children and would like to plan their marriages and their lives. The judge is of a different mind. When Madeline chooses Felix Graham, the barrister with heterodox opinions regarding the law, it is Judge Staveley who approves the match even as his wife is persuading young Peregrine Orme to propose to Madeline again. But it is not difficult for Lady Staveley to accept Felix when the rest of the family approve of him.

Love and its dreams may lead to matrimony, but marriage in Trollope's world is always defined in legal terms as a contract with certain obligations on either side. So when Madeline accepts Felix Graham, preferring mind to matter, as her father puts it, sentiment and law are joined in the same passage:

> Madeline still stood silent before him and still fixed her eyes upon the ground, but very slowly she raised her little hand and allowed her soft slight fingers to rest upon his open palm. It was as though she thus affixed her legal signature and seal to the deed of gift. (ch. 74)

And when Peregrine is refused it is a legal verdict:

> Peregrine stood there, like a prisoner on his trial, waiting for a verdict. He did not know how to plead his cause with any further language; and indeed no further language could have been of any avail. The judge and jury were clear against him, and he should have known the sentence without waiting to have it pronounced in set terms. (ch. 30)

In the Staveley marriage, the obligations between husband and wife, parents and children, have all been punctiliously observed with resulting satisfaction. Not all successful marriages require the same obligations, and what would be misery for some is amicable content for others. Moulder and his wife contrive to live harmoniously because each knows what is expected of the other—the partnership is maintained on the basis of financial security for Mrs. Moulder's life and starched collars and hot dinners for Mr. Moulder. However, Mrs. Furnival yearns for the days when she lived in frugal bliss with her husband, buttering his toast and making his tea. His success as a barrister and member of parliament has separated them and Mrs. Furnival no longer has a sphere of her own, no identity in a familial or institutional sense. Lady Staveley manages an estate, Mrs. Moulder starches collars, and Mrs. Furnival waits disconsolately for her husband to come home to his dinner. Eventually she has to accept marriage on the same terms as Mrs. Moulder, having first begged humble forgiveness for ever having suspected her husband of amorous intentions toward Lady Mason. At Groby Park, that obsessive miser, Mrs. Mason provides the domestic analogue for her husband's Draconian ideas of justice.

It is Sir Peregrine Orme who dreams most passionately and

whose love consumes his mind and spirit with the same obsessive desire that has taken possession of his grandson. There is one marked difference between the two—the love of the old is more serious than that of the young because it lives in the shadow of death. Contrary to all Victorian and comic conventions, an old man's love in Trollope is more poignant than a youth's because there can be no second chance. His heart is broken when Lady Mason refuses to marry him, knowing that love cannot survive the social ostracism of a scandalous marriage. The law may well be interpreted according to the whim of the judge, but "social laws" are inflexible. When they are invoked both Lady Mason and Sir Peregrine are obedient.

Lady Mason's marriage was the most barbaric of all. Left in the wreck of a bankrupt business, she was taken up by Sir Joseph Mason, her father's creditor, to be his wife and housekeeper. She had never been a willing partner to the marriage contract but she had fulfilled her obligations conscientiously. When Sir Joseph failed to provide for their son, her outrage led her to commit a forgery. The contract she had observed so faithfully had been broken by her husband and she therefore felt justified in seeking redress. Lady Mason had defined her institutional and familial identity by her son's right to Orley Farm. Her assumption is false in law and, more importantly, in the expectation that a child can ever be the custodian of a parent's hope and happiness. When Lucius takes possession of Orley Farm he disregards every suggestion from the woman who had managed it competently for him since he was born.

Felix Graham has decided that he can avoid the risks of customary marriage by molding a wife for himself. Mary Snow has been selected and is being educated according to his taste and requirements. Not unexpectedly Mary gives her heart to a sentimental apothecary's apprentice and Felix falls in love with the judge's daughter. When he has to extricate himself from a written contract with Mary's father and a threatened suit for breach of promise, Felix learns the difference between absolute truth and human honesty. He is the link between justice and the practice of law on one side, and love in its social expression of marriage on the other.

At the law conference in Birmingham where theory is propounded by European jurists to the skeptical ears of English lawyers, Felix ridicules common law as a system "which contains many of the barbarities of the feudal times, and also many of its lies" (ch. 18). His words reflect Trollope's own opinions, but even at this point they are challenged by Augustus Staveley, who believes that it is better to effect small changes gradually than to try and reform the whole legal system overnight. The nature of truth and the constitution of honesty are tested throughout *Orley Farm*. Felix has lived by an ideal of absolute truth that is gradually modified by experience: Lady Mason has based her life on a deception that is destroyed by the nature of her son. Honesty and truth are not divine aspirations implanted in man with the soul, but the result of society's unending struggle for order and happiness. Lady Mason's account of the will is plausible, consistent at all points, and yet a lie: John Kenneby's faltering and contradictory recall of signing one or maybe twenty-four documents is honest and the truth. Lady Mason is left an exile and a solitary because her crime makes all compromise with society unfeasible: Felix finds that his legal and social theories have been changed when he accepts marriage and its obligations.

The man who had been unswerving in the service of truth finds that he has to prevaricate and engage in a deal of casuistry when Mary's lover requires a dowry and her father demands a settlement. At Lady Mason's trial he refuses to bully old Mr. Torrington from London who had been called to verify the deed witnessed by Bridget Bolster and John Kenneby. Although his mild interrogation receives nothing but scorn from Mr. Chaffanbrass, his views on the law have ceased to be fixed beliefs and are now expressed as queries:

> He felt as though he were engaged to fight a battle in which truth and justice, nay heaven itself must be against him. How can a man put his heart to the proof of an assertion in the truth of which he himself has no belief? That though guilty this lady should be treated with the utmost mercy compatible with the law;—for so much, had her guilt stood forward as acknowledged, he could

still pity her, sympathize with her, fight for her on such ground as that; but was it possible that he, believing her to be false, should stand up before the crowd assembled in that court, and use such intellect as God had given him in making others think that the false and the guilty one was true and innocent, and that those accusers were false and guilty whom he knew to be true and innocent.   (ch. 69)

Later Madeline tells him pleasantly that her father thinks he should give up his writing and concentrate on his profession, and Felix does not argue. The idealist of the first pages of *Orley Farm* has changed, not without a struggle, and his future is set out for him by the ebullient Augustus Staveley. Felix Graham will never be a Chaffanbrass at the Old Bailey but he will relinquish theory to practice, like George Bertram in *The Bertrams*. As a married man, Felix can no longer afford an individual's idealism. On this occasion, Augustus has the last word:

". . . for Mad's sake, I do hope you will get rid of your vagaries. An income, I know, is a very commonplace sort of thing; but when a man has a family there are comforts attached to it." "I am at any rate willing to work," said Graham somewhat moodily. "Yes, if you may work exactly in your own way. But men in the world can't do that. A man, as I take it, must through life allow himself to be governed by the united wisdom of others around him. He cannot take it upon himself to judge as to every step by his own lights. If he does, he will be dead before he has made up his mind as to the preliminaries."   (ch. 74)

The problem of truth and advocacy is brought to a conclusion that modifies the initial statements. Lady Mason is found not guilty after she has confessed to Sir Peregrine and Mrs. Orme that she had indeed forged the codicil. At this point the reader is called upon to answer the same questions that troubled Felix Graham's conscience. It would be manifestly unjust for Lady Mason to be sent to prison for perjury when the property was being returned and her motives were so righteous in Biblical, if not legal and social, terms. She had wanted no more than an equitable share of the property for her son, which was rather less than Rebekah obtained by fraud for Jacob. Certainly, Joseph Mason desired far more than Orley Farm—he hungered for revenge, and when Lady Mason met his stare in court, he lowered his eyes. If motives were on trial, it would not have been Lady Mason who was found guilty.

If Lady Mason deserves no further punishment, then it is not clear how she could have restored the property and saved herself from public scandal without recourse to Mr. Chaffanbrass and Mr. Aram. At the very least she deserves to be protected from Joseph Mason. In *Orley Farm* Trollope has argued his way to a position that is closer to customary advocacy than he cares to admit. Felix Graham vehemently defended the lawyer's right to make an independent moral judgment, and only reluctantly came to understand why this could never be maintained in practice. One man's honesty tends to be another man's falsehood, and truth, like honesty, can be tested only by rational examination in a social context. Chaffanbrass and Aram are both honest to their client's cause, and John Kenneby's honesty is indubitable, if unreliable as a source of fact. Human fallibility makes the judgment of a group necessary when moral concepts are formulated, and when Felix realizes the imperfection of his own reasoning he no longer demands that every lawyer should exercise his own judgment in deciding the innocence or guilt of a client.

In Trollope's world, the only relationship that requires no compromise is friendship. Lady Mason knows bitterly that she must appeal to men's sympathy to keep the secret of her forgery from the world. She dresses becomingly, appreciates the exact length of time she may allow Mr. Furnival to hold her hand and the proper degree of affectionate respect she must give Sir Peregrine. It is a humiliating masquerade of dress and manner that has been maintained for twenty years in her son's interest. Then the delicate balance between friendship and love that she has established with such care is shattered by Sir Peregrine's passionate declaration of love. Only in Mrs. Orme does Lucy Mason find the emotional communion and friendship that has been denied her. Not all the friendships between women are so rewarding, and the analogue for Lady Mason and Mrs. Orme is Mrs. Furnival and Miss Biggs, who enjoys a marital feud with the same relish as she does a hot toddy on a cold night. Mrs. Orme is the social conscience of *Orley Farm*, speaking for order, kindness, and honesty—the woman that Lady Mason might have been in altered circumstances.

At first nobody could seem less suited for the role of guardian of morals than Mrs. Orme. Nevertheless, she has a sympathy that more than compensates for her intellectual deficiencies. Her language is a ragbag of religious allusions, but she has the power to see herself in Lady Mason and wonder what sacrifice she would be prepared to make for her own son. Her virtue has never been tested and she is grateful. Gently she reminds Sir Peregrine how much he owes to Lady Mason, who could have ruined his reputation had she married him. Later, she stays with Lady Mason at Orley Farm, sits beside her in the court at Alston, and undertakes to tell Lucius the truth about the codicil. If Judge Staveley represents legal justice, Mrs. Orme embodies the "social laws" that may seem confused and arbitrary but are ultimately beneficent.

Scene and character are combined by serial correspondences in *Orley Farm*. Each incident implicates another, every meal is illustrative of general explanation from Mrs. Mason's manic fragments of deviled chicken to Moulder's precise apportioning of Christmas turkey. It is a world of law in which people think and act as legal beings, testing their rights, determining their obligations and duties. This is the perfect example of the structural device of the multiple transaction. Within the sustaining form of the declaration, the plot meshes every incident to the central cause. Thus, Moulder in the commercial room at the Bull Inn is prepared to defend the customary privileges of his class against the presumptive authority of Dockwrath. "The unpleasant transaction" is concluded when Moulder leads the commercial gentleman upstairs, and Dockwrath is left to spend the evening alone. The solution is a compromise that benefits the group at the expense of the individual. Dockwrath has ventured to break a social law and is duly punished with ostracism by society. The same penalty is imposed upon Lady Mason in more tragic circumstances.

Chapter X

The Multiple Transaction—Social Contracts—The Rebels: *Mr. Scarborough's Family, Ayala's Angel*

Trollope argued for the authority of society over the individual—when, as with the English upper class, that society was composed of reasonable people making free decisions. This freedom of choice was limited for women and unattainable for children and the poor. The latter play no part in his world because they are passive agents of society. Poverty was intolerable for Trollope because it first robbed a man of his freedom, thus making him the potential victim of economic circumstances which were inconceivable for the well-to-do. Those who refuse to conform with "social laws" are sentenced to exile, but such laws never imply a creeping uniformity, depressing the individual and crushing all initiative. It is possible, on rare occasions, for the individual to flout the law and recognized conventions in ways that will make the resulting compromise favor him at society's expense. There must always be rebels in society to question accepted forms, and if they act unselfishly and for the public good the likelihood is that society will accommodate their demands. If they act for themselves, disregarding the rights of others, they will most assuredly be cast out of society.

In the two novels describing such nonconformity, Trollope again chose the structure of the multiple transaction. Rebellion could be unconscious as in the person of Ayala Dormer, who places her dream before all the demands of society in *Ayala's*

Angel (1881), or it could be a deliberate act of will as with John Scarborough of *Mr. Scarborough's Family* (1883). In the end both are defeated by society, but not before certain victories have been won that proclaim the power of imagination in one case and intellect in the other. Because Ayala's imagination is a sublimation of love she changes all around her, simply by refusing to obey the rules of conventional courtship. Mr. Scarborough challenges convention in the name of justice, and he achieves much. It is not within his power to alter the characters of his two sons, but he does succeed in seeing how they would behave if he were dead—and he does contrive to put the law on its head. Imagination and intelligence are the two powers that can disregard all social laws.

Mr. Scarborough accomplishes what Lady Mason had sought for her only son by means of a plan conceived long before he even considered marriage. And Trollope apologizes that he must recall a number of incidents that took place before the actual commencement of the action. Time in Trollope is within the living memory of the concerned parties and functions in causal relationship with the central issue. Mr. Scarborough is a man who chafes against all restraints, and particularly against the law of entail that will compel him to pass his property on to his eldest son whether or not that son is fit to manage the estate. Desiring the right to choose his heir in spite of the law, Mr. Scarborough has married the same woman twice, and contrives to hold the documents that can declare his heir to be illegitimate should he so decide.

This occasion arises when Mountjoy, the eldest, has 'run up a fortune in gambling debts to be repaid when his father is dead. Mr. Scarborough decides the time has come to clear the estate of debt by producing the evidence of a marriage after Mountjoy's birth, and to see how Augustus Scarborough will carry himself as heir of Tretton. With Mountjoy now a bastard, the moneylenders must settle as best they can. And when Augustus fails to please his father, Mr. Scarborough produces the proof of the first marriage and Mountjoy is made heir again. At the graveside Mr. Tyrrwhit and Mr. Hart, the money-lenders, fall upon Mountjoy demanding justice:

"You see how it is, Captain Scarborough," said Tyrrwhit; "your father, as has just been laid to rest in hopes of a happy resurrection, was a very peculiar gentleman." "The most hinfernal swindler I ever 'eard tell of," said Hart. "I don't wish to say a word disrespectful," continued Tyrrwhit, "but he had his own notions. He said as you was illegitimate,—didn't he now?" "I can only refer you to Mr. Barry," said Mountjoy. "And he said that Mr. Augustus was to have it all; and he proved his words. Didn't he now? And then he made out that, if so, our deeds weren't worth the paper they were written on. Isn't it all true what I'm saying? And then when we'd taken what small sums of money he chose to offer us, just to save ourselves from ruin, then he comes up and says you are the heir, as legitimate as anybody else, and are to have all the property. And he proves that too. What are we to think about it?"   (ch. 60)

It is a brilliant scheme that outwits all the lawyers and forces the moneylenders to settle for the sums they had advanced without a shilling of interest. It becomes even more satisfactory to Mr. Scarborough when he can persuade Augustus to pay the debts for fear that Mountjoy will bring suit against him when his father is dead. This is the triumph: but the result is the bitter recognition of his sons as unworthy and despicable. Esau and Jacob haunt this work as they do *Orley Farm*, but whereas the sons of Isaac were virtuous in different ways, Mountjoy and Augustus are both reprehensible. Mountjoy is a compulsive gambler who ends where he began, at the gambling tables of Monte Carlo: Augustus returns to his practice of law in London, knowing that he has brought about his ruin by failing to show a modicum of courtesy and kindness to his father. It would have been so easy for him to establish himself as the heir, provided he showed his father some respect. But he possesses the arrogance of his father without the intelligence, just as Mountjoy has inherited the passion without the prudence and acumen.

Age asserting its authority over youth is an underlying

theme of the action, and Mr. Scarborough dominates the work by the energy of an intellect that defies illness and age. He rejoices in the exercise of his mind, probing the motives of those who consider they have a right to his property, dissecting their intentions, just as the surgeon cuts away portions of his body in a futile contest with death. Mr. Scarborough knows that he cannot change the course of events: Mountjoy will gamble away Tretton after his death with the same reckless fury as he did before. The only difference is that Mountjoy can now justify his gambling because Florence Mountjoy has refused to marry him. Nothing angers Florence more than this determination to make her responsible for his ruin. Mountjoy's end is foretold; he keeps a pistol with him to finish his life when his credit is gone.

At the least, Mr. Scarborough has been able to see his sons and test their characters, and finds that he can die comfortably in the certainty of his knowledge. Mountjoy will certainly squander Tretton at the card table but Mr. Scarborough appreciates that his son loves him, and he can delight in having encompassed the destruction of Augustus. The last scene turns on the question of duty, and Augustus is reminded that by offering to pay his brother's debts, thus making him wholly dependent, he had ruined himself. If Lady Mason had been able to deceive her husband into writing the codicil in favor of her son, she would have rivaled Mr. Scarborough in guile:

> "You think you have done your duty," said Augustus. "I do not care two straws about doing my duty, young man." Here Mr. Scarborough raised himself in part, and spoke in that strong voice which was supposed to be so deleterious to him. "Or rather, in seeking my duty, I look beyond the conventionalities of the world. I think that you have behaved damnably, and that I have punished you. Because of Mountjoy's weakness, because he had been knocked off his legs, I endeavoured to put you upon yours. You at once turned upon me, when you thought the deed was done, and bade me go—and bury myself. You were a little too quick in your desire to become the

owner of Tretton Park at once. I have stayed long enough to give some further trouble. You will not say, after this, that I am *non compos,* and unable to make a will. You will find that, under mine, not one penny piece, not one scrap of property, will become yours. Mountjoy will take care of you, I do not doubt. I am not so soft-hearted, and will not recognise you as my son. Now you may go away." So saying, he turned himself round to the wall, and refused to be induced to utter another word. Augustus began to speak, but when he had commenced his second sentence, the old man rung his bell. "Mary," said he to his sister, "will you have the goodness to get Augustus to go away? I am very weak, and if he remains he will be the death of me. He can't get anything by killing me at once; it is too late for that."   (ch. 56)

In this passage all conventions are broken and every obligation due a son is cast aside. The words are precise and measured, they state the cause and impose the sentence without recourse to any metaphor that extends the meaning beyond the stated intention. Throughout *Mr. Scarborough's Family,* the implied contracts between parent and child, lawyer and client, and between the members of a family are examined and defined. The desire of Peter Prosper to disinherit Harry Annesley serves to counterpoint Mr. Scarborough's maneuvers and illustrates the technique of the multiple transaction. Augustus has violated every bond of human society and his punishment is therefore justified. But it is Mr. Scarborough who assumes the right to sit in judgment on his sons. That right is not the prerogative of age or the privilege of wealth, but the expression of his intellect. His last words to Augustus marshal all the relevant arguments for and against his son, and range them in order of precedence. It is as though Mr. Scarborough had made his deathbed a judgment seat from which he could assess the past and determine the future. It is quite within his power to put Harry Annesley on his feet by writing to his uncle, Peter Prosper, and denouncing Augustus as a traducer. Whether by speech or letter, Mr. Scarborough can make his authority felt from Lincoln's Inn to country village.

Mr. Scarborough is dying with a ferocity that terrifies those around him. While he lives, and every day brings the threat of the scalpel and continuing pain, he maintains his authority over his property and his sons. Instead of yielding to the agony of his body, he flaunts his pain, taunting those possessed of health with the dominating strength of his mind. It is a dramatic tour de force, an explosion of intellect, that enables him to change the conventional pity for the dying into a horrified admiration. At every point he justifies himself by right of good intention, and since hell has no place in Trollope's world, intention must be evaluated in terms of the individual and social effect. The law for Mr. Scarborough is no more than a yoke of precedent to keep the independent spirit from straying too far. So he uses legal strategies to defeat the law and crushes an honest attorney in the process.

If Mr. Scarborough has one weakness it is that of applying logic to society and attempting to make convention run to rules. Mr. Grey, the attorney, regards him as a great knave, a man who deserves to be punished because he has set the laws of his country at defiance. But Mr. Barry, Grey's partner, says he is "the best lawyer he ever knew." The narrative advocate speaks of Mr. Scarborough's iniquity, and of his sense of justice in alternative passages. Law for Mr. Scarborough is of the same order as religion, and as unnecessary for the intelligent and well-intentioned:

> Law was hardly less absurd to him than religion. It consisted of a perplexed entanglement of rules got together so that the few might live in comfort at the expense of the many. Robbery, if you could get to the bottom of it, was bad, as was all violence; but taxation was robbery, rent was robbery, prices fixed according to the desire of the seller and not in obedience to justice, were robbery. "Then you are the greatest of robbers," his friends would say to him. He would admit it, allowing that in such a state of society he was not prepared to go out and live

naked in the streets if he could help it. But he delighted to get the better of the law, and triumphed in his own iniquity.... (ch. 21)

The tragedy of defeat for Mr. Scarborough is not death but the recognition that his sons are incapable of fulfilling his will. Society too cannot be subjected to such logical analysis of rational regulation. It is the nature of the human condition to be fallible and inconsequent, and law must reflect the society of its creation. Mr. Scarborough is an exception to this rule and, therefore, though he may influence, he can never wholly change society.

The analogue for Mr. Scarborough is Mr. Prosper of Buston, who decides to disinherit Harry Annesley because his nephew is not sufficiently appreciative of his mumbled sermons, and has even been known to laugh at him. When Mr. Scarborough invites Harry to Tretton, he tells him that the old will accept a great deal from the young, but never ridicule. If Mr. Scarborough is the rage and the passion of age, Mr. Prosper is the vanity and foolishness. One man is dying in torment, the other feigns a mortal illness when his plans to marry Miss Thoroughbung founder over the settlements. Finally, he renounces all authority and dies symbolically, yielding his house and property to Harry and Florence. In their turn, Mr. Prosper and Mr. Scarborough are examined by analogy with Mr. Grey and his daughter, and Mrs. Mountjoy and Florence. The complete abdication of parental authority is made evident in the Carroll family that becomes the responsibility of Mr. Grey and his daughter.

Trollope was always aware of the special relationship between mothers and daughters, often tyrannical and frequently perverse. Harry explains to Mr. Scarborough that his uncle has disinherited him because he did not care to listen to sermons, and the old man replies: "That was an indiscretion, as he had the power in his hands to do you an injury. Most men have got some little bit of pet tyranny in their hearts" (ch. 40). In Trollope's world the desire to dominate others is a universal that men can express more easily than women. The tryanny of men can reach to the furthest limits of society, but a woman is confined to the home. Moreover, because she is herself the subject of so many persecutions, she will become the greater tyrant in the limited sphere accorded her. Trollope knew that the victim will often become a bully, and the slave the harshest taskmaster. In the West Indies he observed that the most brutal overseers had always been slaves.

The problems confronting women in Trollope's world are largely the result of their limited authority and the restrictions imposed upon them. Seldom, if ever, does a woman have the opportunity to fulfill herself in an institutional sense. Mothers might occasionally influence their sons, but they could never control them. Lady Lufton opposed her son's engagement to Lucy Robarts in *Framley Parsonage*, but she could not prevent their marrying, just as Mrs. Launay had reluctantly to accept the marriage between her son and Bessy Pryor in "The Lady of Launay." Daughters were considered the moral responsibility of the mother and convention sanctioned their subjugation to maternal control. It is not uncommon to find mothers making their daughters surrogates for lost opportunities and failed ambition. Those who have had no life will always try to live the lives of their children. This passion to become the daughter can develop into a form of insanity. Thus Lady Anna's mother is quite prepared to commit murder in *Lady Anna* when her daughter insists on marrying the tailor, Daniel Thwaite:

> Do you think that I will stop at anything now;—after having done so much? Do you think that I will live to see my daughter the wife of a foul, sweltering tailor? No, by heavens! He tells you that when you are twenty-one, you will not be subject to my control. I warn you to look to it. I will not lose my control, unless when I see you married to some husband fitting your condition in life. For the present you will live in your own room, as I will live in mine. I will hold no intercourse whatever with you, till I have constrained you to obey me. (*Lady Anna*, ch. 36)

Because a woman's rights were so limited she often felt required to employ the moral authority of religion. Women are more religious than men in Trollope's world because they need moral sanction to act where they have no real rights. There are no male religious fanatics—the crazed Louis Trevelyan in *He Knew He Was Right* demands that his wife should obey him more on legal than on religious grounds. But there are numerous women who use the Bible to countenance their actions and defend their daughters from the horrors of sexuality. The woman who abhorred the sexual demands of her husband, defined as rights, would seek her daughter's chastity and justify herself in religious terms. Mrs. Bolton in *John Caldigate* is married to an elderly man whom she detests physically; in return she determines to protect her daughter from marriage, thus retaining control of the one person she can dominate. When Hester, who has married, asks her mother if she is not still her child, Mrs. Bolton replies:

> No. You are not mine any longer. You are his. You are that man's wife. When he bids you do that which is evil in the sight of the Lord, you must do it. And he will bid you. You are not my child now. As days run on and sins grow black I cannot warn you now against the wrath to come. (*John Caldigate*, ch. 21)

Mrs. Mountjoy in *Mr. Scarborough's Family* is as much attracted physically to her nephew, Mountjoy, as her daughter is repelled by him. She could happily relive her youth in fancy as the wife of Mountjoy, but despite her threats and anger, her taking Florence to Brussels, she cannot prevent her daughter from marrying Harry Annesley. Unless a property was entailed a father could effectively withhold the means of livelihood from a son, but Mrs. Mountjoy has no control over her daughter's money once she is of age. It is within the power of Mr. Scarborough and Mr. Prosper to change their heirs' prospects, but no woman has this right. Therefore women raged the more and invoked religion to remedy their social impotence.

Because Florence is intelligent and resolute she marries the man of her choice, and Harry becomes the squire of Buston. She has had wit enough to choose the true gentleman among her suitors—even Mr. Scarborough approves of the match before his death. Like Mr. Scarborough, her decision has been plagued with difficulties and opposition, but whereas she could choose freely from a host of eligible suitors, his choice is restricted to his two sons, and the decision then becomes one of selecting bad from worse. Reason, as Mr. Scarborough knows, can never function successfully when choice is restricted. He is as much bound to his sons as he is to his dying body. What comforts him is the thought that if age must yield to youth, then youth can be made very uncomfortable indeed if it does not show a measure of deference and respect to age.

Florence is rational and resourceful, the spiritual heir of Mr. Scarborough in her intelligence and determination. Nobody can deflect her from her intention. Mr. Scarborough is more singular, and it is Mr. Merton, the young doctor, who best describes the quality that sets him apart from all other people:

> I think that he has within him a capacity for love, and an unselfishness, which almost atones for his dishonesty. And there is about him a strange dislike to conventionality and to law which is so interesting as to make up the balance. I have always regarded your father as a most excellent man; but thoroughly dishonest. He would rob anyone,—but always to eke out his own gifts to other people. He has therefore to my eyes been most romantic. (ch. 53)

To be romantic is to disregard convention, even reason, in order to express the individual self. For Mr. Scarborough, law is no more than convention masquerading as authority, leading-strings for those afraid to walk without guidance and support. He is governed by a presence that baffles and terrifies others. "You don't understand the inner man which rules me,—how it has struggled to free itself from conventionalities. Nor do I quite understand how your inner man has succumbed to them and encouraged them" (ch. 19). And in response to this challenge, Mr. Grey the attorney, can only reply defensively: "I have encouraged an obedience to the laws of my country. Men generally find it safer to do so" (ch. 19).

Mr. Scarborough embodies an intelligence that can still be of influence despite being shackled by circumstance. The stated transaction of the work is a material failure with Mountjoy restored as heir, but the work does proclaim the victory of will. Certainly, when the score is read, Harry Annesley would not have found it so easy to marry Florence had Mr. Scarborough failed to mediate between Harry and his uncle, and it was no small accomplishment to clear the property of debt by outwitting Messrs. Tyrrwhit and Hart. Mr. Scarborough had simply been too clever for lawyers, his family, and the sharpest moneylenders in London. He had dominated them all with the authority of his intelligence.

Ayala Dormer of *Ayala's Angel* is as singular as Mr. Scarborough—a romantic whose imagination will not truckle to the cash-and-courtship conventions of society. In her own way she is just as anachronistic as the old man playing ducks and drakes with the laws of entail and inheritance. The commencement of the declaration is concerned with the disposition of two orphans, daughters of Egbert Dormer, the painter. Ayala is taken to the home of her rich aunt, Lady Tringle, Lucy to her poor uncle, Mr. Dosett. The charm of fairytale always illumines the plight of pretty orphan girls, but the only romance in this situation is hidden in Ayala's mind. While the rest of society goes matchmaking with an intensity of purpose that casts aside all other interests, Ayala can say defiantly: "I have got nothing, and I expect nothing" (ch. 26). To show such an obvious disregard for society's main preoccupation is as cavalier as Mr. Scarborough's announcing his scorn for all conventionalities.

Lucy and Ayala had been brought up by an adoring father who preached the supremacy of art but still contrived to furnish a charming bijou house in South Kensington and spread his table with blue china. Both daughters had been gloriously happy at home: "At the bijou there had been a republic, in which all the inhabitants and all the visitors had been free and equal. Such republicanism had been the very mainspring of life at the bijou" (ch. 5). This is a constant in Trollope's world: happy children make intelligent and contented adults. It was an opinion that ran counter to Dickens and Brontë, who implied that an excess of misery in childhood would always produce a wealth of virtue should the small unfortunate survive. Harry Annesley's home in *Mr. Scarborough's Family* resembles the Staveleys' in *Orley Farm*, and in *Dr. Thorne* the good doctor maintains that

> the principal duty which a parent owed to a child was to make him happy. Not only was the man to be made happy,—the future man, if that might be possible,—but the existing boy was to be treated with equal favour; and his happiness, so said the doctor, was of much easier attainment. (ch. 3)

The happiness of the Dormer sisters comes to an end when they are packed off to different homes like surplus furniture.

Lucy has already chosen her future husband, the young sculptor Isadore Hamel, but Ayala is dedicated to the vision of an ethereal being, an angel who may, or may not have azure wings, but is unquestionably not of this earth. Art is the expression of the imagination, and Hamel's sculpture is the analogue for Ayala's angel. Ayala's dream is absurd, but it is her reality and receives the same devotion from her that Isadore Hamel bestows on his allegorical figures of Italia United and the Prostrate Roman Catholic Church. And just as Ayala will never compromise her dream by accepting the love of a man, Isadore regards his sculptures as the sublimation of his soul:

> Into them had been infused all the poetry of his nature and all the conviction of his intelligence. He had never dreamed of selling them. He had never dared to think that any lover of Art would encourage him to put into marble those conceptions of his genius which now adorned his studio, standing there in plaster of Paris. But to him they were so valuable, they contained so much of

his thoughts, so many of his aspirations, that even had the marble counter-parts been ordered and paid for nothing would have induced him to part with the originals. (ch. 33)

Later, Hamel finds it much easier to accept Sir Thomas Tringle's advice on the means by which an artist can make a living than Ayala does when called upon to relinquish her dream and accept the world.

Ayala's Angel is a series of marital transactions expressing the main cause of the work—Ayala's necessary compromise between imagination and social reality. For a woman, London is the marketplace where she goes to exchange her beauty and her money for a suitable husband. Frank Houston tells Imogene Docimer that it is her duty "to purchase for herself a husband with her beauty" (ch. 28). And, since he is so poor, he must shop for a woman with money. But there is a difference and Mr. Dosett, who had once been the handsomest of men, knows what it is. A woman could not work, but a man could make his way by industry and talent. The good things of life are not to be despised, but what price should be paid for them? Mr. Dosett had not married for money, and he lives now in a genteel poverty that condemns his wife to an existence of patched towels, haggles over legs of mutton, and little schemes to make ends meet without sacrificing respectability. Poverty is uncomfortable and degrading, capable of tarnishing the most enduring dreams:

> Of the good things of the world, of a pleasant home, of ample means, and of all the absence of care which comes from money, poor Mr. Dosett had by no means a poor appreciation. That men are justified in seeking these good things by their energy, industry, and talents, he was quite confident. How was it with a girl who had nothing else but her beauty,—or, perhaps, her wit,—in lieu of energy and industry? Was she justified in carrying her wares also into the market, and making the most of them? (ch. 39)

Isadore Hamel is converted to Sir Thomas Tringle's philosophy when he finds he can marry Lucy, and by implication, his art will be immeasurably improved in consequence. He looks upon his monumental figures as the necessary prelude to art: "They were the lessons which I had to teach myself, and the play which I gave to my imagination" (ch. 63). Hamel has learned to work as energetically as Egbert Dormer, without necessarily preaching a high aesthetic. His success is assured and Lucy can look forward to a bijou residence and blue china. Guided by Tringle and accepting the exigencies of marriage, Hamel finds a compromise between the demands of the marketplace and the honesty of his art. By analogy, Frank Houston can never really admit that marrying for love requires considerable industry on a man's part if life is not to dwindle into something less than the Dosett frugalities. When he chooses Imogene because he loves her, instead of Gertrude Tringle, whose money he covets, he fastens onto an aged aunt with a small income and plays at being the artist that Hamel has worked to become. Because he is a rational man he knows that love, no matter how irresistible, will go the way of "cradles and cabbages."

Sir Thomas Tringle, an erstwhile governor of the Bank of England, presides over the commercial world of *Ayala's Angel*. Never having experienced any difficulty in getting a beautiful woman to be his wife, Sir Thomas is driven to fury when his daughters marry and Ayala refuses to marry his son. As a man of considerable commercial enterprise he cannot understand why a contract of marriage should be more difficult to arrange than a foreign loan. He accepts money as a necessary part of the contract but is enraged when Sir Septimus Traffick not only demands over one hundred thousand pounds with his eldest daughter, Augusta, but also refuses to set up his own residence, preferring the comforts Sir Thomas can provide. Shrewd and perceptive in most things, he has managed his family like his business with unfortunate results. Travers and Treason, his financial house, flourishes in Lombard Street: his family "were indeed what he had made them, but still were not quite to his taste" (ch. 5). Being generous and fairminded, he cannot understand why adding a codicil to his will on Ayala's behalf should outrage his wife and daughters.

There is a solid financial base to the work in the character of Sir Thomas Tringle. Certainly, he is a far more credible financier than Melmotte in *The Way We Live Now*. Melmotte becomes pasteboard when we are called upon to witness his financial manipulations, and the Great South Central Pacific and Mexican Railway Company has more in common with Dickens' Anglo-Bengalee Disinterested Loan and Life Assurance Company than it does with some of the more spectacular contemporary swindles.[1] Melmotte does seem in a direct line of descent from Mr. Merdle of *Little Dorrit*. The inconsistency of *The Way We Live Now* is that it undertakes to recall a more stable and honorable past while severely criticizing the present immorality of the city. Now this simply does not work in the light of the evidence presented. The gentry, with the exception of Roger Carbury, are as corrupt as Melmotte, yet there is sufficient intelligence and moral strength in the London of the novel for Melmotte to be effectively ruined. We are told of men in the city who have always stayed clear of Melmotte and his dealings, and these are the men who continue to run the city's affairs.[2] But they are not permitted to testify and, as a result, the work is flawed because the evidence is partial and incomplete. Certainly, by 1875, when *The Way We Live Now* was published, the financial speculations of bogus companies were being subjected to unofficial regulation by the Bank of England.

[1] J. A. Banks in "The Way They Lived Then: Anthony Tollope and the 1870's," *Victorian Studies*, 12 (December 1968), 177-200, demonstrates the incongruities between the events of the period and Trollope's depiction in *The Way We Live Now*. It has been a literary commonplace, long in need of revision, that Trollope is a social and historical realist.

[2] The City in *The Way We Live Now* never fully accepts Melmotte. On the occasion of the dinner for the Chinese emperor, the City abandons him:
> The Lord Mayor had even made up his mind that he would not go to the dinner. What one of his brother aldermen said to him about leaving others in the lurch might be quite true; but, as his lordship remarked, Melmotte was a commercial man, and as these were commercial transactions it behoved the Lord Mayor of London to be more careful than other men. He had always had his doubts, and he would not go. (ch. 58).

This is the strength of London that is never made evident in the novel—it is there only by implication.

Sir Thomas Tringle is an honest man who would not be out of place in Walter Bagehot's *Lombard Street*.³ Unlike Melmotte, he keeps to his own set in society and does not mix with people like Sir Harry Albury of Stalham. If Sir Thomas cannot manage his family as successfully as he does Travers and Treason, this is because love, which is quite irrational, complicates every marriage contract. Money, on the other hand, is the very essence of logic. It is typical of the man that he tries to marry his remaining daughter and his wards off in one big wedding, being of the obvious opinion that troubles of this kind, like some debts, are best settled with one payment.

Ayala is both the critique of Sir Thomas Tringle's commercial philosophy and its justification. Imagination without industry and reason will not clothe the back and put food on the table. She is quite appalled, for example, by her aunt's preoccupation with mutton bones and her daily concern with the needs of dinner. Aghast, Aunt Dosett says:

> "You don't hate eating" "Yes, I do. It is ignoble. Nature should have managed it differently. We ought to have sucked it in from the atmosphere through our fingers and hairs, as the trees do by their leaves. There should have been no butchers, and no grease, and no nasty smells from the kitchen,—and no gin." (ch. 21)

To the baffled astonishment of all the women in the work, who have the current rates of the marital marketplace down to the value of the last dimple, Ayala is the magnet for every male within sight. Even Sir Septimus Traffick trots gladly after her in Rome, and young Tom Tringle, the epitome of commerce and cut-rate diamond necklaces, falls desperately in love with her. For women, her charm is inexplicable because

---

³ *Lombard Street. A Description of the Money Market*, intro. Frank C. Genovese (Homewood, Ill., 1962). The ideas of *Lombard Street* were first expressed by Bagehot in a series of articles in *The Economist* during the 1850s and were published as a book in 1870. If Melmotte is derived from Dickens, Sir Thomas Tringle with his abhorrence of stock-jobbers is in the Bagehot mold. There is no question in *Ayala's Angel* that banking should be regarded as a dubious activity.

she is oblivious to what should concern a woman most. When Jonathan Stubbs declares his intention to marry Ayala, his aunt, the Marchesa Baldoni, writes in haste and trepidation:

> She is one of those human beings who seem to have been removed out of this world and brought up in another. Though she knows ever so much that nobody else knows, she is ignorant of ever so much that everybody ought to know. Wandering through a grove, or seated by a brook, or shivering with you on the top of a mountain, she would be charming. I doubt whether she would be equally good at the top of your table, or looking after your children, or keeping the week's accounts. (ch. 20)

It is because Ayala is unlike other women that she moves through society with all the singularity of her name. Where other women are looking for husbands, she seeks only friends, and it is her tragedy that men can never be her friends, only her lovers. Tom Tringle worships her and in the course of his infatuation becomes more vulgar and ridiculous than ever. Ayala has the power of imagination that can enter into the spirit of people and see them as they really are. Thus she can win Aunt Dosett's heart after a fashion unknown to Lucy, by calling her Aunt Margaret, and showing a little sympathy for a woman trying so hard to make ends meet. Yet she is often unable to understand, even to find the words to respond to those around her. Men and women examine and cross-examine; Ayala dreams—and her words fail to correspond with the reality around her.

It is Colonel Jonathan Stubbs of the red hair and less than aquiline nose who finally embodies the angel. From the first, he has sensed Ayala's world of imagination and entered into it with fabulous tales of past loves thrown out of windows and a merry disregard for practical things. But to the end she is reluctant to give up her dream for the sake of a husband:

> She did not want the lover. She was sure of that. She was still sure that if a lover would come to her who would be in truth acceptable,—such a lover as would enable her

> to give herself to him as her lord and master,—he must be something different fom Jonathan Stubbs. That had been the theory of her life for many months past, a theory on which she had resolved to rely with all her might from the moment in which this man had spoken to her of his love. Would she give way and render up herself and all her dreams simply because the man was one to be liked? (ch. 49)

This refusal to accept the Colonel is as inexplicable to women as the secret of Ayala's charm. Lady Albury, who loves the man, is prepared to matchmake on his behalf, even to give him Ayala as proof of her love. But Ayala's dreaming is not fancy: it is a power of spirit that will not compromise with the world.

Eventually, it requires the whole of Ayala's society to make her accept Stubbs, and when she has promised to be his wife, there is still the regret that she may have lost more than she has gained. However, once forsaken, the imagination of her dream is lost, and she must reconcile herself to reality. Mr. Scarborough, too, is defeated by society, since although he can outwit lawyers he cannot avoid leaving his property to a son. The social laws prevail, just as society conspires to make Ayala accept a contract of marriage. The moment she does, her language changes, and for the first time she can examine her thoughts and feelings rationally. So she explains to Jonathan Stubbs, "I knew how to love you, . . . but I did not know how to tell you that I loved you" (ch. 61). Nonetheless, society is changed by the intelligence of Mr. Scarborough and the imagination of Ayala. As Trollope writes in *Mr. Scarborough's Family*, "the reader may judge" whether the transaction can be deemed a success.

Chapter XI

The Extended Multiple Transaction— The Rights and Duties of Barchester: *The Warden, Barchester Towers, Doctor Thorne, Framley Parsonage, The Small House at Allington, The Last Chronicle of Barset*

Barchester is more a condition than a place and time. It is a mesh of rights and duties based materially on the ownership of land and expressed socially in the person of the gentleman. In Trollope's world, the gentleman is the servant of his community, a man of private fortune who is prepared to devote himself to the welfare of those around him. Ideally, in Barchester, the gentleman who fulfills these obligations is a clergyman, but the same function can be undertaken by a local physician like Dr. Thorne. In return for accepting this duty the gentleman is accorded the right of deference and granted a recognized rank in society. This is the ideal, and not all men could embody it. Nevertheless, the implicit acceptance of the ideal is the unwritten law of Barchester. Those who fail to observe it are castigated and driven out, some to foreign exile, some to their death.

Each of the Barchester novels outlines a transaction that is extended by means of character and theme to the other novels. It is like a case with a continuing right of appeal. *The Warden* is concerned with the regulation of Hiram's Hospital and the fate of the Reverend Septimus Harding. This work, as we have seen, follows the pattern of the single transaction, but the subsequent novels in the series construct a variety of parallels and analogues even more complex than the multiple transaction. Questions of individual property, marriage, and authority are extended throughout the social hierarchy in a succession of mirror images. The moral issues of *The Warden* are developed in *Barchester Towers*, which relates the struggle to occupy the bishop's throne in Barchester. As though to challenge the right of the clergyman to adjudicate the morality of society, *Doctor Thorne* shows the ability of the local physician and his daughter to become one with the local gentry. *The Small House at Allington* shows the city joining forces with a corrupt and upstart aristocracy and its effect on Lily Dale. *The Last Chronicle of Barset* draws all the preceding themes together in an omnium gatherum from which the clergyman as gentleman emerges triumphant despite poverty and social disgrace.

The clergymen Trollope admires most are those who effectively render to the community the services that are now generally termed welfare. Frank Fenwick, who befriends the wayward Carrie Brattle in *The Vicar of Bullhampton* and risks social ostracism, is rewarded with a great victory over his critics and the local Marquis of Trowbridge. As the protector of his flock the clergyman must be prepared to withstand prejudice and defend his stewardship in the manner of Dr. Wortle, who refuses to cast out a young couple accused of adultery in *Dr. Wortle's School*, thereby incurring an admonition from his bishop and the censure of his friends. Yet in *Framley Parsonage*, Trollope wrote:

> I have written much of clergymen, but in doing so I have endeavoured to portray them as they bear on our social life rather than to describe the mode and working of their professional careers. Had I done the latter I could hardly have steered clear of subjects on which it has not been my intention to pronounce an opinion, and I should either have laden my fiction with sermons or I should have degraded my sermons into fiction. (ch. 42)

Nothing could be further from the evidence of the novels than this comfortable statement with its concluding paradox.

Throughout the novels, the means whereby men rise in the church are delineated, generally by political preferment or a family connection with the local gentry. Bishops owe their sees to the party in power, and a change in government can alter the tone of the clerical hierarchy. Since "bishops are but men,"[1] they make their appointments to suit their political masters. In the exercise of their professional lives, we hear the clergy preaching their sermons, or witness the often stultifying effect of those sermons on their parishioners. And we are allowed to watch an archdeacon preparing one of those sermons by reading Rabelais in a locked study. There is little that is left to know about the life of Trollope's clergymen except the reason why they ever adopted such a calling. As with Mark Robarts, it is generally because it seemed the natural career for a man with a university degree who wanted to spend his life helping others. Metaphysical speculations are the concern of places like Oxford, where Dr. Arabin spent his time like a schoolboy throwing paper darts at his opponents. When George Bertram in *The Bertrams* questions the nature of the soul and the resurrection of the body, the best he can do is toss off a few rhetorical commonplaces and decide to take up the law as a profession.

As we have seen earlier in the context of institutionalized religion in *The Warden* the Church of England is clearly meant to be not a spiritual force, but a moral regulator for those "conventionalities" that underlie society. It is not only a guide to conduct, but a museum, preserving the traditions of past time.[2] This is of particular significance since the society Trollope depicts has no time beyond that of living memory: the

---

[1] "Men in all walks of life do as others do around them, and bishops are but men." "English Bishops, Old and New" in *Clergymen of the Church of England*, London, 1866, p. 20.

[2] *Ibid.*, "The Normal Dean of the Present Day," p. 36.
We are often told that ours is a utilitarian age, but this utilitarian spirit is so closely mingled with a veneration for things old and beautiful from age that we love our follies infinitely better than our new virtues.

only historical presence in people's lives is provided by the church. Although Trollope insisted that the future of England would be egalitarian and republican, there must be a regard for history in order to maintain social continuity.[3] Thus the clergyman is both a moral exemplar and the custodian of social tradition. As such he is more vulnerable to contemporary challenge than any other member of society. If he is not constantly aware of his moral responsibility to the past, as well as his duty to the present, he will be overcome by the worst of popular enthusiasm in the form of Mrs. Proudie and her toadies.

To speak of spiritual or religious values in this context is merely to note the absence of the unnecessary and irrelevant. There is no reality beyond the world of known things and the moral order that people have created so they might live in safety and content. The vehement demonstration of religious faith is generally the sign of a hypocrite in hot pursuit of life's good things while professing to despise them. When there is genuine enthusiasm and zeal like that of Mr. Saul in *The Claverings*, we accept that marriage and the acquisition of material comforts will modify the most heartfelt conviction concerning the virtues of poverty. Saul will undoubtedly become Paul, converted by good food and a comfortable home. It is obvious that Mr. Crawley's madness in *The Last Chronicle of Barset* is not a temperamental affliction, but the result of poverty and the gross inequity of his position in the church. To reject the world is both ungodly and foolish, as Dr. Arabin realizes in a moment of inner illumination. No man should scorn the comfort of possessions: the test of morality is how he goes about acquiring and using them.

[3] *Ibid.*, "The Modern English Archbishop," p. 4. "We in our English life are daily approaching nearer to that republican level which is equally averse to high summits and to low depths." Trollope accepted a growing egalitarianism and made reference to it in *The Prime Minister* and *Marion Fay*. He also regretted the loss of the picturesque, associating hedgerows and green commons with the dignitaries of the Church of England. The church may be redolent of "the sweet mediaeval flavor of old English corruption" (p. 28) but it is required in a society that is becoming increasingly utilitarian.

In a rational society there is no place for ghosts, premonitions or a religion relying upon supernatural sanctions for its authority. Nobody in Trollope's world is ever haunted or troubled by intimations of immortality. When people make mention of an afterlife it is a conversational cliché used as the occasion demands to comfort or warn. Nevertheless, they are required to abide by a moral code, expressed as social laws. These social laws require occasional attendance at church, particularly in the country, where the gentry set the moral standards in conjunction with the church. Sir Harry Albury of *Ayala's Angel* thought it disgusting when his male guests did not attend service on Sunday morning. Sir Roger Scatcherd of *Doctor Thorne* is not untypical of social attitudes when he prefers to have his old friend the doctor at his bedside instead of the local parson. Scatcherd tells Dr. Thorne that he regrets everything, and the doctor reponds:

> "You should not think in that way, Scatcherd; you need not think so. Yesterday you told Mr. Clarke that you were comfortable in your mind."

Mr. Clarke was the clergyman who had visited him.

> "Of course I did. What else could I say when he asked me? It wouldn't have been civil to have told him that his time and words were all thrown away. But, Thorne, believe me, when a man's heart is sad,—sad,— to the core, a few words from a parson at the last moment will never make it all right." (ch. 25)

Since a clergyman could expect only a token respect for his profession, it is clear that his authority was derived from his role as a gentleman. Without the latter he would amount to nothing more than a Mr. Slope.

The difficulty for the clergyman was to maintain this dual role of active moral exemplar and gentleman. Archdeacon Grantly lived too much in the world, and the magnificent marriage of his daughter to Lord Dumbello, the future Marquis of Hartletop, was a public triumph and a bitter personal disappointment. The grandeur of the Hartletops oppressed even the worldly archdeacon with an excessive presumption of social glory. Not far from Barsetshire, in Brotherton, the local dean managed his affairs more prudently. That astute clergyman had also married his daughter to an aristocrat but knew precisely what was fitting for Mary Lovelace, a clergyman's daughter, and what became the wife of Lord George Germain:

> In her dress, her ornaments, her books, her parties, there had been always something to mark slightly her clerical belongings. She had never chafed against this, because she loved her father and was naturally obedient; but she had felt something perhaps of a soft regret. Now her father, whom she saw very frequently, never spoke to her of any duties. How should her house be furnished? In what way would she lay herself out for London society? What enjoyments of life could she best secure? These seemed to be matters on which he was most intent. It never occurred to her that, when speaking to her of the house in London, he never once asked her what church she would attend; and that when she spoke with pleasure of being so near the Abbey, he paid little or no attention to her remark. And then, too, she felt, rather than perceived, that in his counsels to her he almost intimated that she must have a plan of life different from her husband's. (*Is He Popenjoy?* ch. 3)

Dean Lovelace's transaction of marriage and money is triumphantly successful both for his daughter and for himself. Not only does he establish her in an institutional role that she has learned to defend by right of her money and intelligence, but she is now the Marchioness of Brotherton and mother of the heir. Moreover, the dean has so bullied and cajoled his son-in-law that he has become a model member of parliament and a pattern landlord. Unlike Archdeacon Grantly, Dean Lovelace is always at home in his daughter's drawing room, where he is "worshipped with an exquisite grace." Since it is character that determines fortune, not circumstance, Dean Lovelace's prosperous content must be compared with Archdeacon Grantly's chagrin, and assessed accordingly. Trollope's reader is continually being called upon to make judgments of this kind from analogous situations that may occur within a novel or among a number of them.

It is typical of Trollope's method that the truth is aways ascertained by giving a fuller account of the evidence. The narrative advocate will defend or prosecute the various characters, winning the confidence of the reader by means of common assumptions and digressive comments of general reference. *The Warden* assumes the inequities of clerical preferment, but does not examine the reasons for one man's wealth and another's wretched poverty. In many ways, *Barchester Towers* is an expanded, critical revision of *The Warden*, defining the Reverend Septimus Harding once more as the central moral conscience. At issue is the power invested in the bishopric of Barchester. There are several contenders and one clear victor.

Whenever in Trollope's world an institution is irregularly managed and corrupt, it becomes possible for a woman to assume control. And because women have been so long oppressed, their hunger for power is insatiable. In Mrs. Proudie, Trollope is scrutinizing not the nature of woman but the question of authority in society. Those consistently denied authority will be tyrannical and arbitrary when once given the opportunity to seize power. Mrs. Proudie's rule in Barchester speaks for the condition of the church and the incapacity of her husband, the bishop. She is that most monstrous of Anglican bugbears, a she-priest: a woman who is fanatical in the profession of her faith because her claim to clerical authority is so dubious. Just as Mrs. Proudie can hold sway because of the church's failings, Charlotte Vesey-Stanhope manages her family because her father has renounced all parental responsibility. Both women have made institutional roles for themselves at the expense of society.

Charlotte Stanhope is the quintessence of a moral self-interest, a woman capable of logic without conscience, desiring neither love nor occupation from life beyond the material comfort of her family. The prurient encouragement of her sister's voracious sexual encounters provides her with all the entertainment she requires. Her brother Bertie is despatched to win the hand and fortune of Eleanor Bold. Bertie is charming but parasitic; their sister, Signora Neroni, is like the Scarlet Woman let loose on the men of Barchester. A pander by instinct and inclination, Charlotte and her family embody the worst of the immoral old church: fat livings earned by starving curates for absent clergy to enjoy by Lake Como. The Stanhopes have an attractive decadence and engaging amiability, firmly grounded in a complete disregard for the needs of others.

By analogy, the moral Mrs. Proudie reflects the contemporary revivalist church—so concerned with restraining sex and profanity that it would abolish human nature altogether. As the acting bishop, she controls preferments in Barchester, and those she approves are always the very poor, who cannot afford the luxury of dissent, or enthusiastic hypocrites. Mr. Slope is an able and conscientious ally, but when he falls in love with Eleanor Bold's money and Signora Neroni's captivatingly defenseless body, he can no longer serve Mrs. Proudie.

Throughout *Barchester Towers* sex is in contention with clerical conventions. Signora Neroni, specializing in clergymen, brings men to their knees and then rejects them, deriving enormous pleasure from their miserable frustration. She is delighted when she can bestow a discarded lover like Francis Arabin upon her ostensible rival, Eleanor. Arabin is a virgin who is aroused to the mysteries of sex by the Signora. In so many ways, Arabin is a creation of book-dust and arid controversy who must be taught his duty to the church and to life. Mrs. Proudie demands chaste behavior from her supporters, she trumpets her horror of Signora Neroni's lascivious influence, yet her own victories are never won in the cloisters of Barchester but in the bishop's bedroom. The reader must decide whether the sexual *frisson* that always surrounds Signora Neroni's sofa is really so different from Mrs. Proudie's militant crusade against loose behavior. Signora Neroni, whose every word is a tantalizing invitation, is physically frigid: Mrs.

Proudie, who flinches from the very mention of sex, is a volcano in the bedroom, capable of reducing a man to the shard of his former self.

The church is clearly a fallible institution, reeking of prejudice and injustice. It is, by analogy, an expression of Miss Thorne's medieval garden party at Ullathorne. Here, like the Earl of Eglinton, she attempts to revive chivalry and "The good old times—all times when old are good—" as Byron put it with some confusion in "The Age of Bronze." Trollope shared Macaulay's contempt for mock medievalism and the attempts to create a "Merrie England." Miss Thorne's intentions are of the best: she has always maintained that class distinctions promoted social accord. What she achieves is a fiasco of squabbling and misadventure. It is one thing to preach the virtues of class, it is another altogether to make people content with a class that is not of their choosing.

The only person who speaks for humanity and justice in *Barchester Towers* is Mr. Harding, and in this work there is no ambiguity between the demands of conscience and of duty. They are in accord when he refuses first the wardenship and then the office of Dean of Barchester. By his efforts at Oxford and in London, Arabin is appointed to the latter office. And because children always resemble their parents, there is hope for the church when Mr. Harding can call Dr. Grantly and Dr. Arabin his sons. One man lives too much in the world, the other spends his time "sifting and editing old ecclesiastical literature, and in producing the same articles new" (ch. 53). The two can reach a common humanity in the person of the precentor of Barchester Cathedral.

Mrs. Proudie is the ostensible victor and the battlefield is in her hands, but a number of notable skirmishes have been won at her expense, with Mr. Slope exiled to a London parish, and Eleanor married to the new dean of Barchester, Dr. Arabin.

As with most wars, victory is a debatable question and there are a great many in *Barchester Towers* who claim to have won most. Dr. Grantly rejoices over the downfall of Mr. Slope and Eleanor's escape from his marital aspirations; Dr. Arabin has found new life and purpose with a wife and position in the church; and Mrs. Proudie sits enthroned in Barchester, secure in the weakness of her husband and the failings of the church. But if any man should be accorded the triumph it is Mr. Harding, who can see his daughter married to a man of his taste, and who has not been forced into clerical offices that would offend his conscience. If happiness is the measure of success, then Mrs. Proudie may have won the substance, but Mr. Harding has gained the spirit. A decision in law may be clear-cut and definitive: this is not the case with Trollope's system of equity, which offers conclusions, but also challenges the reader to question the validity of those conclusions.

The only doubt with Mr. Harding is whether he is sufficiently popular to be of real influence in the community. As a man of true humility, his role is a passive one, and his actions are never engagements but withdrawals. Far from grappling with the issues, he prefers to ignore them, and retires to the enchanted world of his music. There is no clergyman in *Barchester Towers* who is capable of serving his community with discretion and vigor. Now, if the function of personal confidant and community leader was no longer within the capacity of the clergyman, another could be found to take his place. In *Doctor Thorne*, the ideal clergyman is not a man of the church but the local doctor.[4] If the church is scrutinized in *Barchester Towers*, then its social manifestation, the gentry, is examined in *Doctor Thorne*. Without the gentry, the church could not survive. Empty churches were tolerated so long as the secular authority of the landlord could receive the religious sanction of the parson. It is not easy to see where the gentry ends and the church begins, with both sharing the same values and observing the same social conventions. Younger sons were given livings and, in the course of time, they could inherit the whole estate. In *The Claverings*, the Reverend Henry Clavering moves gracefully into the family title and Clavering Park when his two nephews die. However, the gentry were not

---

[4] In *Wives and Daughters*, Elizabeth Gaskell makes the moral conscience of society, the local doctor.

producers of capital unless, as with Mr. Scarborough of Tretton, the property had been occupied by industry and town. To be profitable, an estate had to be large; this meant the demise of the small-holding and a gentry often older than the local aristocracy. The newness of the de Courcys is immediately apparent in their use of the particle.[5] The Duke of Omnium buys up every adjoining acre until the only remaining rival to his wealth is the new money from industry and commerce in the form of Miss Dunstable's patent-medicine fortune.

The Greshams of Greshamsbury have held their land from time immemorial, but mortgages can no longer be met and Sir Roger Scatcherd, the railway magnate, is ready to foreclose. The intermediary between gentry and industry is Dr. Thorne, whose illegitimate niece, Mary, is the child of Scatcherd's sister and the doctor's dead brother. It is Mary who inherits the vast fortune of Sir Roger Scatcherd and marries Frank Gresham. This compromise of land and industry is negotiated by her father, who has long been the confidant of Squire Gresham and Sir Roger. The theme of social obligation is argued out by Mary Thorne, who uses language like a lawyer, continually defining terms and noting the implied contracts that necessarily sustain all social relationships. So, when the imperious Lady Alexandrina de Courcy attempts to put

---

[5] Another and less elevated section of the community decided not to bother with the House of Lords at all and, taking a different tip from Sir Egerton Bridges or Brydges, took the matter into their own hands and simply changed their names from Smith or Green to what they supposed they had been in the Middle ages, sometimes adding the particle 'de' in front of them.

De Burghs, De Veres, De Greys and De Beauchamps, all multiplied uncontrollably. A family called Mullins changed their name to De Moleyns. . . . It has since been shown by historical research that, except in a few cases like those of Howard de Walden and Willoughby de Broke, the particle 'de' was never used in the Middle Ages except to denote where a person lived, and was never taken in a surname or written in a document except by accident. So that now practically all names of this nature are seen to be concoctions and, instead of proving their medieval origins, reveal themselves as Victorian gothicisms.

Ian Anstruther, *The Knight and the Umbrella*, London, 1963, p. 81.

Mary in her place, Mary responds with a literal interpretation of de Courcy philosophy that confounds her splendid acquaintance:

> "I agree with Miss Thorne in thinking that, in ordinary circumstances, with ordinary people, perhaps, the lady should have her way. Rank, however, has it drawbacks, Miss Thorne, as well as its privileges."
> "I should not object to the drawbacks," said the doctor's niece, "presuming them to be of some use; but I fear I might fail in getting on so well with the privileges." (ch. 4)

Every relationship is tested and examined, whether it is Sir Roger's claim to be the legal guardian of his niece, or Dr. Thorne's desire to see Mary made an heiress and his equally strong reluctance to have her associate with Sir Roger in his alcoholic frenzies. When Dr. Thorne and Mary discuss the future, it is Mary who abjures sentiment and argues from natural law. The doctor is still pondering the great wealth that could be Mary's if he allowed her to know the circumstances of her birth:

> "Suppose, now, I could give you up to a rich man who would be able to insure you against all wants?"
> "Insure me against all wants! Oh, that would be a man. That would be selling me, wouldn't it uncle? Yes, selling me; and the price you would receive would be freedom from future apprehensions as regards me. It would be a cowardly sale for you to make; and then, as to me,—me the victim! No, uncle; you must bear the trouble of having to provide for me,—bonnets and all. We are in the same boat, and you shan't turn me overboard."
> "But if I were to die, what would you do then?"
> "And if I were to die, what would you do? People must be bound together. They must depend on each other." (ch. 11)

Mary is always "sharp and decisive," with a mind as logical as her language.

For every situation in the work there is a corresponding analogy: Scatcherd and Squire Gresham each have a son, Lady Scatcherd nursed Frank when he was a baby, and the Greshams educated Mary with their own daughters. Beatrice Gresham marries the local vicar, Mr. Oriel, and Mary brings the Scatcherd money to the Greshams with social harmony prevailing, successfully negotiated by Dr. Thorne. And it is already obvious that the real doctor will marry the patent-medicine heiress, Miss Dunstable. Scatcherd and Moffat contest the Barchester election as Radical and Conservative. The Greshams can no longer play their customary role in local politics and it is now a struggle between the enfranchised townsfolk, who prefer one of their own, and the de Courcys, who no longer have enough money to buy votes. The town, with its representative, Scatcherd, is the new and disturbing element in rural electoral traditions. Nevertheless, although there may be deep political and social divisions there is a mesh of social contracts that imposes its own obligations upon people.

These analogous relationships are not for the sake of duplication or symmetry, but constitute the means whereby each situation may be examined from a number of different viewpoints. The structure of the declaration determines the events, but the content of the events is not controlled by any restricting rule of evidence. Letters are used for exposition and examination, adding strength to the character's testimony. What is spoken constitutes one truth; what is thought, another; and that which a character chooses to write is evidence of a different order altogether. Thus, when Augusta writes humbly to Amelia de Courcy, requesting the permission of Courcy Castle to marry a local attorney, Mortimer Gagebee, she does not suspect that Amelia's letters in reply are a means of eliciting information about a husband who will satisfy her own marital ambitions. Letters are of particular significance in the elucidation of intention since they are, in a sense, testimony, as distinct from evidence that is spoken and may be occasioned by the impulse of the moment. If a character cannot commit the truth to paper, then the reader is left in doubt about his honesty. A letter is an occasion when a character is called upon to write under oath. For many, of course, the letter, like a great deal of sworn testimony known to law, simply offers an opportunity to deceive from a distance.

As early as in *Doctor Thorne*, one of the major themes of the later novels begins to emerge as a dominant concern. If the Barsetshire novels convinced Trollope of one thing, it was the relative ineffectuality of the church as a social institution. Certainly, a gentleman could not hope to express the fullest potential of that role unless he went into political life. In his efforts to be of service to others, a clergyman was limited by his calling. But the gentleman as politician was the goal to be sought and respected by all reasonable men. So, in *Doctor Thorne*, the narrative advocate states as a general rule that "when a man lays himself out to be a member of Parliament, he plays the highest game and for the highest stakes which the country affords" (ch. 17). It was a principle iterated at length by all manner of men, and for different purposes, in Trollope's world.

In *Framley Parsonage*, the Reverend Mark Robarts marks the transition from clerical to political life. He is proud to be known as a friend of the local member, Mr. Sowerby of Chaldicotes, and receive an invitation from Gatherum Castle. Politics is the finest game, but not all who play it are honest and well-meaning. Robarts signs a bill for Sowerby, then another, and soon finds that he must repay such a sum for his engaging friend that it will bankrupt him. Robarts longs to be part of political life and has sufficient intelligence to understand that the highest offices in the church are the gift of the party in power.

As the political interest takes shape in these works it becomes increasingly clear that the church is the most inefficient organ of government: a source of patronage that can preserve its inequities because it is partly autonomous but always controlled by a hierarchy of politically appointed priests. Bishop Proudie is typical of those clergymen who have learned to play politics as deftly and unobtrusively as any senior civil servant. Mr. Harding and Mr. Crawley of Hogglestock personify the clergy that has no gift for politics and no private income. In *Framley Parsonage* it is quite within the power of Sowerby, as a member of the government, to bestow a stall in Barchester Cathedral upon Mark Robarts. This is how the church works and it is the reason for its incompetence and corruption.

The lesson Robarts must learn is that a country clergyman's natural allegiance is to the local gentry that pays him, not to a political faction. Robarts was appointed to his living by Lady Lufton, a conservative whose rule in politics is to oppose whatever the Duke of Omnium supports. When the bailiffs are removing Robarts' furniture it is Lord Lufton who pays his debts and welcomes him back into the conservative fold. Lady Lufton has found it difficult to forgive her clerical protégé for going to Gatherum Castle, and is not mollified when her son tells her what Robarts gained there:

> "Prebendal stalls are for older men than he—for men who have earned them, and who at the end of their lives want some ease. I wish with all my heart that he had never taken it."
> "Six hundred a year has its charms all the same," said Lufton, getting up and strolling out of the room. (ch.43)

Lufton too has lost money to Sowerby and knows what it means to be tempted.

In Barsetshire there are no parties bound to a particular doctrine, simply coalitions of local interests. Lady Lufton detests the de Courcys but she will join forces with them as a conservative in order to defend her property against the Duke of Omnium. The political life of *Framley Parsonage* takes place in the great country houses, and is seen as a game of capricious interests more concerned with fox coverts than with foreign wars. Because it is Robarts who is being initiated into political life, there is a lack of clarity about the politics being discussed. With few exceptions, the politicians are designated in a way that denotes their distance from the reader's immediate concern. References to battles of the gods and a scattering of classical allusions are sufficient indication that this scene of activity should not be taken too seriously. *Fram-*

ley Parsonage is not a study in politics, but a novel in which political life brings a young clergyman to the verge of ruin. And no one has been assisted along this perilous route by such an ambivalent guide as Sowerby—a man possessed of honor and intelligence, but depraved by indolence and indigence.

Political power in Barsetshire is determined by the ownership of land, unlike the town of Barchester which will cheerfully vote a Roger Scatcherd into Parliament. Tenants of a property, however, will invariably vote with the landlord, particularly when the landlord is prepared to protect their interests. At the conclusion of *Framley Parsonage*, the Conservative interest is again in the ascendant with the Greshams, the Luftons, the de Courcys, and the Thornes as the new owners of Chaldicotes.

Around Mark Robarts a number of marriages take place which cement political and social alliances. Mr. Sowerby plans to marry Miss Dunstable so that he can save Chaldicotes, but Miss Dunstable chooses Dr. Thorne who finds, to his bemusement, that he is the husband of the richest woman in England. There is no reward too handsome for the true gentleman in Trollope's rational and ordered society. Lady Lufton has fixed on the beautiful and silent Griselda Grantly for her daughter-in-law, but Lord Lufton sensibly prefers Lucy Robarts, and Griselda is married off to Lord Dumbello—after considerable efforts by her father. All these marriages change the landscape of Barsetshire. The Greshams are now the richest commoners in the county, but it is Miss Dunstable's Oil of Lebanon that buys Chaldicotes and the great forest around it. The Duke of Omnium has sought to purchase Chaldicotes but even he cannot match Miss Dunstable's offer. Nevertheless, Omnium still retains the power to nominate his own candidate, and Sowerby, now standing for the conservatives and supported by Miss Dunstable's money, goes down to Lord Dumbello.

Politics are never permitted to dominate local interests, so the mesh of implied contracts is not broken by the flurry of an election. Lady Dumbello greets the new Lady Lufton with the glacial cordiality that is the fullest expression of her charm, and Omnium can gather all his past enemies around him at Gatherum Castle. But Mark Robarts is now content with the landscape of Framley Parsonage, and to live under the wing of Lady Lufton. He renounces the prebendal stall, endures the accusations of the *Jupiter*, and strives to be a clergyman, not an aspiring politician.

The London of government offices and cheap boarding houses reaches out to Allington, where Lily Dale falls in love with Adolphus Crosbie, a young civil servant and friend of Bernard Dale, heir to Squire Dale. Lily loves Crosbie passionately—of all the young women in Trollope's world she is most capable of an obsessive adoration that casts out every rational thought. When Crosbie is snatched up by the de Courcys and married off to the mature Lady Alexandrina, Lily has a complete mental and emotional breakdown. Her devoted admirer has always been Johnny Eames, but she shares more than the family name with her uncle, Squire Dale. Not only is action consistent with character in Trollope's world, but children resemble their parents and often duplicate their fate. Old Mr. Dale had once fallen in love with a woman who wisely refused to marry him:

> And in that matter of his unrequited love he had been true throughout. In his hard, dry, unpleasant way he had loved the woman; and when at last he learned to know that she would not have his love, he had been unable to transfer his heart to another. (ch. 1)

In exactly the same fashion, Lily refuses Johnny's proposals, and all others. Just as the squire has remained single as if to reproach the woman he loved, Lily elects to be a professional old maid. The institutional role she chooses is no more rational than her infatuated worship of Adolphus Crosbie. It is not just a single life but an old maid's existence inscribed in her diary and reflected in her thoughts. It is a covert and unreflecting way of punishing the lover who rejected her.

Lily's inability to compromise with her feelings and society is more than a perverse idiosyncracy, it is a family trait that is also evidenced by her cousin Bernard. He despairs when

Bell, Lily's sister, refuses him and marries the local doctor. Rejection is the recurring theme in *The Small House at Allington*, from Lady Dumbello's spurning of Plantagenet Palliser's suit to Johnny Eames' escape from Jemima Roper. Adolphus Crosbie finds that his aristocratic alliance has dwindled into a small domestic purgatory. It is as painful for Lady Alexandrina as it is for him. She now appreciates the life of an unloved middle-class housewife:

> "You do not know what my life is in that house. He never speaks to me,—never. He comes home before dinner at half-past six, and when he has just shown himself he goes to his dressing-room. He is always silent at dinner-time, and after dinner he goes to sleep. He breakfasts always at nine, and goes away at half-past nine, though I know he does not get to his office till eleven." (ch. 37)

The lamentations continue but her mother shares a similar domestic misery, and all she can suggest is that they go into exile together. In Baden-Baden they share the lot of the misfits who have been driven out of society.

The analogue for the de Courcy household that ends with the Countess in Germany and the dissolution of the family is Mrs. Roper's boarding house. Here, every trap has been set for Johnny Eames but he refuses to spring them and at last it is the unfortunate Cradell who, like Adolphus, is left with the lady and a mountain of debts. Eames does not succeed in marriage, but his patron, Lord de Guest, helps him to higher office in the income tax bureau and leaves him a bequest in his will. Although still yearning for Lily, Eames has not done at all badly for himself, and, in a sense, he knows it.

The Last Chronicle of Barset is the reprise of all the previous themes and concludes Trollope's study of the church as an institution in society. Trollope would write again about clergymen, but he had now examined the function of the church to his satisfaction, and it had failed to meet his criteria of efficiency and economy. As a calling, the church could never fulfill a man's highest aspirations to be of service to his community—that role belonged to the politician. The church's shame was that it employed gentlemen like Mr. Crawley, fine scholars, dedicated to their faith and their community, and paid them a wage less than a navvy's. Yet it was expected that these clergymen should dress like gentlemen, live like gentlemen, and set a standard that could be emulated by their parishioners. There is considerable irony in the frequently quoted passage wherein Archdeacon Grantly speaks of "the perfect level" on which he can meet Mr. Crawley: they are both gentlemen. Had Mr. Crawley ever been given the salary befitting a gentleman, the accusations of theft would never have been brought against him. To demand that a man live like a gentleman and then deny him the means to do so is capricious and unjust. The church is guilty on both counts in the case of Mr. Crawley.

Mr. Crawley's career in the church has been a long ordeal of social humiliation. His scholarship is not rewarded with a commensurate office, rather it is relegated to the bricklayers of Hogglestock and the school he maintains for their children. The despair of his life is to witness what his calling has done to his wife, who spends her days fending off tradesmen, or begging for the means to feed her children. Mr. Crawley is proud, intelligent and scrupulously honest, and, in the opinion of his wife and others, poverty has brought him to the verge of madness. When he is charged with stealing a cheque for twenty pounds, the whole country debates the cause of a clergyman who could also be a felon. His announced disgrace reaches out through the community, with Mrs. Proudie determined to have him sentenced without trial and Lady Lufton and her daughter-in-law equally resolute in their belief in his innocence. The tragic ambiguity of his situation is that he is not even certain himself of his innocence.

For years, Mr. Crawley has relived the past, going back in his thoughts to that point where he had found his calling and rejoiced that he might be called upon to share the poverty of Christ or St. Paul. Now he understands that the world of St. Paul, where poverty was commendable in a religious, is not Barsetshire.

And he would recall the circumstances of his poverty,—how he had been driven to accept alms, to fly from his creditors, to hide himself, to see his chairs and tables seized before the eyes of those over whom he had been set as their spiritual pastor. And in it all, I think, there was nothing so bitter to the man as the derogation from the spiritual grandeur of his position as a priest among men, which came as one necessary result from his poverty. (ch. 12)

These are the ingredients of madness, and the man's sufferings are compounded because he has learned to doubt his own reason.

Mr. Crawley is saved by the same circumstance that initially rescued Mr. Harding from obscure poverty. Mr. Harding's position in the church has been assured ever since his two daughters married an archdeacon and the dean of Barchester. Now Mr. Crawley's daughter, Grace, has captivated the archdeacon's son, Major Grantly. When the latter insists on making her his wife, it is intolerable that an archdeacon should be related by marriage to a perpetual curate in debt to his butcher. Therefore, when Mr. Harding dies, his living at St. Ewold's is passed on to Mr. Crawley. It is by such means that the virtuous occasionally flourish, and the inefficiency of the church is guaranteed.

Johnny Eames is the link between Allington, Barchester, and the Dobbs Broughtons of Bayswater. He is still single when three deaths draw the Barsetshire novels to a close. Mr. Harding dies as peacefully as he has lived and is buried by his friends in the cathedral cloisters. His gentle passing is the analogy for the suicides of two people who have lived by sham. Dobbs Broughton has always been the quintessence of brummagem, a man of whom Johnny Eames could state: " 'Clap him down upon the counter, and he rings dull and untrue at once' " (ch. 24). Dobbs Broughton blows his bains out at the entrance to Hook Court when his small financial empire begins to crumble, and he suspects his wife of being unfaithful. Unfortunately, Broughton is not of equivalent stature to the women we have studied in so many varied situations. Mrs. Proudie has staked her authority and reputation on forcing Mr. Crawley from Hogglestock as a convicted thief and putting Mr. Thumble, her pet, in his place. All this she has done in the name of preserving morality among the clergy of Barchester. But this time the bishop will not move in accordance with his wife's direction, and the debate becomes one of authority and duty, argued out with such bitterness that there is only one possible fate for the vanquished. Mrs. Proudie demands that she be permitted to send Mr. Thumble to Hogglestock:

> "This will not do at all," she said. "My dear, do you know that you are forgetting yourself altogether?"
> "I wish I could forget myself."
> "That might be all very well if you were in a position in which you owed no service to any one; or, rather, it would not be well then, but the evil would not be so manifest. You cannot do your duty in the diocese if you continue to sit there doing nothing, with your head upon your hands. Why do you not rally, and get to your work, like a man?"
> "I wish you would go away and leave me," he said.
> "No, bishop, I will not go away and leave you. You have brought yourself to such a condition that it is my duty as your wife to stay by you: and if you neglect your duty, I will not neglect mine."
> "It was you that brought me to it."
> "No, sir, that is not true. I did not bring you to it."
> "It is the truth."
> And now he got up and looked at her. For a moment he stood upon his legs, and then again sat down with his face turned towards her. "It is the truth. You have brought on me such disgrace that I cannot hold up my head. You have ruined me. I wish I were dead; and it is all through you that I am driven to wish it." (ch. 66)

The Extended Multiple Transaction 1

Throughout this interrogation, Mrs. Proudie can find no adequate defense. Her guilt is made evident with the bishop's recognition of the truth. Slowly, she goes to the room where all her victories have been won, clasps the bedpost and dies on her feet. It is deemed accidental, but with no further reason to live, Mrs. Proudie still has sufficient will to die.[6]

Barsetshire has already echoed to the clamor of elections, and in the great houses schemes are under way to pull down a party and put another in its place. The power of the church was clearly limited to the countryside. In the city, the empty churches, even the abbey itself where Mr. Harding sheltered on his flight from the archdeacon, proclaimed an institution that was respected but never obeyed. Power resided in another part of Westminster where the authority of parliament was the final expression of law. Like Austin, Trollope saw the function of formal authority as the ultimate source of legal validity, and was comforted in the knowledge that there was no power beyond that of parliament. Here a man could know the meaning of authority and accept its concomitant responsibility. The ability to govern and to serve, to lead and to follow, was the test of the true gentleman. In the Palliser novels, where Trollope pursued all the implications of this view, he chose to repeat the structure of the Barsetshire series and to use the form of the extended multiple transaction.

[6] Women had always been regarded with the deepest suspicion in the Church of England where any female presence smacked of Rome. William Sherlock in *A Short Summary of the Principal Controversies between the Church of England and the Church of Rome*, London, 1687, p. 84 wrote: "And if intercession be annexed to the Priesthood, I desire to know, how the Virgin *Mary* comes to be so powerful a Mediatrix, and *Advocatress*; for we never heard of any she High Priest before." Bishops' wives were always a ready subject for criticism and gossip, particularly when they had social aspirations. Thus, when Bishop Watson desired to denigrate Archbishop Cornwallis, he did so with reference to the noble cleric's wife: "I had no opinion of his abilities, and he was so wife-ridden I had no opinion of his politics." *Anecdotes of the Life of Richard Watson*, London, 1817, p. 70.

Chapter XII

The Extended Multiple Transaction—Privilege and Power in Politics: *Can You Forgive Her? Phineas Finn, The Eustace Diamonds, Phineas Redux, The Prime Minister, The Duke's Children*

To be elected to the House of Commons in Trollope's day was to feel oneself seated on the throne of the world. Beyond England were the colonies and an empire that other countries could only envy or imitate. Quite simply, a member of parliament belonged to the most exclusive, the most responsible and influential club in the world. Trollope had longed to be part of it all, standing for Beverley in 1868 and then spending weeks in the gallery of the House, listening to debates and noting how the fate of a politician could turn upon the challenge of a single question. This was the source of power and privilege, with honors and appointments at the disposal of the ruling party. The man who did not wish to write M.P. after his name was devoid of ambition and deficient in a sense of duty.

The Palliser novels are primarily concerned with the question of parliamentary election: who should stand and for what reasons. A Ferdinand Lopez in *The Prime Minister* desires to be a member so that he may better serve his own social and financial interests, Plantagenet Palliser takes the highest office so that he may work for his country. And it is possible that although a man's intentions may be altruistic, his nature will preclude him from office. Palliser possesses every quality save that of popularity, and because of this deficiency he cannot ensure the loyalty of his colleagues and the support of his party. In his official election address, Trollope made his loyalty to Mr. Gladstone his main recommendation for election.[1]

The game of "hunt the character" in the Palliser series has always provided an engrossing occupation for some critics and historians. Sir Shane Leslie, for example, in his preface to *Phineas Finn* takes it for granted that "Phineas was based on a political adventurer called Sadleir...,"[2] and James Pope Hennessey is equally as dogmatic in the assertion that his own grandfather provided the model.[3] In *Trollope and Politics* John Halperin has linked character to historical figure, providing an interpretative key to the novels. The difficulty for Halperin is that Trollope so seldom meets the necessary criteria for verisimilitude. Thus we have a continuing reliance on composites such as "The Disraeli-figures of Daubeny in *Phineas Redux* and Sir Timothy Beeswax in *The Duke's Children*."[4] If the Palliser novels are *romans a cléf*, as Halperin would seem to insist, then there must be a greater degree of exactitude.

There is no question that Gresham is *like* Gladstone, and Turnbull is *like* Bright, but this is not stating that Trollope's fiction is a veridical imitation of reality. Rather it would seem that the mimesis is deeper and considerably less exact than a form of synthetic and synoptic historical commentary. What Trollope is concerned with in his work is not reproduction but, and only the French term suffices here, the *vraisemblance* of reality: not facts as such, but general truths that in the case of character become general likenesses. *Vraisemblance* re-

---

[1] The best account of Trollope's campaign at Beverley is given by John Halperin in *Trollope and Politics*, London, 1977, pp. 112-130.
[2] Preface to *Phineas Finn* by Sir Shane Leslie, Oxford University Press, 1973, p. v.
[3] James Pope Hennessy, *Anthony Trollope*, Boston, 1971, p. 280.
[4] Op. cit., Halperin, p. 160.

quires that the truth shall be ascertained from the comparison of a number of things.[5] It resembles legal reasoning in its quest for rules and their general application from a rational scrutiny of events.

Trollope satisfies the reader's "taste for the emotions of recognition" as Henry James expressed it. This recognition is based not on the precise correlation of fiction with historical event, but on the *vraisemblance* derived from the comparison of the fiction with generally known things. Throughout Trollope there is a demonstrated accuracy of social reference concerning class, manners, and dress. A small study could be made from the novels of the contemporary significance of touch—the pressure of the hand, or the finger tips, denoting several degrees of amatory inclination. A veritable album of styles in women's hairdressing and gowns could be compiled from the same source. Then there are the resonant incidents that recall historical figures without defining them: Sir Roger Scatcherd, who made his money and title from railroads, is reminiscent of Thomas Brassey, and it is tempting to find a source for the artistic Dormer sisters in Elizabeth and Alice Thompson, especially since Elizabeth marries a famous soldier and becomes Lady Butler. But it would be unwise to press these resemblances any further than the observation that a historical model can be found for almost every character in the novels. This is not to classify Trollope as a historian but to recognize that fiction will always make the reader accept history on its own terms.

A diversity of opinion and a reliance upon analogical argument are always Trollope's modes of ascertaining the truth. He deplored the interest of women in politics and opposed the female suffrage, yet the Palliser novels are as much concerned with women in political life as they are with men. In his public lectures, Trollope pooh-poohed women's demands for higher education, but in *The Last Chronicle of Barset*, Major Grantly expresses Grace Crawley's remarkable attrac-

---

[5] "Vraisemblance: Apparence de la vérité. La décourverte du vrai dans la plupart des choses dépend de la comparaison des vraisemblances." Littré et Beaujean.

tion for him in one sentence: " 'She is simply the best educated girl whom it has ever been my lot to meet' " (ch. 3).[6] Lady Glencora, with Marie Goesler in mind, observes that men always prefer clever women, particularly if they know how to use their cleverness. It is Lady Eustace's tragedy that she is not quite clever enough, despite her repertoire of romantic poetry suitable for all private occasions. In *Can You Forgive Her?* politics provides a background, but the work is primarily an account of the transactions between marriage and money undertaken by three women.

Alice Vavasor is passionate and rational, and her life has alternated between the scholarly John Grey and her violent and attractive cousin, George Vavasor. But she knows that it would be impossible to make a satisfactory life for herself with a man who is keeping and starving a mistress, and who thinks nothing of assaulting his sister. So she molds John Grey into a politician with Plantagenet Palliser's help, and if she can never experience Mrs. Greenacre's high rocks, she can at least look forward to valleys that are rich and various. For Glencora Palliser there is the choice of a husband who will be offered high rank in government, or Burgo Fitzgerald, the man she loved as a child and worships as a woman. Glencora, like Alice, chooses an institutional role instead of personal and sexual fulfillment—nevertheless, Glencora's decision is a bitter one because she was never given the freedom to choose in the first place. She recognizes immediately that Alice would have been the perfect wife for Palliser, just as Alice is fashioning John Grey into a lesser Palliser. In Paris, he compiles statistics and Alice not only assists him but provides him with some computations of her own. Unfortunately, Glencora is

[6] Trollope deplored the movement for avanced education for women in his lecture, "Higher Education of Women" (1868), and offered a number of comic portraits of feminists in his novels. This has been taken literally by a number of critics. Thus, Frank Pierce Jones in "The Role of the Classics in the Emancipation of Women," *Classical Journal*, vol. XXXIX, no. 6, March, 1944, p. 332, writes of Grace Crawley: "Her Greek was real enough but it had no particular meaning in her life and offers no clue towards understanding her character." On the contrary, it seems one reason why Major Grantly was so attracted to her.

intelligent enough to know herself and appreciate that she can never give anything more to her husband than money and children:

> "I do so wish you had married him!" Glencora said to Alice that evening. "You would always have had a pocket-book ready to write down the figures, and you would have pretended to care about the eggs, and the bottles of wine, and the rest of it. As for me, I can't do it. If I see a hungry woman, I can give her my money; or if she be a sick woman, I can nurse her; or if I hear of a very wicked man, I can hate him;—but I cannot take up poverty and crime in the lump. I never can believe it all. My mind isn't big enough." (ch. 68)

Again, in *Phineas Finn*, women are confronted with the same problem of establishing an institutional role for themselves that does not deny all hope of personal fulfillment. Lady Laura Standish loves Phineas and would gladly have made him her husband had he been something more than a young Irish politician with a precarious seat in the House. Instead she marries Mr. Kennedy and her discontent drives him to madness and death:

> She had married Mr. Kennedy because she was afraid that otherwise she might find herself forced to own that she loved that other man who was then a nobody;—almost nobody. It was not Mr. Kennedy's money that bought her. This woman in regard to money had shown herself to be as generous as the sun. But in marrying Mr. Kennedy she had maintained herself in her high position, among the first of her own people,—among the first socially and among the first politically. But had she married Phineas,—had she become Lady Laura Finn,—there would have been a great descent. (ch. 55)

At the conclusion of *Phineas Finn*, Lady Laura's only satisfaction is to see her own misery eclipsed by her husband's. Men can experience political life directly; women, indirectly, and their resentment provides a chorus of discontent throughout the novels. Lady Glencora announces at some length why she would make a more successful prime minister than her husband. When she is forced to leave her husband and live with her father in Germany, Lady Laura speaks of her altered situation to Phineas:

> "But I am nobody,—or worse than nobody."
> "And I also am going to be a nobody," said Phineas, laughing.
> "Ah; you are a man and will get over it, and you have many years before you will begin to be growing old. I am growing old already. Yes, I am. I feel it, and know it, and see it. A woman has a fine game to play; but then she is so easily bowled out, and the term allowed her is so short."
> "A man's allowance of time may be short too," said Phineas.
> "But he can try his hand again." (ch. 80)

The game is indeed lost for Lady Laura, but even though Phineas has been turned out of office and has lost his seat because of his stand on Irish tenant rights, he can still hope for a second innings. As is not the case for most women, it is always possible for a man to have another chance. Just as Palliser gave up the chancellorship of the exchequer and returned to become a member of cabinet and future prime minister, so the reader is satisfied by Lady Laura's words that Phineas Finn's case is not settled—it is pending appeal. Moreover, he enjoys a popularity that Palliser does not. When a man is popular, his friends will not forget him, and for the term of his temporary exile in Ireland he is made an Inspector of Poor Houses in Cork.

Phineas has always loved honestly, recognizing that a woman like Lady Violet Effingham could secure his political career with her rank and fortune. When Marie Goesler offers him her money and her hand, he remembers that he is betrothed to Mary Flood, whose charms as a wife are equivalent to the pleasure he takes in his new position. But since he is a man, he can always return and offer his hand again. In the last episodes of this inconclusive work there is the assurance that several matters are still waiting to be resolved. Marie Goesler has the Duke of Omnium at her feet, Lady Laura is in exile, and Phineas is banished to Ireland. It is not the end of his career. He has acquired something far more valuable than money and a wife in England—he has become popular. This is the golden key in Trollope's world that will enable even a poor young Irishman to attain high office. His success is dependent upon his character, for:

> He was a man who was pleasant to other men,—not combative, not self-asserting beyond the point at which self-assertion ceases to be a necessity of manliness. Nature had been very good to him, making him comely inside and out,—and with this comeliness he had crept into popularity. (ch. 40)

Although concerned with politics, there are few occasions where a political issue is debated at length. Rather it is the process of arriving at decisions that is examined, and the composition of those factions that passed for parties in Trollope's life. The works do provide a remarkable gallery of women who determine the fate of the men who sit in the House and debate the issues of the day. And if there is anything that should reveal the Palliser novels as unhistorical, it is this pervasive influence of women in a period of English history when their authority in political life was minimal. The major political issues are all prefaced and queried by women who implicitly challenge the assumption of a free and democratic assembly.

In *Phineas Redux*, the cause of church disestablishment is to be debated by Daubeny and Gresham. Phineas Finn invites Madame Goesler to attend, and she replies:

> "What a pleasure! To hear a man speak for two hours and a half about the Church of England. One must be very hard driven for amusement! Will you tell me that you like it?"
>
> "I like to hear a good speech."
>
> "But you have the excitement before you of making a

good speech in answer. You are in the fight. A poor
woman, shut up in a cage, feels there more acutely than
anywhere else how insignificant a position she fills in the
world." (ch. 32)

Now because events in Trollope's world are always the logical consequence of character, this resentment becomes a dominant motive force. Causation is more often an affair of women than of men in these novels.

Palliser must resign as prime minister when it is discovered that his wife has encouraged Ferdinand Lopez to stand for Silverbridge, and Phineas Finn is saved from the gallows when Marie Goesler provides the evidence that acquits him of having murdered Mr. Bonteen. Indeed, Mr. Bonteen is bludgeoned to death not because of his political rivalry with Phineas Finn but as a direct result of his warm friendship with Lady Eustace. Continually, a man's career in politics will be determined by a woman, whether it is John Grey entering parliamentary life to please Alice Vavasor, Mr. Kennedy resigning his seat because of his marriage, or Frank Greystock preferring Lucy Morris to a seat in the House.

Lady Glencora's life is a struggle against the frustrations of her marriage and her conviction that she could be a better prime minister than her husband. There is a considerable affinity between Lady Glencora and Mrs. Proudie. Unfortunately, Lady Glencora's idea of a prime minister is a century and more out of date, and more redolent of Robert Walpole than of the age of Gladstone. In her own words, she would make the office a fount of patronage and bribes, dispensing honors for a price and pensions in return for support. It is frequently quoted passage, but one that is seldom examined as a statement of political policy:

"They should have made me Prime Minister, and have
let him be Chancellor of the Exchequer. I begin to see
the ways of Government now. I could have done all the
dirty work. I could have given away garters and ribbons,
and made my bargains while giving them. I could select
sleek, easy bishops who wouldn't be troublesome. I could

give pensions or withhold them, and make the stupid men peers. I could have the big noblemen at my feet, praying to be Lieutenants of Counties. I could dole out secretaryships and lordships, and never a one without getting something in return. I could brazen out a job and let the "People's Banners" and the Slides make their worst of it. And I think I could make myself popular with my party, and do the high-flowing patriotic talk for the benefit of the Provinces. A man at a regular office has to work. That's what Plantagenet is fit for. He wants always to be doing something that shall be really useful, and a man has to toil at that and really to know things. But a Prime Minister should never go beyond generalities about commerce, agriculture, peace, and general philanthropy. Of course he should have the gift of the gab, and that Plantagenet hasn't got. He never wants to say anything unless he has got something to say. I could do a Mansion House dinner to a marvel!" (*The Prime Minister*, ch. 56)

If this passage demonstrates one fact, it is that Glencora understands neither her husband nor the political process. She voices the popular and simplistic interpretation of government that seizes on the exceptional and regards it as the general rule. As she once told Alice Vavasor, she has a ready sympathy and shrewdness, but lacks the intelligence to cope with general and abstract problems. Nevertheless, her resentment of women's political inferiority darkens her life and blights her husband's career. She speaks as one oppressed, and her cry for justice is as heartfelt as that of Mr. Bunce, Phineas Finn's landlord, who goes down into the streets to fight for the charter. And although Sir Thomas Underwood in *Ralph the Heir* may find Ontario Moggs' banner, "Moggs, Purity, and the Rights of Labour," a source of amusement, it is Moggs who eventually wins a seat in parliament. As the wife of the prime minister, "Prime Ministress" in her own words, Glencora had tasted power, but she could never appreciate the responsibility of privilege. When Palliser asks her what she wants when he has been turned out of office and replaced by Gresham, she says:

"Nothing;—except being the Prime Minister's wife; and upon my word there were times when I didn't like that very much. I don't know anything else that I'm fit for. I wonder whether Mr. Gresham would let me go to him as house-keeper?" (*The Prime Minister*, ch. 78)

Plantagenet Palliser makes an impossible leader of a coalition government, and yet, as his pleasure in the office grows, the awareness of his deficiencies confronts him at every turn. Palliser, like Septimus Harding, is a study of failure that transcends the everyday criteria of success to achieve a special kind of triumph. He is by nature stiff, awkward, and unduly sensitive. Just as Mr. Harding could not endure criticism from *The Jupiter*, Palliser is crushed by an editorial in *The People's Banner*. Phineas Finn says that "He is not by nature gregarious or communicative, and is therefore hardly fitted to be the head of a ministry" (ch. 27). But the ability to communicate and to persuade is the very essence of political life. Certainly, a politician must learn to be able to refuse without making enemies, but, when men seek favors from Palliser, as is customary with a prime minister, he cannot simply deny the request; he must deliver an outraged homiletic address on honesty. A man who deserts his colleagues to discuss cork soles with Lady Rosina de Courcy is hardly suited for the first office in government.

The Prime Minister traces the fortunes of Palliser and Ferdinand Lopez. No two men could be more dissimilar, yet they are brought together by Lady Glencora. The analogical relationship is set against the demands of politics—one is too inflexible and too sensitive to succeed, the other takes his life when his schemes bring him to financial and social ruin. Politics demands something more from a man than Lady Glencora imagines. Above all else, there must be honesty and the trust of friends. At the end it is Mr. Gresham who becomes prime minister and no one questions his fitness for that office—not even Glencora.

Phineas Finn succeeds as man and politician because of those gifts that ensured his popularity. His wife, Marie Goesler, is a woman of wit, wealth, and high intelligence, and it is obvious that without financial embarrassments, he will hold office under any liberal government. But for Plantagenet Palliser it is more difficult to acquire the same harmony between his personal, familial, and institutional identities. In *The Duke's Children*, Palliser, now Duke of Omnium, has learned at last that the privilege of politics is to serve. He is now a statesman who knows that a political career should be the goal of every gentleman, not for reasons of glory or reputation, but that he may have the power to help others. At the breakfast table with his two sons, he warms to a statement of his political creed:

> "As far as my experience goes, the happiest man is he who, being above the troubles which money brings, has his hands the fullest of work. If I were to name the class of men whose lives are spent with the most thorough enjoyment, I think I should name that of barristers who are in large practice and also in Parliament."
> "Isn't it a great grind, sir?" asked Silverbridge.
> "A very great grind, as you call it. And there may be the grind and not the success. But——" He had now got up from his seat at the table and was standing with his back against the chimney piece, and as he went on with his lecture,—as the word "But" came from his lips—he struck the fingers of one hand lightly on the palm of the other as he had been known to do at some happy flight of oratory in the House of Commons. "But it is the grind that makes the happiness. To feel that your hours are filled to overflowing, that you can barely steal minutes enough for sleep, that the welfare of many is entrusted to you, that the world looks on and approves, that some good is always being done to others,—above all things some good to your country;—that is happiness. For myself I can conceive none other." (*The Duke's Children*, ch. 25).

Quite simply, no other career can offer a man the opportunity to do so much good for so many others. It is a profession of service that surpasses Phineas Finn's concept of duty, and makes the clergyman seem ineffectual by comparison.

Despite his joy in political life, Palliser has never known happiness as a man. *The Duke's Children* shows how he must compromise with his children in order to find personal and familial happiness. Palliser married not for love but to please his uncle, knowing that Glencora was less capable of resisting than he. Her life ends when he resigned as prime minister and became a member of the opposition. She dies in the arms of her friend Marie, but not before she has sought compensation for her own loveless marriage in the happiness of her daughter. Glencora is mourned by her husband, who finds that his wife has left him with a daughter who feels entitled to marry the man of whom her mother approved.

The man who could speak of a growing age of egalitarianism to Phineas Finn, and who once told John Grey that he took no pride in being born to a dukedom, is now faced with the reality of his abstractions. Glencora could never look beyond the mundane events that touched her life: Palliser could not live except by statistical tables. He did not lack judgment, but he was devoid of sympathy and the sense of common humanity that made Phineas Finn as popular with Mrs. Bunce as with a duchess. Now, Palliser's daughter wants to marry a young Conservative, Frank Tregear, and his heir declares his allegiance to the same party. Not only does Silverbridge want to desert the Liberals, but he has fallen in love with an American, Isabel Boncassen. All this in spite of the plans Palliser has made for his daughter to bring an aristocrat into the family, and Silverbridge to make Lady Mabel Grex, of an ancient and decayed line, the future Duchess of Omnium.

As Palliser learns to become a father, and when he is reconciled to his daughter's marriage and Silverbridge's American wife, it is as though his feelings and his personality are at one with his political creed. It is not within the power of any man to change the past, but it should be possible to protect children from the mistakes of their parents. Glencora is vindicated when Mary marries the man of her choice and Silverbridge rejects all the old traditions of rank in his own marriage. The compromise Palliser has reached is that between his pride and the happiness of his children: " 'Perhaps, after all, it is well that a pride of which I am conscious should be rebuked. And it may be that the rebuke has come in such a form that I should be thankful' " (ch. 74). And with the loss of pride and the accession of a new understanding, Palliser is returned to office as president of the council.

In all his novels devoted to English society Trollope created a rational world, the ideal universe of law in which cause and consequence exist in a state of logical accord. The form he used was derived from a legal declaration, but within its formal structure he set up the dynamic of opposing visions of life. Law was set against popular fiction, and both contended with the world of known things. The critical mode of enquiry was the discovery of the truth by means of comparison. The goal was a just society governed by free and rational decisions. Truth is made known not from a single voice in the novels, but as a synthesis of many disparate attitudes and convictions. The writer who embodied so many of the prejudices of his day, from antisemitism to racism, would always permit the evidence of a contrary opinion.

Trollope is essentially a judicial writer in his willingness to hear all opinions and then let the final decision rest with the reader. One phrase is repeated throughout the novels: "The reader must judge for himself." This requires more than a passive acceptance of the narrator's interpretation of events: it calls for the active participation of the reader in the elucidation of character and the moral verdict to be reached. The peculiar pleasure of Trollope is derived from a discourse between the reader and a rational fiction that is never violated by the unexpected or coincidental. When asked once to define the special quality of Trollope, the Philadelphia jurist Henry Drinker spoke of his "deep reasonableness." It is this reasonableness in an unreasonable world that has always comforted and reassured Trollope's readers.

Index

The American Senator, 132
apRoberts, Ruth, 152 n.3
Archbold, John Frederick, 13-17, 19-24, 82, 105, 112
Australia and New Zealand, 60-61
An Autobiography, 5-8, 11, 18, 21-22, 28, 31, 37 n.17, 38-39, 41, 44-45, 53, 68-79, 89-90, 94, 96, 111, 113
Ayala's Angel, 44, 80, 100, 172, 182-189, 194

Bagehot, Walter, 187
Barchester Towers, 55, 88, 134, 142, 191, 196-199
Beale, Constance, 42-43
The Belton Estate, 107-109
Bentham, Jeremy, 16, 46
The Bertrams, 53-55, 168, 192
Blackstone, Sir William, 13-15, 25, 46, 84
Brontë, Charlotte, 10, 41, 72, 86, 183
Bryant, Margaret, 106
Bulwer-Lytton, Edward, 23
Burke, Edmund, 4-10
Burton, Richard, 53-54
Butt, Sir Isaac, 36, 157 n.1

Carlyle, Thomas, 101
Can You Forgive Her?, 45, 70-71, 80, 92, 109, 112, 215-216
Castle Richmond, 37, 120, 125
"Christmas at Thompson Hall," 110
Cicero, The Life of, 5, 77

"The Civil Service as a Profession," 50
Clarke, John, 105
The Claverings, 193, 199
Clergymen of the Church of England, 143, 192 n.1, 193
The Commentaries of Caesar, 5, 16
Cousin Henry, 38, 114, 144-157

David Copperfield, 44
Dickens, Charles, 3, 41, 71-72, 86, 91, 93, 183, 186
Doctor Thorne, 85, 183, 191, 194, 199-203
The Domestic Manners of the Americans, 4-6, 56
Drinker, Henry S., 82-83, 225
The Duke's Children, 103, 213, 222-224
Dumas, Alexander, 93

Eisele, Thomas, 85, 105
The Eustace Diamonds, 84 n.4, 131
An Eye for an Eye, 125

Field, Kate, 42, 44
The Fixed Period, 47, 51, 84 n.3
Framley Parsonage, 76, 179, 191, 203-207
Freeling, Mrs. Clayton, 6
Freeling, Sir Francis, 6-9, 11-17, 20-24, 30, 49, 82
Frye, Northrop, 19

Gay, Susan, 32-33

Griffin, Gerald, 118
Great Expectations, 72

Hall, N. John, 51 n.9
Halperin, John, 213
Hart, H.L.A., 101, 128
Hay, Douglas, 14
He Knew He Was Right, 43-44, 84, 102, 180
Hennessy, James Pope, 213
Heseltine, Rose (Mrs. Anthony Trollope), 43
Hill, Sir Rowland, 49, 51 n.7
Hine, Reginald, 129-130, 132
Holdsworth, Sir William, 21
How the "Mastiffs" Went to Iceland, 32, 141-142
Hunting Sketches, 39 n.19, 40 n.23

"The Irish Beneficed Clergyman," 132
Is He Popenjoy?, 131, 195

James, Henry, 214
John Caldigate, 93, 180

The Kellys and the O'Kellys, 116, 124-125, 131
Kept in the Dark, 110
Kincaid, James, 133

Lady Anna, 97, 179
"The Lady of Launay," 179
The Land-Leaguers, 116, 126-127
The Last Chronicle of Barset, 71, 80-81, 191, 193, 207-211, 214-215
Leighton, Gertrude, xii, 25 n.33
Lever, Charles, 115
Lloyd, Dennis, 95, 105, 151-152
Lord Palmerston, 76-78, 97, 104

Maberly, Colonel, 9, 11, 27, 69
MacCormick, Neil, 95
The Macdermots of Ballycloran, 112-130, 157
MacDonagh, Oliver, 9
Maitland, F. W., 82
Marion Fay, 74, 80, 85, 98, 193 n.3
Mill, J. S., 97
Miss Mackenzie, 45, 89, 112

Newbolt, Sir Francis, 82-83
North America, 65-66

An Old Man's Love, 99
Orley Farm, 15 n.21, 83, 156-171, 174, 183

Palmer, John, 6-7
Phineas Finn, 106, 213, 216-218
Phineas Redux, 213, 218
"The Present Condition of the Northern States of the American Union," 65-66
The Prime Minister, 40 n.23, 93-94, 98, 104, 110-111, 193 n.3, 212, 219-222

Rachel Ray, 97
Ralph the Heir, 73-74, 86, 95-96, 220
Raz, J., 101
Richardson, Samuel, 42

Mr. Scarborough's Family, 37, 84-85, 103, 173-183, 189, 200
Scott, Sir Walter, 113
Sir Harry Hotspur of Humblethwaite, 112
The Small House at Allington, 71, 86-88, 93, 98, 191, 206-207
Sokol, Ronald, 105
South Africa, 61-62, 101-102
"The Spotted Dog," 119
Stewart, Dugald, 76
Stump, Samuel, 46
Surtees, R. S., 40 n.21

Index

Taylor, Sir Henry, 11-13, 50, 70
"The Telegraph Girl," 102
Thackeray, 73, 79, 90
Thompson, Flora, 28
The Three Clerks, 8, 12, 22, 30, 36, 38, 49
Tracy, Robert, 23 n.31
Trollope, Anthony (childhood), 3-5, (training at General Post Office) 6-25, (Ireland) 26-32, (Egypt report) 33, (hunting) 39-41, 97-98, 125, (attitude to women) 42-46, 102-104, 145-146, (as administrator) 48-52, (on revelation and inspiration) 55, (landscape) 56, 120, (on race) 56-57, 62, (on ideal society) 67-68, (definition of the gentleman) 69, 74-76, 79-80, 190, (religion and sermons) 94-95, 98, 127, 130-131, 160
Trollope, Frances, 3, 6, 113

Trollope, Henry, 3, 6, 8
Trollope, Thomas Adolphus, 4-5, 6, 8, 45

Uren, J. G., 29-30

La Vendée, 84 n.3, 113-114
The Vicar of Bullhampton, 191

Wakefield, Edward Gibbon, 63
The Warden, 128-143, 145, 161, 190, 192, 196
The Way We Live Now, 99-100, 117, 125, 186
Wellman, Francis, 91
The West Indies and the Spanish Main, 42, 57-60, 64-66
White, James B., 85-86, 89, 105
Whitehead, Alfred North, 75
Windolph, F. Lyman, 82
Dr. Wortle's School, 131, 191

LIBRARY OF CONGRESS CATALOGING IN PUBLICATION DATA

Lansbury, Coral.
　The reasonable man.

　Includes index.
　1. Trollope, Anthony, 1815-1882—Criticism and interpretation.　2. Trollope, Anthony, 1815-1882—Knowledge—Law.　3. Law in literature.　I. Title.
PR5688.L36L3　　823'.8　　80-8560
ISBN 0-691-06457-1　　　　AACR2

GPSR Authorized Representative: Easy Access System Europe - Mustamäe tee
50, 10621 Tallinn, Estonia, gpsr.requests@easproject.com

www.ingramcontent.com/pod-product-compliance
Lightning Source LLC
Chambersburg PA
CBHW061442300426
44114CB00014B/1794